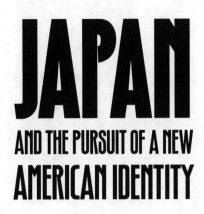

JAPAN
AND THE PURSUIT OF A NEW
AMERICAN IDENTITY

JAPAN
AND THE PURSUIT OF A NEW
AMERICAN IDENTITY

Work and Education in a Multicultural Age

WALTER FEINBERG

Routledge
NEW YORK LONDON

Published in 1993 by

Routledge
29 West 35th Street
New York, NY 10001

Published in Great Britain by

Routledge
11 New Fetter Lane
London EC4P 4EE

Library of Congress Cataloging-in-Publication Data

Feinberg, Walter, 1937–
    Japan and the pursuit of a new American identity : work and
education in a multicultural age / Walter Feinberg.
        p.   cm.
    Includes bibliographical references and index.
    ISBN 0-415-90683-0
    1. Industry and education—United States. 2. Industry and
education—Japan. 3. Academic achievement—United States.
4. American achievement—Japan. 5. Industrial productivity—United
States. 6. Industrial productivity—Japan. 7. Identity
(Psychology) 8. Culture conflict. I. Title.
LC1085.2.F45   1993   92-31372
                                                                  CIP

British Library Cataloguing-in-Publication Data also available.

Contents

For Alicia and Keith

Acknowledgments

This book required the talents of many people for its completion. First my thanks go to all of the people from this country and Japan—teachers, school administrators, factory workers, executives and managers, parents, political leaders, students, university faculty and many others—who patiently described their experiences in American and Japanese society. Except for Kenichi and Hiroshi, the fictitious brothers, whose concerns are expressed in the opening of Chapter One, all the others mentioned are real people who gave generously of their time to help me with this project. Of course all names and initials have been changed so as not to reveal their identity. My translator and interpreter, Reiko Hattori, was also a superb informant who explained many of the practices of Japanese society. In Ms. Hattori I had the good fortune of working with a person who knew both American and Japanese culture intimately and could help me see a bit deeper into the nature of everyday life in Japan. Chieko Fons and Taiji Hotta were similarly helpful in providing detailed historical, economic and sociological background, as well as aiding in translating material. Ms. Fons's research on the changes undergone by Japanese teachers before, during and after the war provided important contextual information[1] and Mr. Hotta's careful reading of an earlier draft of the manuscript was especially helpful in deepening my analysis of certain educational and economic practices. Kirk Masden's familiarity with the Japanese literature on education was helpful in introducing me to some of the important debates occurring in Japan. Students in semi-

[1]Chieko Fons, *Long Engagement: Life Stories of Japanese Teachers who Taught Before, During and After the War* Champaign, Il: Doctoral Thesis, 1990.

nars that I taught at the University of Illinois raised useful questions about earlier drafts of this book.

Special thanks to Professor Naotaka and Kayoko Watanabe who have been important friends and colleagues. They were indispensable in setting up many of my interviews in Japan and in helping me to understand Japanese academic life. Thanks are also due to the administration and faculty of Nanzan University for their exceptional hospitality during the time I spent there. My colleague Alan Peshkin provided some useful methodological advice as I undertook the field work. The Japanese Educational Studies Association invited me to join its keynote session for its fiftieth anniversary, an honor that I cherish. Its members helped me think through material that has been incorporated into Chapter One. Some of the ideas in Chapter Seven were presented to the American Philosophy of Education Society in my Presidential Address.

Suzanne Rice and David Blacker have served as important sounding boards and excellent critics, as has Kevin McDonough. They have read the entire manuscript in a number of different versions and have had a significant impact on my thinking. They have suggested new and useful avenues to pursue and have been extraordinarily diplomatic in letting me know when I needed to rework material. Their suggestions about matters of organization, presentation, argumentation and style have been invaluable. I am also grateful to Belden Fields for his insightful comments on Chapter Two and for his useful comments on my treatment of political theory, and to Eric Bredo for his comments on an earlier draft of the manuscript. Also, my editors, Michael Apple and Jayne Fargnoli helped me to identify many of the rough spots and encouraged me in the final phases of the project. They are indeed the kind of demanding editors that every author should wish for. Thanks also to Jessica George for proofreading the manuscript.

The University of Illinois, through the resources of the Research Board, the Bureau of Educational Research, the Department of Educational Policy Studies and the College of Education, provided support for certain phases of this project, as did the Hewlett Foundation. An early stage of the project was partially supported by The Japan/United States Friendship Commission. My thanks also to Barbara Duncan for her help in the technical production of the manuscript.

As always, I am more than indebted to the support, encouragement and love of my wife Eleanor whose own professional work as a clinical psychologist provided support for some of my thoughts on dependency and whose careful comments on the entire manuscript were important in its refinement.

Introduction

I. The Evolution of the Project

This project has evolved from a concern with the relationship between school and work to a concern about the character of a democratic identity in a multicultural world; in this Introduction I want to trace some of the different points in that evolution. I began this project in the middle of the 1980s, shortly after governmental and industrial leaders declared that a crisis existed in American education, and placed the blame for America's emerging trade gap and declining industry squarely on the public schools. To support this claim, they pointed to the high achievement of Japanese students and the great strides of Japanese industry. They argued that a steady decline in the test scores of American students was a sign of deteriorating schools, and that this was responsible for the declining competitiveness of American industry. The high scores of Japanese students and the high performance of Japanese industry was taken as proof that good schools create good workers.

The argument was influential in inspiring the educational reform movements of the 1980s. However, many questions remain. For example, Japanese students scored well on tests long before their country's steel, automobile and semiconductor industries became world leaders. Their thirteen-year-olds have often scored first in mathematics since at least the early sixties, yet only recently has Japan become an industrial superpower. Given that the thirteen-year-olds of 1960 were already in their mid-thirties when American leaders declared a crisis, why was such a long lead time required? Was it just that Japan needed all that time to recover from the Second World War, or that workers must be in their mid-thirties before school achievement effects increased productivity? Or is it that the skills needed to perform in the workplace have changed? Moreover, while the test scores of American students has steadily declined in absolute terms over the last two decades, American students have long been near the bottom in mathematics in comparisons with industrial nations. This was the case even during the early 1960s, when education was supposed to be fueling our nation's high productivity. If students' performance changed little over time compared to the performance of students in other countries, why should their absolute score be of such concern? And if our students consistently test poorly, why has American productivity historically been so high?

After the initial volley of concerns voiced by the business and political community, many educational changes were mandated, but they have had little effect on test performance or on productivity. For example, since the reform movement of the eighties began, test scores of American students have varied little from year to year—some years they go up a point, and the newspapers applaud, other years they go down a point and the newspapers proclaim a crisis—but during this time productivity and quality has increased significantly in the automobile and other industries. Moreover, while test scores remained relatively stable, the overall balance of payments varies considerably from year to year and even from month to month, with an overall downward trend. In Japan, too, the stock market rises and falls, and industries come and go without any apparent connection to how well students perform on standardized tests. Clearly there must be some kind of relationship between school achievement and economic fortune, but these all-too-obvious examples suggested to me that it is not a simple one, and that the link between them is mediated by many cultural factors, some of which likely have little to do with school.

To understand these cultural differences, I drew on people who are connected in one way or another with the increasing number of Japanese "transplants," as the Japanese companies with branch plants in the United States are called, and who therefore have experienced both American and Japanese society. These people represent but a slice of Japanese culture, and should not be treated as reflecting the range of differences that are to be found in Japan as a whole. However, they are familiar with life in large-scale Japanese industry, and this is the segment of Japanese society that has attracted the most attention and the most concern in this country. Moreover, the Japanese connected with these ventures are a very influential segment of Japanese

society, and they represent for many other Japanese the most important avenues of security and opportunity.

The development of one of these plants was the occasion for initiat-
ing this study. The Japanese children who came into the American
community as a result of the decision to build the plant were placed in
the public schools, and also attended a Japanese culture and language
school on Saturdays. The Saturday school was largely financed by the
state to attract the company to its borders. Almost all of the Japanese
children who came with their parents would return to Japan after a
few years in this country; the Saturday school was a way to ease the
transition back to the Japanese classroom. The political leaders of the
state felt that the school would be an important factor in the decision
about the plant's location, and, given the intense competition for the
plant, it may well have made a difference.

This school provided a focal point for new parents coming into the
community. With the generous cooperation of the administration, I
was introduced to the mothers whom I interviewed, first in the school
and later in their home. With the aid of an assistant, whose flawless
English was matched only by her native Japanese, I was allowed into
an intimate conversation about Japanese life and education. Often, as
we sat drinking tea, I would ask a lead question in English, and my
assistant and the mother would follow it by a conversation in Japanese,
which would then be summarized for me in English. I would follow
the translation with another brief question and their conversation
would continue. Later, in Japan, I continued these conversations with
other mothers who had returned from the United States and whose
children were readjusting to the requirements of Japanese schools.

Since some of the top Japanese executives were on the Board of the
Saturday school, it also provided my first introduction to the corporate
culture. The engineers, executives, and managers spoke about many
of the unique features of the Japanese workplace and about their
experiences with both American and Japanese workers. When they
addressed issues of productivity and quality, they spoke not only
about the skills required by the new technology, but also about the
cultural differences that exist in the American and the Japanese enter-
prises. And sometimes they spoke about their own experience of
learning and working in Japanese society.

When the Japanese construction company broke the ground for the
factory, I began to speak to its managers and engineers about their
contact with American workers; when the transplant hired a consulting firm to screen and test job applicants, I spoke to its director to
find out about the kinds of skills the company needed; as other Japa-

nese mothers came to the community, I interviewed them, and was told about the cultural interaction between family, school and work in modern Japanese society. As I spoke to American workers, teachers, political leaders, and community members who were working with the Japanese, I heard about their (culturally mediated) interpretations of Japanese life at home, school, and work.

Eventually the encounter with this community extended to Japan, where the first group of American workers from this plant was sent for training. There I learned about the character of their training experience and about the workers' impressions of Japanese society. When I was in Japan, I spoke to other Japanese mothers who, having been in the United States, had now returned and were readjusting to Japanese society. I also interviewed young women, about to graduate from college, who spoke openly to me about their hopes and expectations. I interviewed owners and executives of large and small companies about their experience with American and Japanese workers, and I spoke with many others about their encounter with these two distinct cultures. All of these people became my informants, collaborators in my own education about school, work, and culture. In reporting on these interviews I have disguised people and their affiliations as much as possible.

By this time, the central question of the study had changed. I was still interested in understanding the connection between school achievement and industrial productivity, but I was asking it in a different way. I asked: What does the achievement of Japanese students and the productivity of Japanese workers mean for Americans, and why does it carry the meaning that it does? I was led to ask this question for many reasons, but perhaps the most important was the feeling that economic issues had become secondary, and that behind all of the attention given to Japan was a concern about our own identity and moral character. My question thus became: What is it about the nature of our own self-understanding that leads us to see Japanese performance in the way that we do?

To understand the significance of this question, consider the fact that while we attribute the reliability of Japanese automobiles to something about Japanese character and personality, which we often see as threatening, we take the finely engineered German cars and the safe Swedish cars for granted without attributes of national character that carry racist or nationalist overtones. While we voice public concern about Japanese investment in American industry and real estate, little concern is raised about similar investments by the British, Germans, French, or Canadians. While the President seeks an educational strategy that will enable our children to surpass the Japanese in mathematics and science by the year 2000, he does not consider the easier goal of surpassing the students of France, Belgium, Hungary, Scotland, or any of the dozen or so nations that stand between the scores of our children and those of the Japanese. Perhaps a more reasonable strategy, if one believes that being number one is important, would be to try to move from number twelve to number eleven, and from there to number ten or nine, seeking to overcome, say, Finland in 1993, Wales in 1995, Scotland in 1998, and so on, until some years after the turn of the century, we take on number one—Japan.[1] Yet we hear virtually nothing about the achievement of children in Finland, Wales, England, Scotland, Canada, France, or any of the other Western countries that rank ahead of us. We seek only to leap from number twelve to number one. The position of the Japanese is an American obsession.

Clearly there is an element of racism in this concern about Japan. However, there is racism on both sides of this issue, as demonstrated by the misguided Japanese politicians who blame America's problems on Blacks and Hispanics in the work force. Yet to dismiss the overemphasis on Japan as just a matter of racism and nothing more would be to lose the instructive moment in this encounter. Moreover, to focus just on the racism alone is to minimize the real admiration that many Americans feel for the Japanese. The mixture of our admiration and resentment projected onto the Japanese creates the opportunity to learn about the cultural source of our responses—our own identity as a people—and our emerging possibilities. It is precisely such learning that serves, in the classical sense of the term, as education. This then becomes the larger project of this book.

II. Images of Self and Other

Japan stands as a symbolic complement to our own self-image, reinforcing our idea of the way we are and the way we ought to be. The recent achievement of the Japanese highlights and threatens this idea. With the exception of the period during the Second World War, the Japanese along with other Asians have been perceived by us as passive, imitative, obedient, and dependent, the seemingly perfect complement to our self-image as assertive, creative, self-reliant, and independent. Our image of the Japanese is part of our image of the "Oriental" in general, an image that is powerfully expressed by Song in the play *M. Butterfly* as he explains to the Judge how he was able for twenty years to convince his Western male lover that he was a woman:

> Rule One is: Men always believe what they want to hear. So a girl can tell the most obnoxious lies and the guys will believe them every time—"This is my first time"— "That the biggest I've ever seen"—or *both*, which if you really think about it, is not possible in a single lifetime. . . .
>
> Rule Two: As soon as Western man comes into contact with the East—he's already confused. The West has sort of an international rape mentality towards the East. . . . Basically, "Her mouth says no, but her eyes say yes." The West thinks of itself as masculine—big guns, big industry, big money—so the East is feminine—weak, delicate, poor . . . but good at art, and full of inscrutable wisdom—the feminine mystique.
>
> Her mouth says no, but her eyes say yes. The West believes the East, deep down, *wants* to be dominated—because a woman can't think for herself.[2]

As the Japanese now become associated with big money, big industry, and perhaps even big guns, our image of them as passive, dependent, and feminine becomes unsettled, as does our own self-image as independent, strong, generous, and masculine. Racism here is a desperate attempt to maintain the traditional sense of place and personhood in a world where established racial hierarchies and traditional stereotypes are destabilizing.

The admiration we have for Japan is not completely separable from such racism, but here the racism involves a mixture of fear and admiration. In the midst of this instability and the blurring of traditional boundaries, the Japanese seem to maintain a stable sense of themselves and of the various roles each is destined to play. Some Americans believe that place, personhood, and authority are signs of Japan's moral superiority serving as a spotlight to accent the real reason for our fading fortune. To seek a quick technical fix to school performance through the establishment of competitive, nationwide standardized tests or merit pay for teachers is to seek to reaffirm our own traditional identity as competitive and individualistic, and it is also to reaffirm the legitimacy of universal standards that define the educational race and allot the prizes. Yet once the legitimacy of these traditional forms have been challenged, they cannot be returned in the same way. Whereas once such tests were accepted as natural indicators of talent and merit, they are now on contested ground—legitimated but not exactly legitimate, at least not in the way they once were.[3] Hence identity is an issue to be dealt with, not just a nature to be born to. The task that this book undertakes is to address the problems of education as an issue of democratic identity formation, and to do so by exploring the challenge that the Japanese present, and our response to it.

III. Democracy and Markets

We the citizens of the United States see ours as first and foremost a democratic nation. We speak easily of our role as the leader of the free world. We applaud the decline of communism throughout the former Soviet Union and Eastern Europe. Many Americans are capitalists too. They believe in the free market, and they also believe that freedom consists in people being able to buy and to sell what they wish. Most citizens do not believe that one must choose between freedom and markets, between democracy and capitalism, holding that the former is a condition of the latter. Yet if we were forced to choose, I believe that most would choose democracy.

Most people know that however unclear the ideal, democracy insists that economic freedom be tempered by political equality and they know intuitively that the two may commingle but that they are not always the same. We cannot sell our opinions to the highest bidder. Our children, our bodies, our reason, and our souls are not for sale. Markets do have limits. A choice for democracy may not be a choice for riches, but it is indeed a choice for selfhood—both our own and others. There are limits to the tie between markets and democracy, between political and economic freedom. Markets can and sometimes do exist without political freedom—without democracy. And democracies exist where market forces are constrained by politically determined needs. We are in danger of losing this distinction and of wrongly thinking that to achieve democratic freedom we need only market-oriented capitalism. Indeed, in emphasizing the importance of private consumption, capitalism may sometimes constrict the sphere of public, democratic discourse.

This is not the first time we have made such a mistake. Indeed, there is no gilded era, no moment of grace, no Garden of Eden when everyone sought democracy. Many of the Founders themselves were large property owners and merchants and they wanted to stay that way. Yet, in their drive to win popular support for their cause, they appealed to a broader popular base, and in doing so, they articulated the need for public discourse—the foundation of any democratic society. The difficulty with maintaining democracy today is not that the mechanisms for public discourse have vanished. It is that the means for controlling such discourse have increased so greatly. A country where the top one percent of the population controls as much wealth as the bottom ninety percent would be suspect as a democracy at any time and in any place. Yet when that one percent lives at a time when powerful and costly television messages can reach hundreds of millions of people in a split second, and political imagination can be easily controlled by glib sound bites, then the inequality has serious and potentially devastating consequences unless ways can be found to increase the possibilities for more equitable control of information. Markets and democracy can likely coexist, but they are different, and the one does not necessarily entail the other.

IV. The Connection between Democracy and Education

I therefore see our highest ideal of political identity as democratic at its foundation. We know our rights, and we want to be able to express them and to have them recognized by others. We also know that, whether we like it or not, the condition for the recognition of our rights is the recognition of the rights of others. Yet where do we learn to be democracy, and what do we learn when we learn to be democratic? Do we learn democracy at home?—perhaps, if we are lucky. But democracy also rightly teaches that parents should be autonomous, whether or not they are good role models for democracy. Do we learn democracy in the neighborhood, among our peers? Certainly we may indeed learn to respect others like ourselves by playing and working with them. Yet what if our peers are not democratic? Suppose the older and stronger child bullies the younger one. Where then do we learn to be democratic, and where, even if our peers are democratic, do we learn to respect those who are different from us, as democracy is supposed to teach people to do? Our present patterns of housing, with race divided from race and rich divided from poor, make the lessons of democracy less than complete when taught only in the neighborhood. Perhaps we learn democracy in the workplace— a prospect that this book will explore in detail. Yet workplaces may be democratic, but democracy is not their main business. Their business is business, and if served by democracy then all well and good. But democracy is not a required course in the workplace. Churches are democratic—at least some of them. But then again, some are not, and democracy teaches that neither churches—those that are and those that are not democratic—are to be interfered with. And where, if anywhere, do we learn that?

The role of public education for the development of a democratic identity has been seriously neglected in recent years; in this book I want to reconsider its importance in this regard. Yet, in speaking for the role of the public schools, it is important not to minimize their problems and their flaws. I speak of the public school as a place where we might learn to reflect upon our identity as a democratic nation and as a place where such identities could be renewed. However, the schools I speak of are not the schools that are the objects of radical disappointment and conservative scorn. Public schools often do not serve democratic ends.

Yet renewal is ultimately a public project, one that must reach toward a common good, publicly defined. If we think of such a good as the product of an elite, then the public good can be determined by graduates of wealthy private schools and a few excellent public ones. If, as I believe, such a good must be democratically defined, then it must be the focus of education in all public schools. I am not especially optimistic that this can happen, given our present economic and political structure, but if it is to happen we must at least have some idea of what it is that we presently lack. Unhappily, much recent educational discourse has lost sight of the public-forming responsibility of public education.

Certainly the public schools are flawed, but to some extent their flaws are contingent. Some teachers are narrow-minded, but this need not be the case. Many schools are concerned more with keeping order than furthering education, but it is possible to change this if we know what it means to truly educate a child, and if we can see the factors that are inhibiting such education. We are not inevitably programmed to be educational masters and educational serfs. And if schools are not equal enough, if the rich children get better teachers, smaller classes, better equipment, and a richer curriculum, as they indeed do, there is nothing that says things must inevitably stay this way.

There are three quick reasons that could be given for neglecting the public role of public education. The first is that public schools have not met their promise and have not served to promote a more egalitarian and democratic society. I believe this answer is accurate, but that there are different ways of responding to it—a progressive and a conservative way. The conservative asks us to believe that things are as they should be and that the inequalities of the schools are but a reflection of the inequality to be found in nature. The progressive says otherwise. Unequal schools squelch potential and inhibit talent from rising to the top. I disagree with the conservative and take my stand with the progressive—but I stand only partway with the progressive. I believe that unequal schools inhibit talent, but there is more to education than enforcing the rules of the natural lottery.

The second reason for the neglect of the public schools is that a new conservative discourse has taken hold that has no real conception of a public. It understands that there are nations and markets, but nothing sandwiched in between. Political discourse is the feedback that takes place between the poll results and the sound bite. Schools serve national and market forces—not political discourse.

The third and perhaps most difficult reason to address is the tension that exists in classical democratic theory itself. Western democracy seeks the public good, but it does so through maintaining that each of us, each and every individual citizen is a separate unit—a pleasure-seeking animal—with little need or regard for each other. Some draw the implication from the tension that the "public good" is really only a label indicating the compromise each of us must make with others in order to serve our interest. Hence, the public here is ultimately reducible to an aggregate of individual interests. One of the central questions in this book is whether the Japanese present a different and perhaps more appropriate model of a public.

A lot of attention has been directed at public education even if it has not been directed at its public-forming role. We have had an "education president" and a Secretary of Education who became a czar. We have had reports and findings, studies, and investigations. We have had educational crisis and counter-crisis, and the patient continues to linger but is not well. It is not well for a very good reason: the patient, if not the sickness, has been misdiagnosed. The patient is education. It is not job training or even nation building. Its sickness is that it has lost its own sense of purpose. It has a disease of spirit, not of body. It is sick because it has come to mistake the molding of a collectivity—ready to act as one and to think as one—for the job of developing opportunities for public discourse.

Of course there are a hundred and one questions entailed in this claim. Just what is a public? Given so many different groups, traditions, races, ideas, and opinions, can there ever be a public in this country? And if there can be, then do we want it? Must we place our *many* in subordination to our *one*? These questions point not to the problem with the idea of a public as such, but rather to the question of how a public can be constituted in a multicultural age, and this is really the question about the character of intercultural understanding that this book seeks to address. It does not deny the ideal; it asks how it is achievable in a multicultural age. To clarify the ideal is to make it more achievable in more places. We are after all more likely to hit the target if we know what the target is, but knowing what it is does not mean that we will hit it all the time.

V. The Limits of the Present Debate

The ideal of the education of a public seems to be lost in the present debate about the future of American education. One view sees the state as simply a mechanism for distributing educational resources, leaving to parents alone the choice of where their students should go to school and what they should be taught. Another emphasizes the potential economic benefits of schooling, and proposes a curriculum that would improve students' ability to support themselves and to contribute to the nation's economic well-being. Those who advocate this view want to narrow the offerings of the school, eliminate the so-called frill subjects, increase the number of required subjects, and require the same subjects in every school. They want to make schools across the country increasingly similar to one another in terms of curriculum content, and they want this content to have a cash value. Those who emphasize the economic benefits of schools do not see any conflict between their view, which calls for constricting the offerings of the curriculum, and the view that advocates the widest possible choice for parents. This is because they assume that all parents and cultures hold economic success as their major educational goal, that they all share the same meaning of such success—the private accumulation of wealth.[4] Thus they advocate providing parents with more choice as they seek to reduce the variety of alternatives from which parents might choose. A third response is to accept the role of education as a public-forming body, but to assert that the meanings and symbols that constitute this public are already fixed, and that the role of the school is to teach students to identify them.

VI. A Democratic Public

The question raised in these pages is whether there is still a possibility for a view of a public and of public education that is wider and more inclusive than those that I have sketched above, and if so, how that public can be connected to a defensible conception of democracy. The way this question is answered has inevitable implications for the way in which a public is viewed. What I seek is a public that is more than a receiver of state resources, more than an agent in a market, and more than a cluster of individuals who happen to consume a common set of symbols. I want to argue that the concept of a public makes sense in more than just a utilitarian way, and that among the most important facets of public education is its relationship to that public as both recipient of its support and a condition of its growth and maturity.

How shall we go about developing a concept of a public for public education? How shall we seek what some have come to suspect may no longer be there to be found? My strategy is to seek it in the latest condition for its loss—the conservative discourse about schools. This strategy is predicated on the belief that a conception of the public can be reconstituted by closely examining the conservative's appeal to the idea of markets and nations. I seek this public in the struggle that has been so useful in making this case—in the concern expressed when American markets and jobs have been lost to the Japanese. I see in the conservative response a misunderstanding both of the conditions of this struggle and of the advantages that have been attributed to the Japanese, but I believe that we can find in this discourse some of the fragments required to reconstruct a self conscious democratic public.

1

An American Identity Crisis

Introduction

The small store that Kenichi and his wife own is one of fourteen shops on the residential block near the University. The shop sells groceries to the local housewives, and is a meeting place for exchanging a few friendly words and keeping up with neighborhood events. It is also a place for different generations to keep in touch with one another, as young mothers with babies exchange a friendly word or two with older shoppers and receive advice about how to treat the baby's cough or some other small problem.

By United States standards, the entire process is shamefully inefficient and expensive. The aisles of the shop are too small for full-sized shopping carts, and the store supplies only arm baskets for its customers. Because the store is too small for the tens of thousands of people who live in the area, many similar grocers can be found within a few blocks of one another, each served by different wholesalers who frequently buy from different manufacturers. This complicated and inefficient marketing structure makes it difficult for Kenichi to sell exotic, foreign goods, like cookies or soap from the United States, and Kenichi is certainly not getting rich. However, through working long hours and holding down costs, he is able to hold his own.

At twenty-eight, Kenichi's brother Hiroshi is one year older and works for the Toyota automobile company, assembling cars for the Japanese and the foreign market. The plant that he works in has many robots and is highly computerized. Hiroshi works on the line in a six-man team and is largely responsible for the quality of the paint job.

He is proud of his company's reputation for quality and efficiency, and has been pleased to see his salary increase as the reputation and the sales of Toyotas have grown abroad.

While both Kenichi and Hiroshi are comfortable by Japanese standards, they are also dimly aware of a distant threat to their way of life. The trade negotiators from the United States have been complaining about the large number of Japanese cars that are being sold in that country, and threats have been made to place more restrictions on the sale of Japanese automobiles in the United States. The Americans are concerned about the efficiency of the Japanese automobile industry, and believe that it threatens the home industry. Hiroshi is worried about these talks, and does not understand why a great country like the United States, which he once saw as the guardian of free trade, should want to punish Japanese automobile workers for their efficiency.

Kenichi has also been feeling the pressure of these talks, and is concerned for his very survival as a businessman. Americans want larger and more efficient retail outlets so they can better market their goods in Japan. Since he is not employed in an industry that guarantees lifetime employment, he feels even more vulnerable than his brother. He can understand why the United States might be concerned about Toyota, but why should it worry about his small grocery store? And why do the negotiators' complain about the inefficiency of the Japanese system of distribution? Why is this any of their business? Of course it makes it more difficult for some American goods to be sold in Japan, but anyone who knew the culture could figure out how to market a product. Could the Americans be so ignorant of the Japanese culture? Surely someone must be smart enough to figure out how to market razor blades and toilet paper in Japanese grocery stores.

Both Kenichi and Hiroshi now stand as a threat to the American way of life: the one for his great efficiency, the other for his "devious" inefficiency. Oddly enough, though, Americans believe that it is Japan's superior schools, its more advanced science and math education, that provide Japanese industry with more efficient workers, yet both Kenichi and Hiroshi went to the same school, took the same courses, received similar grades, and graduated within one year of one another. If the school produced just the right amount of efficiency in Hiroshi, how did it also produce just the right amount of inefficiency in his brother Kenichi?

II. The Nature of the Identity Crisis

A. THE USES OF "JAPAN"

The story above is told to illustrate a basic theme of this book. Our problem with Japan is not, contrary to recent opinion, a problem of efficiency, productivity, or schooling—and this book is not written, as so many have been, to reveal the great secret of Japanese success in school and work. If Japan has an efficient work force in some sectors, it also has an inefficient one in others. The conflict is not in fact with Japan, and it is not, at its foundation, an economic conflict. Ours is an identity crisis, and in this crisis Japan serves a number of different roles.

First, Japan is seen by some as a warning, signaling the consequences of a disintegrating national identity—second-rate nationhood and a lowered standard of living. Second, Japan serves as a model for taming marginality, cushioning the demands of different interests, reaffirming the importance of role identity, and tempering what some believe are the disintegrating effects of equality. Those who appropriate Japan in this way believe that the Japanese "economic miracle" was accomplished by respecting traditional gendered roles. Where work remains gendered, women remain free to raise the children while men work hard to support their families. Hence, Japan is used to highlight the unfortunate consequences that are thought to result as we stray from traditional genderized roles.

Third, many believe that the Japanese have shown that education is the secret to maintaining a unified national identity, and that we can use education to reestablish national commitment and pride.

B. THE SPLIT BETWEEN CAPITALISM AND PATRIOTISM

Our identity as Americans is contorted by two conflicting forces. The first is the separation between economic and national boundaries occurring in response to growing, global, economic interdependence. For example, business is exporting industries and jobs to other countries, thereby weakening the relationship between industrial and national well-being. What is good for General Motors is no longer necessarily "good for the USA." The second force is the rise in particularism and the narrow association of individuals with their own racial or ethnic group or with a developing gender identity. Thus, as identity is stretched beyond traditional national borders, it is constricted by appeals to ethnic identity, local culture, race, and gender. While many Asian countries, such as Korea, have not escaped the disintegrating tendencies of modern society, some believe, correctly or incorrectly, that Japan is both modern and harmonious, and they also believe that Japanese education has played an important role in maintaining national identity, communal loyalty, and economic growth.

Some have exploited this issue using the specter of Japan as a way to get this country in line—but the problem here is that the identity crisis is a crisis within traditional American ideology itself. It involves a split between patriotism and capitalism. The one seeks to manufacture a single, coherent identity with strong boundaries between the inside and the outside, while the other, working within the context of expanded international markets, requires open, porous relations with other cultures and other countries. Japan is, then, both a threat and a model precisely because it is having success in both areas. It is, it seems, maintaining its strong national identity while apparently thriving as a capitalist society. The recent interest in Japanese education is in part motivated by the hope that it will unlock the secret of this unity.

When it was the case that large oceans and small, cumbersome, commercial fleets made foreign goods too costly for local consumption, American capitalism and patriotism seemed to work together. When it was also the case that other nations' productive capacities were crippled by war, the United States could serve as the cheerleader, guardian, and chief benefactor of a "free" market. United States industrialists could then hold firmly to an identity that was completely "American" and completely capitalistic. Capitalism and patriotism were one, and for the most part schools maintained and passed on this identity. To the traditionalist, capitalism and Americanism should still be one seamless cloth. Change threatens not just the union of country and capital, but also the very fabric of social life—and especially the strong distinctions that capitalism seeks between public and private, male and female, dominant and subordinate.

The conservatives and liberals have responded to the rise of Japan somewhat differently. The conservatives would like to make capitalism and patriotism one again, and to restore the crucial boundaries that constituted the "American" identity—but this is difficult. The flaw here is that patriotism, as love and respect for country, expresses the feeling that the country provides the conditions for nurturing material, emotional, and spiritual well-being. Yet this is a difficult feeling to maintain where there is a growing gap between rich and poor. Some conservatives, justifying new, cheaper sources of labor,

seek to weaken the tie of industry to its national base by exporting
jobs to other countries, and some in the work force feel betrayed by
their nation and its leaders. Others, responding to the needs of service
industries and agriculture—industries that are anchored within the
borders of the country—for inexpensive labor argue for looser immigration requirements. Yet along with immigration from Mexico, Cuba,
Haiti, the Philippines, Korea, Cambodia, and other Third World countries sometimes come new and unsettling interpretations of the
"American" experience, interpretations that challenge the conservatives' preferred story of "America". Some now say that "exploitation"
is said to be the other face of "progress"; Columbus is called an
interloper in a foreign land, and the white "majority" is but one of the
world's minorities.[1]

C. THE SPLIT BETWEEN UNIVERSALISM AND PARTICULARISM

Japan presents a different kind of problem for liberal theory. Today
the liberal commitment to equal opportunity and color-blind education
confronts the liberal concern for cultural integrity. If schools emphasize the child's native culture and language, she may not acquire the
skills to compete in the larger world. However, if the school only
teaches the skills required by the dominant culture, it threatens the
integrity of the local culture and cuts the child off from her roots.
Hence the liberal is uncertain about whether a universal identity needs
to be nourished, or the identity of a particular ethnic or racial group.
Should modern public education serve the particular needs of a culturally diverse society, or should it view diversity as something that the
schools should strive to overcome? Do we want more diversity or
more uniformity? To highlight the successful features of Japanese
education is to take a side in this debate, and to choose more uniformity—a choice that is reflected in recent attempts to streamline the
curriculum and to develop a national system of assessment for both
teachers and students.

D. THE SPLIT BETWEEN SAVING AND CONSUMING

These problems cut across traditional political ideology, and reach
deeply into questions about the nature of the American identity. Many
Americans feel that Japan has appropriated not only our business but
our "work ethic" as well. Japan is now seen as the country where

people postpone present satisfaction and momentary pleasures for long-term and future gain. The Japanese are savers. We Americans are consumers. Yet saving is supposed to be an American virtue, once taught to generation after generation of schoolchildren, who were assured that hard work and frugality pays well. Not everyone was always virtuous, but there was little doubt about what counted as virtue. The message is no longer so clear.

In a society where economic and political policy is directed toward making as many goods available at the cheapest possible price, and where jobs and economic well-being depend on people buying more and more goods, lessons about the inherent value of savings are difficult for children to take seriously. Public schools may still teach about the virtues of hard work and patience, but public lotteries depend on convincing people that the easy life costs only a dollar and a short trip to the supermarket. Conservatives complain about "value clarification" programs in the schools because, in refusing to teach right from wrong, such programs are encouraging ambivalence about what to count as a virtue. Yet value clarification requires no greater admission than what is already obvious from the practices of American political and industrial life. American values are ambiguous. In addition to virtue, Japan offers clarity.

Our attitude toward the Japanese reflects the split that has developed in our own ideas about virtue. We admire their ability to rein in their desires and to exercise frugality, often for the benefit of a wider community. For example, many Japanese buyers are willing to pay higher prices for rice if it means that the Japanese farmer will stay in business.[2] Yet we also applaud when the Japanese break ranks and begin to act like "modern" consumers complaining about high prices—when they begin to act like us.[3]

III. The Nature of the Fragmented Self

Identity is more than the sum of a person's immediate interests. It involves the way people think about themselves, what they care about, the kinds of commitments they make, and the point of view they take. Identity also involves what we can take for granted and what requires explanation. For example, when an American Supreme Court justice resigns, the British news service will explain his role in interpreting the law, whereas American broadcasters simply report the resignation. Knowledge of the function of Supreme Court justices is taken for granted when addressing people who identify themselves as Americans but not when addressing people who identify themselves as British.

Yet even our apparently bedrock identities as an American or a British citizen are not fixed. Some Spanish-speaking United States citizens, for example, have begun to write U.S./American to indicate their larger hemispheric commitment, and to highlight their objection to the hegemonic aspects of United States influence in the region. Their identity as "U.S./Americans" is contextualized by a more primary, but still-emerging identity as "Americans." Identity involves markers like "U.S./American" to determine who is part of the primary group and who is outside of it.[4]

We are born with certain characteristics that contribute to our identity—"U.S./American" "White" "working-class" "male," or "American" "Black," "professional" "woman." But note how the series, and the pairing—"Black," "professional," "woman"—work against more traditional expectations and say that it is no longer appropriate to think of just White men as professionals. In other words, note how incidental once-widely acknowledged taken-for-granted (at least by White middle-class males) core features of selfhood have become. And note too how my descriptors—whether I say "U.S./American" or "American"—say much about my sense of who I am and how conflict-laden issues of self-identity are becoming.

We can know many different facts about a person, and these may often fit traditional stereotypes, but these stereotypes alone will not enable us to draw inferences about the associative qualities that cluster together to form a particular self. The standard formulas for womanhood and manhood are now negotiable. A woman can love a man, but she may also be attracted romantically to another woman. She may be single and yet be a mother. A husband may prefer housework—his wife the heady competition of the executive suite or an evening playing basketball. A wife may go off to serve in a war while her husband stays home to mind the children. She may take the car to the mechanic and have it serviced by a woman and he may take the children to the hospital, where they may be treated by a White, male nurse and a Black, female doctor. Moreover, many of our birth "features" are as much social as they are biological. A baby may be born Black, but she can also be born African-American, and whichever one it is, her skin color may actually be a shade or two lighter than some Italian-Americans who are counted as White.

Many will argue, quite correctly, that to depict America as a place where birth no longer counts is an idealized view of our society, and that most men and women still occupy traditional roles. Bank presidents are largely White, Christian men who were born into wealthy families, and domestic help is disproportionately Black women who were born into poor families. True enough, but it is the critical spirit of the observation that speaks to the point being made here. The fact that the vision is seen as "idealized," a goal worth furthering, illustrates that traditional role clusters are losing their normative force, and I think, indicates a withering of the ideological basis for supporting them.

The right of individuals to choose—the basis of Western democracies—has reached its reflexive, ideological limit, at least for upper-middle-class professionals. It has become the right of individuals to choose the kind of chooser they want to be. It is no longer "cool" for a man to have his pick of any woman he wants. He must also decide whether he is to be the kind of man who treats women as objects to be *picked,* and he may also need to confront his own sexuality, and decide whether he wants to confine his sexual relationships to women. We have been given the freedom to choose, but the consciousness of this freedom makes it *mandatory* that what we do be seen as a choice. We can be traditionalists, but that too is a choice. It is not *just* the way "normal" people are.

We are fragmented selves not because of what we choose, but because we know we must choose, and because no one cluster of roles can be used as the single template out of which all selves of a certain kind are derived, or from which they deviate. The tug between nature and culture, fact and interpretation, genetics and environment is being decided ideologically in favor of openness and choice.

This fragmentation, this openness and unpredictability of self is nerve-racking to some, and these people feel the need for more uniformity and predictability. To them, Japan provides both a model and a threat. It has the coherence and the will that we lack. Japanese schools are impressive not only because students perform at a high level on traditional academic tasks but, more importantly, because that performance indicates an acceptance of standard roles and norms. Japan represents order, structure, and a taming of choice and openness.

IV. The Myth of School Failure

For more than ten years the United States population has been hearing that the problem with U.S. industry lies with our schools and with the poor education (the correct word is training) of our young. This is simplistic. Were the problem truly a problem of worker productivity, a case might be made for the failure of the schools. To make such a case convincingly, however, one would need to put aside the undercapitalization that occurred in the 1970s or the multibillion-dollar Savings and Loan theft of the 1980s or the underinvestment in research of the 1990s—all of which deprived the most powerful economic machine in the world of the resources required to develop new and appealing consumer products. One would also have to ignore the fact that, with the exception of Japan, the relation between national productivity and students' scores on standardized tests is unclear. Sometimes students score high and productivity is relatively low, and sometimes it is otherwise. Little unambiguous evidence exists to support the claims that in developed nations school performance is directly related to either absolute or relative productivity. And even where correlations exist, as they do in Japan, it is probably because both high performance and high productivity are indicative of a strong identity with the goals of the school and the workplace.

A better, although not completely persuasive case, could be made that schools in the United States are doing a reasonable job in maintaining some semblance of order and civility in a society that has allowed every other significant socializing agency a free hand. Take the one activity that occupies more time of more American students than any other—television watching. The child who graduates from high school will have spent many more hours in front of the TV than in school. Television controls the child's time more than school, the family, or the job. Yet, when researchers examine the effects of television, the guiding question is "Does it do any harm?" While we know that harm does occur in schools, it would be a national scandal if school research were determined to show—as much of TV research is—merely that schools do no harm. We have higher expectations for schools. We expect them to do some good.

The example is intentionally provocative and clearly skewed—but it is not frivolous. Schools are effective when other socializing institutions are functioning properly. When children can count on adults outside of schools to teach them how to obey the rules by playing games, or to respect property by fixing things that are broken, then the schools can refine and use such lessons to teach more specialized and complicated skills. When communities are impoverished, then it is much more difficult for the schools just to teach these skills, because they must perform many other functions as well. It is difficult to evaluate schools when other healthy adult-child relationships have been eroded, and when appeals to private greed threaten to diminish every public facility from museums to outdoor theaters and libraries.

If we do not care to look at that erosion, then we will blame the schools for the inadequacies of the society at large. This, however, is like blaming the tenant farmer for failing to grow crops on soil that the landowner has depleted.

The flow of jobs, capital, and talent around the world is certainly not unrelated to the quality of education. The narrow focus and straightjacket approach to education of the Japanese secondary schools probably serve to keep more talented people out of Japan than most other factors (barring outright immigration discrimination) and in the long run may hurt its development. Moreover, the high quality of university and graduate education in the United States and some European countries is the single most important source of the migration of talented people to these areas, a migration that unfortunately places great stress on the poorer nations of the world.

Putting aside such obvious examples, we have a very limited understanding of the relationship between schooling and worker productivity. The recent concern to "improve" education as a way to improve industrial efficiency is an attempt to mend a fracturing national identity, but this simply has the effect of playing out the tension between patriotism and capitalism in the debates over schools.

Those who wish to penetrate foreign markets rightfully advocate that more foreign languages be taught in the public schools. It is indeed good for businesspeople to know the language of their customers. Ironically, often these same people wish to promote a uniform national identity, and insist that English receive recognition as the official national language. Thus immigrant students who already speak a foreign language are to be discouraged from using it in school. Bilingualism threatens national identity. Yet if we cultivated the cultural insights available to immigrant children—if we treated that cultural resource with the same consideration and respect that we treat the resource of the child who has a special gift for mathematics—our industrialists and businessmen might not be so mystified by foreign markets. The concern is that if schools emphasize children's unique cultural heritage, they will be unable to develop the sense of nationhood that comes through learning to appreciate common symbols and meanings. The concern assumes that the meanings of these symbols are absolute and nonnegotiable.

V. Postmodernism and the Identity Crisis

Our identity crisis has roots in a basic principle of Western thought—that the individual exists prior to the collective, and has priority over it. The principle places constraints on collective action, by requiring that such action arise as the voluntary response of individuals as a result of an uncoerced deliberation regarding their own best interest. Unlike the Confucian tradition, where membership in a collective is taken for granted, collective action in the West is not simply a condition of life. It is supposed to arise as a conscious and deliberate individual choice which could have been otherwise.

One expression of this idea is found in the model of capitalism. Part of the appeal of capitalism is the belief that it enables the pursuit of collective goals even as it acknowledges individual uniqueness. "Unique" individuals accomplish collective goals because, beneath the difference, we are all essentially the same. We seek the same thing—wealth and comfort—and are motivated by the same desires—pleasure and profit. To know this is to know that, by allowing each individual to pursue selfish goals through an unrestricted market, the collective good will be maximized.

One problem with such "knowledge" is that as soon as it is announced, capitalism can no longer claim to be simply *descriptive* of individual behavior—it is constructive of it. It requires traditional consciousness to be reshaped in accord with the principles of profit and productivity. If children are not attuned to the rewards of wage labor, for example, the schools must bring them into line through the use of grades and other extrinsic rewards. The same holds true for distant populations with household and family-based production systems. Capitalism requires efficiency, and efficiency means that production be removed from the family to the factory—a move which affects the character and composition of the family itself.

To reveal that capitalism does not just describe reality but that it shapes it, is to challenge its influence as scientific and impartial, and to raise the suspicion that, in the name of individualism, it operates as an instrument for collective conformity.

This suspicion is the actual but hidden bedrock of postmodernism. While postmodernism claims to have decentered the individual self and hence reduced its prominence, it relies on a healthy suspicion of collective and socially constructed practice for its critiques. Postmodernism has not rejected individualism as its foundation. It has simply rubbed the bedrock sufficiently smooth to enable our "decentered" individual identity an opportunity to slide away—if we choose to take it.

Postmodernism turns the inbred suspicion against collective practice into a criticism of the remnants of Western individualism. Yet it is not individualism *per se* that it is really after, but its many impostures.

It works by revealing their ideas and practices to be disguised "social constructs" that have been imposed on individuals. Hence if one wants now to critically assail ideals like romantic, heterosexual love or human rights, it is sufficient to point out that each is a social construct—a kind of text that is given a restricted interpretation. The alternative is not a better ideal or a truer concept. It is another interpretation—a different social construct. We should not expect the alternative to be "better" according to some set of neutral, rational standards. According to the postmodernist, rational standards are themselves "social constructs" serving paternalistic ends and dominant groups. Moreover, there are no metaconstructs by which we can decide among the competing alternatives.

While postmodernism is often taken as a devastating critique of individualism, it actually rests on a refined notion of individuality. To turn all meanings into contested domains is to force the issue back to the individual who must choose between the different contestants. More important, it is to render problematic the norms and meanings encrusted in traditional institutions like schools and workplaces. Hence traditional canons of Western literature are dismissed as "works by dead White men," or "Thanksgiving" is presented to children as a day of mourning for certain groups.[5]

As the meanings of these institutions are contested, some worry that national harmony and goodwill are diminished and the prospects for effective collective action are threatened, and this, of course, just at the time when more collective action seems to be in order. In privileging the margins are we playing chicken with our own national identity and selfhood? But then *whose* is "our own" national identity and *whose* conception of selfhood is at risk?

VI. The Japanese Advantage

The Japanese have not, it seems, heard about postmodernism. They still accept institutional meanings and trust established sources of authority—or so it appears from this side of the Pacific. Confucianism has had its influence in Japan as well as in China.[6] Confucianism taught the primacy of the collective over the individual, and encouraged mutual respect and obligation from different elements in society. The authority of the group holds sway over the wishes of the individual, and people are expected to anticipate one another's needs as they pursue a common goal.

Respect for the parent is transferred to teacher and supervisor, and loyalty to the family translates into loyalty to the firm. Many believe that this explains the recent emergence of Japan as an economic superpower. However, given that these characteristics would have, under different circumstances, been used to explain how "the dead hand of tradition" stifles innovation and achievement, the belief is best taken as another sign of our own self-doubt rather than as a sufficient explanation for the success of Japanese industry. It represents the concern that is presented by the specter of Japan, that is, its ability to hold on to a coherent national identity is the moral alternative to our own fragmentation.

Neither Japanese nor Western culture is all of one piece. Japan, for example, has a well-developed literary tradition that celebrates the loner who abandons society for the sake of an inner harmony.[7] And "My Station and its Duty"[8] was an ideal developed to justify the British class system by emphasizing its call for service and mutuality. That this ideal was articulated at the same time that the self-consciousness of the working class was heightened is, however, a sign of the continually waning influence of the concept of mutuality as an institutional bond.

While neither Japan nor the United States is monolithic, each operates on certain dominant tendencies. More common in this country than the ideal of mutuality is the Madisonian principle that individual interests are basically antagonistic, and that effective governments are those that find ways to institutionalize the distrust that arises from those antagonisms, and to check and balance them. Madisonian distrust and the energy that comes from competing interests rubbing against one another have often been thought of as the source of the great, American, industrial and political machine. This political ideal has been extended beyond the realm of government, to relationships within industry and between business and labor. The worry now is that the friction is finally wearing through and crippling the machine of industry and state.

If friction is the metaphor that dominates our self-discourse, harmony, or what the Japanese call *"wa,"* is the metaphor that controls Japanese discourse. Thomas Rohlen's book, *For Harmony and Strength*, took its title from the motto of the Japanese bank which he studied; it described the way this firm becomes the center of its employees' lives both on the job and at home. *Wa* requires that conflicting identities be brought into line, and that problems be resolved within the framework of the group. The importance of *wa* in Japan indicates that the sharp line that Americans seek to maintain between public and private, work and family, is blurred by the Japanese, and it is often difficult to tell "where group or public life ends and where private life begins."[9]

Yet *wa* is not simply coordinating behavior to accomplish a task determined outside the group, nor is it a bloodless, static set of hierarchical relationships that cannot accommodate human needs and feelings. It is, as Rohlen defines it, "A quality of relationship, particularly within the working group, and it refers to the cooperation, trust, sharing, warmth, morale and hard work of efficient, pleasant and purposeful fellowship."[10] Rohlen likens it to teamwork, but the concepts are not quite the same. As one author on Japanese baseball put it: "If you ask a Japanese manager what he considers the most important ingredient of a winning team, he would most likely answer '*wa*.' If you asked him how to knock a team's *wa* awry, he would most likely say, 'Hire an American.' "[11] However, American baseball players are not, as a group, generally short on teamwork. *Wa* and teamwork intersect but they are not the same.

Wa involves more than coordinating individual activity to achieve a common goal—the ideal of teamwork. It also involves the insertion of the company and its goals into what we would consider the private and emotional lives of its members. And it requires members to come to share a common history and sense of obligation and respect. In the bank that Rohlen studied, members were "often reminded that the present state of Uedagin [the name of the bank] development . . . is the result of the efforts and sacrifices of previous generations. These predecessors are in the position of ancestors . . . and to them a great debt of gratitude and respect is owed by all who presently benefit from their efforts."[12]

This message, which is communicated to new members through initiation ceremonies, as well as in day-to-day contact with more senior members, is intended to establish an identity with the firm. This identity is much deeper and stronger than that implied by our concept of "teamwork." It roots the company in the same system of respect, obligation, and obedience that holds traditional families together, and, through the company, members are taught that they advance the social well-being by serving its specific need. The company has more than an instrumental purpose, and its members are taught to relate to it in more than instrumental ways.

With the increase in part-time and temporary employees, the practices that Rohlen describes are becoming strained, but they still reflect important components of the Japanese identity. Few Americans employed by sizable companies relate to the firm in this organic way. We frequently separate who we are from where we work, and feel it inappropriate to be reminded of the sacrifices others made in building the firm or told that we should be grateful for their past efforts. It is even difficult for parents or schools to convey such messages, because to do so seems to tread on individual autonomy and choice, and thus to violate a cherished notion of equality.

We tie individuality, equality, and independence together into a tight and tidy bundle. Our individuality depends on being equal with others and independent of any ties that we do not choose for ourselves. In other words, our identity as individuals depends on being able to do what we want to do—not what we are told to do. And this ability requires a loose set of obligations whose renewal is continually renegotiated. Marriage and careers are both subject to this loose binding, and the ability to change both serves as the condition for independence. We are most free when we are able to express that which is most truly our independent selves. Yet to some Japanese, this looks less like freedom and more like an impossible burden. As one highly respected Japanese scholar writes, commenting on our *Declaration of Independence:*

> It is in fact highly doubtful that all people are created equal, and even if they are, it still remains to be asked just how they are equal. Rather, it is fair to suggest that Americans promote equality precisely because of what is in fact an extremely naive belief in universal equality as self-evident truth. It is in this belief that a uniquely American optimism manifests itself, and it is this belief that provides the groundwork for American-style individualism. If everyone is equal, then each individual must make his or her own way, relying on nothing but his or her own ability. No one else, not even parents can be depended on.[13]

Although this description overstates the reality, it is an approximation of the ideal. It is the reason postmodernism is perceived by the Right as such a threat. It enables a weakening of traditional norms and concepts by doing no more than showing that they are social constructs. Individualism may, as de Toqueville once argued, lead to a longing for comformity, but he should have added that it will not allow conformity to rest comfortably once it has been revealed for what it is. The Japanese have an easier time with a socially situated identity, and many would likely find the "insights" of the postmodern rather humdrum. What, after all, is there in this world that is not a social construct?

Many commentators believe that the crucial difference between

Japanese and Western identity is to be found in the difference between a situational and a principled morality. If accurate, the difference indicates more than the simple idea that the Japanese make their moral judgments in terms of the interests and opinions of the group, and that we Americans seek more universal grounds for our moral decisions. It indicates a difference in what is accepted as the object of a moral decision, and it reveals the conceptual difficulty that the Western ideal of individualism must face. An example can illustrate the issue.

An older Confucian scholar asked a Western acquaintance if he could help him understand his youngest son's odd and disturbing behavior. His son had just finished his first year at the university, and after taking a course in Western philosophy he came home "babbling about the authority of reason and announced that he would no longer simply obey his father but would follow his own rational understanding of what is right." He would, of course follow his father's orders whenever they accorded with the rational thing to do, but otherwise reason was his new authority. The father asked the Westerner how he would manage such a disrespectful son. The Westerner responded he would hesitate to count it as disrespect because he did not believe that one person needed to obey another person in order to respect him. The father was bewildered and speechless.

The Westerner may not understand that it is the disengagement of respect and obedience that is the father's problem. The father rejects the idea that there is a single, abstract, universal standard that can be used to make impartial judgments about right and wrong. It is not that he objects to considering different reasons for a certain course of action. He is not stubborn and is often persuaded to change his mind. Certainly reasons have their place—but not the cold, abstract, objectless "reason" that his son pronounced. Reason must have a beneficiary—it must have an object. What is the object of this "reason"? Who is its beneficiary? Is it some abstraction like "mankind," and how does that abstraction serve to settle specific disagreements between different groups of people? He suspects that the object of this reason is his own son and his growing ego. The evidence is not just *what* the son said. It is that he said it at all—that he was willing to challenge the unity of the family and to set himself apart from its authority without so much as discussing the matter first. Respect involves obedience because it affirms the importance of the family as the object of concern and deliberation, and it acknowledges the father's experience in upholding the traditional values of the family.

For the father, respect, loyalty and commitment are what hold a family and a community of families together. Without these communities and the families that comprise them, "mankind" and "universal reason" are just empty abstractions. It seems that his son has chosen to give up family and community for "reason." But then just what is the grounding of reason? What goals does it work for? Whose interests does it serve? If *I* am reason's ultimate seat of authority, then how can I come to respect others and to serve communal goals? The modern Western tradition, and especially its embodiment in American civilization, has largely avoided this issue, believing that progress requires changes in traditional patterns of thought and behavior, and that obedience and respect can be decoupled. And while neither Confucianism nor tradition-minded fathers nor authoritarian families have the influence in Japan today that they once had, the ties between rationality and community remain strong.

VII. The Lost Community

Once we see the individual as the seat of rationality, then just how do we assure collective action when such action is needed? The practical answer, as Alasdair MacIntyre has critically noted,[14] has been to separate moral rationality from technical rationality, placing the first in the hands of the individual and the second in the jurisdiction of the bureaucracy. Thus each individual is allowed her own council regarding right and wrong, while bureaucratic institutions are given responsibility for mobilizing collective action in industry and government. This approach works as long as bureaucratic decisions are accepted as amoral and as long as people allow institutional experts to determine what is and what is not a private, moral issue. As some of the consequences of collective action become prominent—environmental depletion, weapons of mass destruction, campaigns of genocide—the separation between moral and technical rationality, between individual morality and collective action, is increasingly difficult to maintain. Yet the Western intellectual tradition has few resources for bridging the gap that is created between an appeal to the individual's self-interest and action which is in the interest of the larger community.

The most prominent response to this gap serves as the foundation for capitalism. It was Adam Smith who argued that a kind of invisible hand allowed all our most self-serving actions to work for the betterment of the group. Yet to the extent that Smith's formulation was accepted by his contemporaries, it was not because greed is the mother of all good things, but because he could assume a community with a shared set of ethical definitions and moral norms.[15] Smith elaborated the principles of capitalism in his course on political economy, the second of the two courses that he taught while occupying the Chair of Moral Philosophy at the University of Glasgow. The first was the course on moral philosophy.

While he argued the controversial thesis that greed served the common good, the nature of that good—the quality of the human virtues— or the moral value of virtues such as benevolence, went without questioning. Underlying Smith's statements about the intrinsic relation between self-serving and other-serving was a strong sense of the community of humankind. Hence while opening a door for self-directed action, he knew exactly where he wanted that door to lead— to a world of mutual regard and well-being.[16] And he believed that reason would truly take us there. Contemplating the reasoning of a man faced with the loss of his little finger he asks whether,

> To prevent . . . this paltry misfortune to himself, would a man of humanity be willing to sacrifice the lives of a hundred millions of his brethren, provided he had never seen them? Human nature startles with horror at the thought, and the world, in its greatest depravity and corruption, never produced such a villain as could be capable of entertaining it. . . . It is not the soft power of humanity, it is not that feeble spark of benevolence which Nature has lighted up in the human heart, that is thus capable of counteracting the strongest impulse of self-love. It is a stronger power, a more forcible motive, which exerts itself upon such occasions. It is reason, principle, conscience, the inhabitant of the breast, the man within, the great judge and arbiter of our conduct. . . . It is he who, whenever we are about to act so as to affect the happiness of others, calls to us, with a voice capable of distinguishing the most presumptuous of our passions, that we are but one of the multitude, in no respect better than any other in it.[17]

Reason, for Smith, is thereby grounded in our common understanding about the proper behavior toward our fellow human beings.

After the human-made catastrophes of this century and the genocidal destruction of hundreds of millions of people, it is impossible to share Smith's optimism. Yet it is useful to remember that the inventor of capitalism worked with a belief in a set of shared norms. By placing these norms in the breast of each individual rather than in the shared understanding of a community, he provided the leverage that individual entrepreneurs needed to break free from established religious constraints. In other words, human nature places a limit on self-interest and therefore we need not distrust individual initiative. Yet if, as is likely the case, what Smith saw as human nature was the result of a certain kind of community affiliation, then contemporary Western society has the opposite problem—to harness initiative to a renewed but expanded communal identity. Ironically, while Smith worked to free individuality from communal bonds, it was those very same bonds that enabled him to believe that an individuality so freed would enhance the common good.

Without such communal bonds it is difficult to know what reasons would compel otherwise autonomous individuals to act for the good of the community. Smith assumed a shared community of shared meanings, values, and interpretations which we cannot assume. Without such a community, we are left with a society of individual choosers whom we hope will see a congruence between their interests and the interests of the group. Conservatives sense this flaw and believe that it belongs only to the cultural "anarchism" of liberalism. They believe that selling more television sets, VCRs, and automobiles (hopefully American) is in everyone's interest, and hence they seek to fuse together the new capitalism with the new patriotism. Yet patriotism cannot contain capitalism and new interpretive forms—new modes of identity are arising.

VIII. Conceptions of Self and Community

The ideal of community—of people working together to accomplish a common end ready to serve individual members in time of need— is a part of the American psyche and is memorialized in images of town meetings, community barn raisings, and immigrant self-help groups. These images represent a central feature of the American ideal—one where individuals voluntarily come together for mutual aid and enrichment. We are individuals first and as individuals we create communities. The images are reformulations of the social contract. When we create communities, we do so out of our own desires, and in reaching out to others we are to be commended. Yet precisely because we are first individuals who may choose or not choose to be members of communities—it is thought that we should suffer no approbation should we choose not to engage with others in a communal context. As long as we pay our taxes and obey the law we are meeting our obligations. This is the minimal notion of citizenship, but as the minimal notion it is also often seen as a sufficient one—anything more is viewed as intrusive and in danger of violating individual rights. Given this conception of the individual, just why anyone should actually choose to take up membership in a large community is somewhat unclear, but presumably it has to do with long-term material goals and a need for companionship.

There are a number of problems with this conception of self and community. First, social contract theory may be a useful theoretical device for justifying certain forms of institutional power, but it is not a very comprehensive account of what actually happens between individuals and their communities. There are no social individuals who stand in some fashion outside of groups deciding whether or not to take up membership in them. We are born into social configurations and our choices are reflections of those configurations. We choose as members of groups, not as isolated, dispassionate individuals; my membership already influences the kind of alternatives I accept as true choices. Contrary to the post modern image depicted earlier, if I am born poor, Black, and female, it may be difficult to see medicine or law as truly a choice for me. I choose from the point of view of a social position and not from the point of view of an isolated individual.

A second problem involves the recent failure of traditional individualism to provide the intellectual foundation for a conception of cultural freedom. Traditional individualism was intended to liberate people from the economic and political constraints of established authority. One of the real insights of postmodernism is the recognition that traditional individualism has little to do with the need for cultural expression and serves in modern times to support institutions that repress lifestyles that are out of step with the drive for collective economic action. The increase in corporate codes, the constant testing of children to determine their future ability to work in the corporate sector, the increasing criminalization of drug use, and the encouragement of "the vague sense that each of one's actions today *might* form part of a record that *might* be used for or against one in the future— these signify a *regularized* politics of normalization through observational judgment and anticipatory self-policing."[18] With the institutionalization of general repressive measures, and the "self-policing" features of *voluntary* choice, the repressive possibilities of individualism are revealed.

A third problem with traditional individualism is that it treats the self as basically fixed and essentially uneducable. Individual wants are reduced to the desire to seek pleasure and avoid pain; hence all individuals can be motivated through the manipulation of appropriate external stimuli. What an individual wants, however, is essentially unconnected to what that individual is. All individuals are seen as essentially the same: they seek to maximize satisfaction or, in some theories, to minimize dissatisfaction. Self-understanding is largely restricted to knowing what kinds of objects will achieve this end[19] and whether one has the drive, ability, and desire needed to acquire these objects. This view of the self is responsible for the unfortunate doctrine of the fixed nature of intelligence that dominated educational research for much of this century. More important, however, it reflects the doctrine of the fixed self that assumes selfhood is essentially independent of community. Yet one can also see in this doctrine some of the very characteristics of Americans—especially students and workers—that have drawn the most criticism from liberals and conservatives alike. Students, it is said, study what they are interested in rather than what the nation needs. Workers care only for their paycheck and are indifferent to the quality of their work. Whether the criticisms are accurate or not, what they see is certainly not inconsistent with the view of selfhood and community implicit in Western notions of individualism.

The Japanese appear to offer a communal conception of the self, where individual efforts are self-consciously related to the wider social consensus, and where individual expression and desire are contained by communal norms. In contrast to Western conceptions of self and community, the boundaries between selves within a given community are relatively weak, whereas the boundaries between different groups are quite strong. It is, according to the Japanese scholar, Takie Lebra, a conception of self where belonging is a stronger value than independence, where collective coherence is valued and uniqueness is not,[20] and where the boundaries between my self and my group are largely open and fluid. It is a self that is especially sensitive to other human beings, and is preoccupied with social relationships.[21] This means, among other things, that the Japanese are likely to reject strong judgments of right and wrong, and to distribute responsibility among a number of different actors.

For example, Lebra tells us that "The Japanese tend to hold everyone involved in a conflict responsible for it. The Anglo-American compulsion for a court trial that determines one party to be guilty and another innocent is in remarkable contrast to the Japanese ideal that mutual apology and compromise be attained between the parties."[22] The Japanese thereby tend to soften judgments and their morality emphasizes compassion and tolerance arising because human frailty requires tolerance and compassion.[23] Empathizing with the suffering of others especially when the suffering is undertaken—as is the case with one's mother—to benefit one's self, is a cardinal virtue.[24]

This empathy is used by corporations to deepen the loyalty of their employees. Yet it would be a mistake to assume that the new employees are simply being brainwashed to obey the orders of a single, unyielding authority. Although relations are indeed hierarchical, and great significance is given to status, authority is relatively diffuse and "the authority holder is no more autonomous than those subject to him."[25] This is borne out by descriptions of the slow and arduous process of consensus-building that takes place in many Japanese industries among people of different rank.

IX. Identity and Social Reproduction

Radical educational scholars have often viewed identity issues as arising from structural features of the workplace, features which they believe are largely fixed by the requirements of capitalist society.[26] Radicals differ somewhat on whether or not schoolteachers and students are simply passive recipients of the structural requirements of capitalism, or whether they actually speak back and offer resistance to their assigned roles.[27] Whatever position one takes on this issue, there is general agreement within this group of scholars that capitalism requires more or less acquiescent, passive workers at the lower end of the occupational hierarchy. This they see as a requirement of capitalism itself, and they see little hope of changing things under capitalist economic systems.

This may be so, but the image presented of the Japanese workplace, an image in which workers are given responsibility for improving quality, where group participation is encouraged, and where consensus-building is emphasized, implies that there is a new, more active role for the worker, even under capitalism—indeed, necessitated by capitalism. If this image is accurate, and if one believes that the school's role is to create the future work force, then it would appear that both the reproduction theorists and the resistance theorists need to reexamine their positions. The optimistic capitalist would say that capitalism itself is now the engine for progressive change, not just economic change but social and educational change as well. Is the optimistic capitalist right?

To those concerned with improving efficiency, productivity, and quality, the Japanese seem to have opened a new chapter in industrial relations, providing a more skilled and cooperative work force. To those concerned with democratic process, the Japanese seem to provide an outlet for group decision and participation. While few argue that we can or should adopt the practices of Japanese schools or industry wholesale, many believe that there is much that we can be learned from Japanese education. The intent of some of the following chapters is to explore that belief and to examine whether and how the Japanese experience is compatible with improving American education, industry and democracy. Yet this is not a book about Japan. It is about our identities as Americans, and the direction that education and work may play in reconstituting and reproducing those identities.

I have chosen our recent discourse on Japan as a way to open up a discussion about the conception of education that would make sense for us. Japan is not, it seems, encumbered by an Asian version of the American individualism. Japanese images of nature, and of people's place in nature, tend to be harmonious and friendly. The landscapes are tame—the mountains, streams, and rivers are inviting, the gardens manicured, and even the carp in the ponds are trained to come when called by a hand clap. The guiding philosophy of Confucianism emphasizes a system of obligations, obedience, and duty, where a natural harmony is presumed and where the achievement of a similar harmony is the goal of all social relationships. Its guiding belief systems, Buddhism and Shintoism, speak to the family of the Japanese nation and to its unity with the natural order of things. Identity is easy because membership in the group is so important. It is not "the squeaky wheel that gets the oil." It is rather "the nail that stands out," in the words of a famous Japanese saying, "that gets hammered in." The Japanese are a people shaped by centuries of tradition.

Of course without the recent economic success of the Japanese, these qualities would hardly attract notice. They would remain but the quaint characteristics of a far-off and exotic land. However, the Japanese have been successful, and it is easy to see in that success our own failures—our diminished ability to compete and our fragile self-identity. We know that we cannot in any way be Japanese, and yet we see in the Japanese some kind of sign, as vague as it may be, of our own lost possibilities. The success of Japanese students, their single-minded pursuit of academic achievement, and their unquestioning acceptance of their identity as Japanese are taken to explain their country's emergence from the "dustheap" of a defeated nation to the status of an economic superpower. This image of the Japanese has served to clarify for many the aims that should govern the American school—academic achievement for international competition, and the development of a unified national identity. These two goals have become the focus of educational thought in the United States. The first—education for international competition—is the concern of what

I call the economic conservatives. The second, education for national identity, is the concern of the cultural conservatives. It is the purpose of remaining chapters to examine these goals within the context of the requirements of a democracy in a multicultural age.

Because its traditions are so different from our own and because it has provided much of the reason for the renewed interest in schools in this country, Japan can be an important component in this reexamination, providing a clearer sense of our own considered reactions to a tradition that is more collective than our own, but that sees itself as no less committed to democratic values.

2

Japan and the
American Quest for Moral Authority

I. Introduction: Moral Authority

Classical Western individualism has a credibility problem when it comes to the question of moral authority. We are told that authority is moral when it guides action by impartial, universal principles—principles which one is willing to apply to oneself as well as to others.[1] We are also told that for an authority to be moral it must be chosen freely without coercion or indoctrination. To act morally means to respect the basic autonomy and independence of individuals. This means that each one of us is to be allowed to act out of our own understanding of the good, even if that understanding places our own individual interests above all those of others.

The problem with this common formulation is that it fails to explain how moral education can take place. If, as Western individualism assumes, we all act out of self-interest, then how do we ever come to accept the authority of impartial, moral principles, principles which are moral precisely because they are indifferent to self-interest? If a teacher convinces a child to be generous because "a favor given is a favor returned," then she is teaching the child to do the right thing, but for the wrong reason. She is teaching the child to be generous to others because it will eventually benefit oneself. The child who is given to skepticism and doubt has no reason then to act morally. If, however, the teacher asks the child to do the right thing because it is "the right thing to do" or because "it will help another person," she is assuming the child is already morally motivated and hence needs no fundamental moral education. Granted the child may need to learn some relevant information. To be honest, she will need to know who owns what; to be brave, she will need to know what danger involves, and to be truthful, she will need to understand the facts of the case. However, this is technical, not moral knowledge.

Another problem with the traditional formulation is that it does not capture everything that we mean by "being moral." We expect moral people to do the right thing for the right reason, but we expect more than that. We also expect them to care about doing the right thing, and to identify the needs of others with their own. The wisdom of Solomon in the story about two women who each claimed to be the mother of a single child is not in the application of the "right" principle. It is in using "the right principle" to discover who cared *merely* about principle and who really cared about the *child*. Solomon acted wisely because he chose the person who was acting morally. That is he chose the person who cared about the well-being of the child.

No matter what traditional moralists tell us, our idea of morality is not encompassed by the image of an impartial, machine-like judge rendering morally right decisions with computerlike accuracy. We expect our moral authorities to have links with us through their identification as members of a common community. We worry when we think these links are in a state of disrepair, but we are also uncertain about how far it is appropriate to go in repairing a fraying moral chain.

The problem of disrepair is perhaps more acute in societies like the United States, where philosophical individualism was developed without the overlay of shared norms. De Toqueville, writing from the standpoint of declining aristocratic society, observed the danger of American individualism, and its potential for encouraging neglect of the public sphere—albeit, one governed by elite norms—as the dilemma of American democracy. In his classic *Democracy in America*, he defines individualism as a "mature and calm feeling, which disposes each member of the community to sever himself from the mass of his fellows . . . so that after he has thus formed a little circle of his own, he willingly leaves society at large to himself."[2] Individualism, he tells us, "saps the virtue of public life."[3]

II. The Quest for Moral Authority

Japan is forcing Americans to face the possibility that individualism is an inadequate foundation for moral development. For example, in a front page article entitled "Profile of Today's Youth: Many Just Don't

Seem to Care," *The New York Times* described the reaction of a young clerk in Columbus, Ohio to a radio report of a flood in southeastern Ohio, and the heavy loss of life and property that resulted: "The cashier looked up at the radio and said: 'I wish they'd stop talking about it. I'm sick of hearing about it.' "[4] The item is newsworthy precisely because it highlights the dangers of extreme individualism—the complete absorption with oneself and the inability to identify with a larger community. To the *Times* reporter, this response reflected a more pervasive attitude of indifference toward public affairs among youth between the ages of eighteen to twenty-nine. Quoting a recent survey on the attitudes of youth, the *Times* notes that it is a generation that "knows less, cares less, votes less, and is less critical of its leaders and institutions than young people in the past." While the claim that young people care less today than they did in the past may be challenged, the indifference to the public good described in the article is an example of the tendency de Tocqueville worried about.

We may disapprove of the young clerk's indifference, but there is little that a commitment to individualism enables us to say about it. As individualists we believe that each of us has the right to think and feel as we will, and we are reluctant to impose on others a set of public values, partly because we are unwilling to license them to impose a different set of values on us. We want others to be motivated by appeals to the needs of others and to the public good, but it is often easier to motivate one another through appeals to self-interest.

Japan has become an object of envy partly because we believe that it has found a way to connect people to one another in the service of a larger public good. It seems to supply the communal force that we worry our own brand of individualism lacks. This belief is reflected in some of the opinions expressed when I interviewed community members in a town where a large Japanese factory was about to be built. Predictably, reactions are mixed. "The Japanese bring more jobs," but "they also strain the community resources." "Revenues are increased," but then "so too are expenditures." "They were once our enemy" but "let bygones be bygones."

The most interesting response is the view "that the Japanese were arriving to give Americans back their commitment to the work ethic." Some recall a time when "American products were the best in the world," and believe that the decline in American workmanship is a sign of a larger decline in our sense of community. Some blame American industry and the indifference of the American company to its workers. Others blame workers and the litigious nature of contemporary American society. Yet a common theme among most was a nostalgic sense for a lost community of work. A political leader spoke of an older America where people worked together. He recalled an earlier farming era where, if a hardship occurred, say if someone broke a leg, he would not feel it was automatically his boss's fault or that compensation was necessarily due him. He observed "those are the kinds of things that I think personally we had traditionally with Americans fifty or sixty years ago, we have kind of been slipping away from but the Japanese will help restore it through our working force." Here the Japanese company is accepted as the moral savior bringing back the very values that we "exported" to Japan after the war. Yet these are not the values of individualism. The problem of America's lack of competitiveness when compared to the Japanese is seen as a problem of community.

Sam Herman is a training officer for a government-supported job program. He believes that the Japanese companies have a greater concern for the well-being and happiness of their workers. And in expressing this belief he describes the moral force that he attributes to a community of caring workers and managers.

> The Japanese philosophy is that it takes all of us to build a product, to be proud of that product, to have the quality of that product [as a high priority] so that we can all go on for many years building it and we'll all be happy. They want that guy on the line, the lowest paid individual out there, to be as concerned about quality and making a good product. It sounds like sure, doesn't everyone understand that, but I'm not so sure that really takes place today in America. I'm not sure whether the guy who puts the nuts and bolts on things really cares about whether someone buys another one. The Japanese philosophy is if you do your job, we'll keep you for life and you'll work your way up in the company. I keep hearing the Japanese keep talking about harmony of the workplace and that is really what they are talking about. We want people who will be happy working for us. Have you ever heard anyone [in America] caring whether the workers are happy? We don't talk here about happy workers. We want to know if they are here or not here. We don't talk about whether the workers are happy. [The Japanese] don't want anyone who is not happy and being happy is being totally involved. (brackets mine)

Herman spoke nostalgically of his father, who, he said, had worked for a large corporation throughout his life, never complaining about the company, and feeling that its advancement was his own as well:

My Dad worked for [a large national company] for forty-two years. I don't think that you are going to see too many people in my generation and in the generation after me working for a company for forty-two years or even twenty-two years. My dad always felt that as long as he did a good job, he felt very certain that the company would never let him go. You know he had that harmonious feeling about the company. He always believed, and maybe this was just my dad, but he always believed that when something went wrong at a location that he was at, that it wasn't the company. The company was going to take care of him. It was that supervisor of his that screwed him up, someone that wasn't following company policy. He believed that the company's policies were super and proved it a couple of times, astonishingly. I mean he went to the home office and said, "hey, I've been here twenty-five or thirty years and this is what they are trying to do to me and is this right?" And . . . people said "no, that's not right." He believed in that philosophy. I don't hear that anymore. *(brackets mine)*

To Herman, the modern American corporation fails to provide workers with the security that they once expected. The result is a lessened identification with the corporation and a diminished loyalty. The Japanese company would rebuild the lost community of work and provide a new moral education. In this community people will be reunited with one another through their involvement with work and their commitment to quality.

Herman's sense of history is somewhat distorted. In the union hall where the factory's construction workers meet is a large mural commemorating a long and bitter industrial strike that could have taken place around the time that his father was "happily" working for the company. Nevertheless, the values Herman projects onto the past are those that minimize abstract formal principle and emphasize the importance of familial virtues such as benevolence, harmony, and benign paternalism. It is these values that he sees the Japanese bringing with them to his community.

To others, the Japanese would not only bring familial virtues into the factory, they would also bring them back into the home. For some mothers, the Japanese would provide a model for parents to reestablish control over their children. Moral authority is not the authority of abstract principle. It is the authority that is exhibited when a child obeys a parent because of the essential trust entailed in the parent-child relationship. To mothers, the problem with American workmanship is but another instance of this lost trust:

> For example, when I ask my son to wipe the table before supper, he asks me where the cloth is, what do I do, etc. He has to be told everything before he can do it. [The Japanese children I have known] took the cloth and wiped the table the best [they] could. My son would take the cloth and barely scrapes the top and finds nothing wrong with it.

Another mother adds that Japanese products are of superior quality, because they all try their best. "I have been having problems with the ironing board. I have been trying for a new ironing board but haven't come across one that is decent. And I am not talking about cheap products. And the iron, a Sunbeam iron, which costs more than you wish to pay for an iron, drips and it takes forever to get hot." As with Herman, these mothers felt that the Japanese would reteach Americans the lost work ethic.

Both Herman and the mothers conceive the work ethic as a communal product. It is more than simply a way to gain a profit or to reestablish American industry as number one. At issue is the need to reestablish the connectedness which Americans once felt but which they feel no more. For them, work should be a way to connect oneself to a larger community. In Herman's eyes, work is an expression of mutuality and care that should exist between worker and company. To the mothers, work is the moral link between themselves as consumers and the producer. It is an expression of moral character.

Clearly, these visions are informed by distorted memory and incomplete information. They overlook the bitter struggle between union and management that occurred when men like Herman's father were working, and they neglect the fact that Japanese irons are likely to be assembled in Mexico or China. Nevertheless, the idea of community and connectedness is a powerful educational ideal, one which American individualism has difficulty legitimating either in the school or in the workplace.

III. Individualism and the Limits of Rationality

Some of the most significant and popular academic books have recently decried the overemphasis on individualism and have called for a commitment to more communal goals. For example, the philosopher Alasdair MacIntyre argues that our radical individualism has left us bereft of a shared communal language that can be used to resolve moral and ethical disputes. In place of a moral community we rely either on bureaucratic morality, which emphasizes efficiency in the service of arbitrary ends, or on therapeutic morality and its stress on what "feels good." While a sense of individuality may be intensified because we are no longer confined by the traditional roles of a communal-based morality, we have lost the capacity to engage in a reasoned moral discourse.[5]

MacIntyre contrasts this modern version of morality and self with the way in which he believes identity was established in traditional society. In such societies different roles carried with them specific obligations, and it was through these roles that a person's identity was established. Once established, a person's action could be judged by an entire community because the community recognized and sustained the standards appropriate to a given role. The soldier who runs from battle, the captain who abandons ship, the father who leaves the family for another woman, fail morally because they fail in meeting the responsibilities entailed in their role. In taking on a role, they have made a promise to fulfill the virtues appropriate to it. In rejecting the virtues they have broken the promise. In contrast, modern Western society separates the individual from her role, making morality an act of conscience, not a consensual understanding of the community. In doing this, according to MacIntyre, the individual becomes the sole arbiter of standards and the sustainer of her own identity.

For MacIntyre the problem rests with our idea of rationality itself. We wrongly hold rationality to be tradition-free, and we ground it in a recently developed, Enlightenment conception of the individual. This means that individuals have special insight into right and wrong, and that the purity of the individual conscience is the important factor in determining the virtue of action. Values and virtues are therefore a matter of want, and desire and reason are left to address the best and most efficient means to achieve these values. Once we reduce morality to the simple desires of individuals, and view reason as their servant, then moral authority becomes problematic. It is either an arbitrary expression of a deeper power motive, or it is rooted in a single expression of human nature that is knowable through science and predictable and manipulable through scientific methods and bureaucratic structures. In either case, individualism leaves us in a situation in which "moral authority" is not moral. For MacIntyre morality—the real morality—is communally anchored in tradition.

MacIntyre's philosophical thesis was developed by Robert Bellah[6] and his colleagues in a book on American society in which they argued that many Americans long for communal ties, but that this longing is submerged by our public affirmation of individualism. While we want to belong and to be acknowledged as members of communities, our language of justification is individualistic, and this influences the way in which we understand communal relations and the reasons why we enter them.

While the American mothers in my interview complained about the loss of their own moral authority, such separation is one of the important values of American life and contrasts significantly with the more familial Japanese. In this country, the loss of the parent's moral authority is a part of the preparation for the separation of the child from the parent's home and one of the nightmares of many Americans is that their children (or later, their parents) will return home to live. Americans are expected to leave home and, as Bellah and his colleagues point out, much of childhood is preparation for doing so.[7] An emphasis on self-reliance and independence is at the core of the experience of growing up for many people, and the sign of adulthood is a reexamination of one's basic commitments and choosing new ones. Hence, as Bellah relates, Americans are expected to choose their church, their spouse, their career, their life-style, and their sexual orientation and to do so with considerable distance and independence from the choices of their parents or their community.[8] In contrast, Japanese are expected to live at home or, in the case of corporate employees, in a company dormitory, until they are married, and it is still not unusual to have three generations living in one household. Given the material living conditions in Japan, it is not surprising that the values of the family or of the workplace continue to have a strong moral force.

The Japanese orientation to connectedness and to communal ties—especially in the workplace—highlights our own commitment to individualism and independent choice. The contrast is sharpened precisely because the valued commercial outcomes of individualism—efficiency, productivity, ingenuity, and so on—now appear to be uncomfortably more closely related to Japanese collectivism. If there is, as MacIntyre and Bellah suggest, an underlying longing for community and a need for the moral values that communal commitments entail, the Japanese success has certainly increased our awareness of it, but it is unlikely that commercial success has created the need.

IV. The Possibility of Moral Incommensurability

The philosopher Ludwig Wittgenstein created a figure he called the duck/rabbit to illustrate the influence of different points of view on the perceptual "fact." When looked at one way, the figure forms a duck with an elongated beak. When looked at another way, the beak becomes ears and the figure turns into a rabbit. Something quite similar happens when we look at moral authority and the situation of Japan. Sam Herman and the community mothers see the Japanese as more moral, because they believe the Japanese have a strong sense of community and feel mutually responsible to one another. They do not especially feel that the morality of the Japanese is essentially different from our own. We are both ducks or we are both rabbits, but the Japanese are not a duck to our rabbit. This provides a largely optimistic view—American morality is repairable and the Japanese have come to show us how to make the needed repairs.

Although MacIntyre himself is pessimistic about the degree to which the fiber of American morality can be restitched, his ideas lend themselves to a certain conception of education that stresses shared symbols and values. If American students are all taught the same stories, presented the same heroes, and provided with the same information, our moral life would be renewed.[9]

Sam Herman, together with the community mothers, expresses a need for stronger communal forms of social life, believing that the Japanese can lead the way by shining the light on our own communal past. Yet in truth, the Japanese likely express the limits involved in unreflectively grafting one conception of morality onto another, and any search for renewal will need to understand this limit. The difference begins with a different conception of the boundaries between self and other.

Within the Japanese conception of community, there is more at stake than people like Herman or the mothers realize. Our own way of life places limits on our ability to appreciate and accept strong communal forms. For example, even MacIntyre fails to realize just how much his role-based traditionalism reflects a strong individualism. True, virtues accrue to role and roles are the reflection of a communal consensus, but responsibility is still allocated to individual roles and those who occupy them. This simply reiterates the basic assumption of individualism, only it does so by clothing each individual in a suit of role-embroidered virtues. The role is the thing and somehow these roles, when functioning properly, congeal to form a unified community.[10] The community endures because there is a common basis of rationality that all people can accept. It does not endure, however, because anyone consciously seeks to care for it. MacIntyre's is a communitarian view, but it is still a relatively weak one—based still on Western individualistic premises.

Consider the following as an alternative. On a visit to a well-regarded Japanese public university, I was told by my host, a bright, young, highly visible, internationally known scholar, that he had been approached informally by the head of the department at another, more prestigious university concerning his possible interest in a position. The approach was informal and I was asked to keep the news confidential for a while because the university making the offer had not yet contacted the associate professor's present dean in order to inquire about the hardship such a move might present for his college. The practice—which is more than symbolic—represents a concern for the organization and a recognition that all of the parties involved— the professor, the department head, and the dean—have a reciprocal and collective responsibility. What is striking is the extent to which the different parties accepted responsibility for maintaining the communal relations of the group. This way of acting requires that the group be seen as somewhat more than a means to one's own individual ends, or even, in MacIntyre's terms, that individuals be fulfilling roles that are grounded in a shared set of values. It requires that there be a mutual acknowledgment of the structures that maintain these values.

This is not to say that Americans do not conform to group norms. It is rather to suggest that the conception of conformity may have a different meaning in the two societies. For Americans, one conforms to that which is not an immediate and spontaneous expression of self. If, however, the self is constituted through the group—as the Japanese see it—then it is hard to understand just what conformity means. If a consensus truly grows out of a group in which one fully identifies, then is conformity even possible?

Americans may have some connection with this conception of the group when it comes to clubs or family, but for many workers, according to Bellah and his colleagues, the workplace is fundamentally instrumental. At least for many educated, middle-class men and women it has become, as Bellah and his colleagues note, the place where a person can fulfill his or her individual potential.

> The demand to "make something of yourself" through work is one that Americans coming of age hear as often from themselves as from others. . . . Work traces one's progress through life by achievement and advancement in an occupation.[11]

Realizing one's potential means moving beyond others, separating from them and excelling beyond them. Bellah and his colleagues use one of their subjects, Brian, to illustrate the instrumental character of work and the way in which our language about work has been separated from a sense of social responsibility.

> Brian's definition of success revolves around an open-ended career on the upswing, empty of a calling's sense of social responsibility. "I want to keep progressing to the point where I remain challenged," he testifies. "Where I come as close as I can to performing at the absolute limits of my capacity. That's success." That is also the voice of a utilitarian seeking its separate identity in the exercise of its own growing powers, ever freer of restraints by others and ever farther out in front of them.[12]

Of course there are many jobs that do not have the characteristics of a career, and where growth and challenge do not exist. In such cases the workplace is even more of an instrument serving not one's potential, but one's daily material needs.

The different ways of conceiving the relationship between self and other is reflected in the work situation of Japan and the United States. For example, Americans would find some of the questions asked by Japanese personnel officers—such as whether one is an eldest son— overly intrusive, an inappropriate transgression on one's private life. Nevertheless, this is an important issue for a Japanese company, for if there is anything that can compete with the hold of the company on the individual worker in Japan, it is the responsibility involved in being an eldest son living with one's parents; companies may probe into the private lives of prospective employees to avoid potential conflicts. Once a person is hired into a major company and given the status of lifetime employment, the company begins to incorporate that person into its community, its philosophy, and its history and symbols system. Rohlin describes this process as it occurred in the Japanese bank that he studied: "Uedagin, for example, is not regarded in everyday thought as primarily a legal entity or a complex money-making machine, but more as a community of people organized to secure their common livelihood."[13] Some companies even have a common grave where employees may be buried,[14] and on a questionnaire, seven out of ten employees listed the company as at least equal to or more important than their personal life.[15]

> Membership, therefore, means sharing in the community of interests and endeavor. When a person enters the bank as a member, he discards his independence . . . and accepts the burdens of responsibility as a participant. It is also understood that in return Uedagin assumes the position of provider for the individual's

security and welfare in the face of whatever problems may arise. This general agreement, lacking detail and specifications, is implicit. It is the actions of both parties that illustrate it, and it is their actions that over time confirm or deny it, preserve or destroy it. This is obviously different from the usual contractual relationship found in most Western employment situations.[16]

Indeed, because employees are hired for life in major corporations, the company is able to expend considerable time and money on a training program, which may well last a few years. However, more important perhaps than the development of technical skills, which the new member has theoretically a lifetime of employment to acquire, is the development of an ideological commitment to the philosophy and the practices of the corporation. The company expends an extraordinary effort introducing new members to its shared history and symbols, and incorporating them into the spirit of the company. Rohlen's description of the initiation ceremony of new members into the bank gives a sense of just how deeply the company will influence the lives of its members. Involved in the ceremony, for example, are not only the recruits and the relevant company executives, but also the parents of the new recruits.[17] Rohlen notes that after those assembled sing songs affirming their commitment to the company and to Japan, and after reciting together the principles and catechism of the company, the new recruits are introduced to the company's president, who welcomes them, thanks their parents for raising them, and lectures them on the responsibilities of adulthood and their need to pay back their parents for the sacrifices they have made to raise them. When the president finishes, the master of ceremony then calls the role of the new members "including the schools from which they have just graduated."[18] Thus, just at the time when most Americans are completing their separation from their parents and their school, the Japanese are reaffirming the relationship in a new form.

Much of the behavior within the Japanese company involves maintaining the communal relationship that is first expressed in the initiation ceremony. For example, the long hours that workers and their bosses spend drinking together after work is an important way to smooth over feelings ruffled during business hours, and a way for worker and boss to display their more human side to each other. The frequent weekend get-togethers—typically without families—is a way to reestablish communal solidarity by reaffirming shared symbols and common histories.

Usually American workers need not think about the shared symbols and common history of the group. They are there to accomplish a common goal, but once that is accomplished they are free to go their separate ways, and are under no obligation to acknowledge more than is needed to perform their day's work.

Education for membership in a community is one of the most important functions of both the Japanese school and the Japanese workplace. When children are expected to clean their own school rather than just their desk area, concern is being expressed for the condition of shared, semipublic space, and in this way students learn about responsibility as members of a community. When company training requires future executives to experience work on the assembly line, it is recognizing that common experience makes the difference between holding a job and being a member of a working community.

Yet there are costs as well as benefits to the Japanese emphasis on harmony and community. As Rohlen observes: "Both the safest course and the highest virtue lie in keeping still about personal opinions that contradict public ideology."[19] It would not, of course, be unusual to find American employees who believe with their Japanese counterparts that the safest course is to keep quiet when personal opinion counters the public position of the firm. Karen Silkwood's case suggests the high costs that may be paid for the whistle-blower who insists on contradicting the public stance of the company. The difference is that in the latter case silence is demanded by the company, not belief in the company.

V. Communal and Individual Identities

Americans are Madisonians. They reject the idea that any one person or group can have the interest of the whole at heart. They do not necessarily reject the value of community, but, because the dominant cultural metaphor is friction, they cannot just assume that everyone else shares the desire for community and harmony. Lines of responsibility are drawn more sharply, roles are more precisely defined, and duties more clearly spelled out because everyone must operate with the assumption that everyone else is likely to subordinate harmony for self-interest or self-protection.

This collective distrust is not, however, based merely on self-interest. Because no one can adequately represent the whole—indeed, because no one can have adequate knowledge of the whole—progress is accepted as an emergent quality arising out of the friction created by the conjunction of two or more competing interests. To work in what I call a "culture of friction" like our own means that no matter how strong the longing for communal ties may be, individualism is still a dominant factor in behavior on the shop floor. In one interview, an American worker, now in his eighth month of training in a factory in Japan, explains the difference:

> Many American workers will find it difficult to be self-motivated and put the company's desires and needs ahead of their own personal desires and needs. Each Japanese member of the work force is so conscious of what the other workers think of him that a lot of discipline is in the group. The other group members on their own will tend to guide a person back to the ideals he should be holding in order to be a member of the group. I think that would be very difficult in the U.S. to rely on the group as a source of motivation, because a certain percentage of American workers, quite frankly, could care less about what his fellows will say about him. I don't think there would be that trust of the American worker of management. I don't think he has a reason to because in many cases management has been as much or maybe at most at fault, and lack of good management/labor relationship is bad. It's a two-way street any way you look at it. I think management creates as many problems as the workers create.

To work in a culture of friction means that some values that are prized in a culture of harmony like Japan will always be suspect. Consider the following response by an American worker to the "benevolent" requirement of the Japanese management that gloves be worn on the shop floor. The factory is in Japan where he is being trained for almost a year before returning to the States to take up a position in a new American factory.

> Ed: We have to wear gloves for everything we do. I spend more time taking my gloves on and off in tool grinding than I do anything else. I can't wear gloves when I'm using a precision measuring instrument. I've got to take my gloves off. But when I'm running the machine, I've got to wear my gloves. So, it's constantly run a machine, take off your gloves, measure, put your gloves back on, you know. Before I got into the machines one time I was working on a die and it had some slivers in it. I had been wearing these cotton gloves that are a loose mesh. Well, I got a sliver in this loose mesh and I went and pulled the glove off and I told my trainer. I said "see, these gloves aren't any good because this sliver got in the mesh and then when I went to pick up something, then

it got me, see." His solution to that was wearing two pairs of gloves.

WF: Not getting new gloves. Could you bring your own gloves in if you wanted to? Are these company-supplied gloves?

Ed: Most of us are used to working without gloves [back in the United States]. You have to have a little bit of common sense yourself and know what you can pick up and what you can't pick up without gloves.

WF: But that sliver would have gotten you more, right, if you didn't have a glove on?

Ed: No, I don't think so.

WF: Or, if you had had a better glove, it wouldn't have gotten you at all, right?

Ed: Things like gloves give people a false sense of security, and especially with these panels, like picking up big panels of sheet metal. You know, a cotton glove, if that panel slips and goes down your hand, it's going to be just like a knife edge going down. We'll they don't let you wear the cotton gloves picking up panels, then they've got big mittens for you to wear. It's real hard to pick up sheet metal panels with what's almost like a catcher's mitt.

   They are so afraid of us getting hurt *over here*, I think, is the big thing. I'm afraid of getting hurt over here, too, cause everything is so different, you know, the doctors and hospitals. It would just be a mess if you got your finger cut off or something over here, you know. It isn't like going to your home town hospital and getting fixed up, you know. *(emphasis added)*

Ed is not a dissatisfied worker. He is simply expressing the dominant themes of a culture of friction. He likes his job and his future prospects with the company. He simply does not believe that the management knows best and, more significantly, he does not accept the possibility that the company has his own best interest in mind. The requirement to wear gloves is not just a mistaken expression of "Oriental" benevolence. An American worker injured in Japan would be a serious inconvenience to the company, and he believes that the desire to avoid this inconvenience is the reason for the regulation.

Of course, the culture of harmony and the culture of friction hold a number of values in common. Yet because the cultural assumptions in which the values are embedded are different, the values themselves take on a different character. For example, Japanese workers are frequently commended for the pride they take in their work. Yet Japanese pride is often different from American pride.

Consider the apocryphal story of the Honda worker who walks down the street and wipes the dirty windshields of parked Hondas. The story suggests that the pride extends beyond one's own activity to one's membership in a company that produces the cars. The story may indeed be apocryphal, but it does reinforce a frequently observed difference between American and Japanese workers. Whereas Americans tend to identify themselves in terms of the role they perform—plumber, lawyer, and so on—Japanese tend to identify themselves in terms of the company that they work for. Lebra and other commentators hold that the Japanese are much more sensitive to the requirements of social interactions, and more likely to identify fully with group norms.[20] This identity is more than simply a widely shared, subjective feeling. It is reinforced by language and patterns of social interaction. For example, when a group of businessmen meet for the first time it is the custom to exchange business cards. After the exchange is completed there is a minute or so of silence while everyone studies the cards and takes note of the companies represented, their relative size and importance, and the positions within the companies of those attending the meeting. This information will be used to then determine what honorific forms of speech are appropriate, who bows to whom, and other patterns of interaction. Hence, one's identity, as established through the company, is acknowledged and legitimized by others. Moreover, this ritual links different companies with one another in a system of formalized responses based on a shared conception of hierarchy and place, and reflects the behavioral displays that are expected from members of each company.

In Japan, then, pride is not so much an individual matter as it is the result of membership in a certain group, and indeed, too large a display of individual pride can be a source of embarrassment. Japanese are quite unlikely to speak about their own individual contributions and are taught early not to make conspicuous individual displays. In American schools, for example, Japanese children will often experience embarrassment when asked to participate in show-and-tell, because in doing so they are forced to talk about themselves and what they individually own. They see this as boasting. Even Japanese mothers, who are known worldwide for the energy they put into their children's education and upbringing, will rarely talk about the accomplishments of their children for fear that they will be seen as bragging. And many of the problems experienced in school by Japanese children returning from the United States result from exhibiting individual wants and needs. An example would be waving one's hand vigorously to command the recognition of the teacher. Yet there is much less reluctance in talking about the achievements of one's group. For example, a university professor will describe his largely unknown university in ways that display its uniqueness and its superior merit as, for instance, "the best private Buddhist women's university in this city." Pride, which is largely absent in expressions of individual identity, is an important element in one's collective identity.

For Americans, especially blue collar workers, collective pride, pride taken from the name of the firm, is largely viewed as inappropriate because it seems to substitute the accomplishment of the collective for one's own individual merits. Consider the remarks of an American automobile worker.

> I can look out there and I can see umpteen thousand cars and say that I was responsible for them. I've taken pride in everything I've done. I've always tried to give eight hours work for eight hours pay. I hate to hear people complain about the company did this to me, the company did that to me. My aspect has always been pretty much that they're paying me for what I'm doing, so I'm going to do the best I can. Some people can, you know, get their inner sanctum through their athletics or anything. Mine is doing the best on my job.

This worker's pride is largely independent of the company he happens to work for. It is a matter of how he views his own performance and whether he is meeting his own internal standard. Yet it is also largely independent of the performance of his fellow workers. He does not like to hear them complain because he feels that they all know what the deal is. Nevertheless, the mere fact that they work together does not mean that they form a significant part of his moral community. He would prefer not to hear their complaints, but there is little indication that he feels the need to do something about them.

Contrary to some recent suggestions,[21] individualism does not abandon moral authority. However, it does require that communities be formed as voluntary associations that are renewed continuously through individuals' choice. Communities that are forced have an artificial character and are perceived to border on military organizations. Thus American workers view the "groupiness" of the Japanese workplace with some suspicion, and are sensitive to signs of resistance among workers who otherwise seem to be "toeing" the company line. The following quote is from an American worker who has been training in Japan for more than half a year.

> We have a lot of outings over here. It's just all the men. The wives hardly ever come. It's the men and us and maybe an interpreter and that's it. If they want to be entertained by me when I'm back in the States, I might invite them over to my house with my family but I don't make it a habit of going out to bars with them here and I'm not going to do it in the States either. There are going to be special parties, like out at restaurants for their going-away parties and stuff like that. I'll do the same thing in the States but so many of these men, you see them walking out of restaurants and bars and stuff at eight or nine o'clock at night and you know they haven't been home yet. They still have on their suit and tie, and haven't been home to the family yet. They've been hanging out with the guys they work with.
>
> It's almost like a military. They all participate if there's a company athletic event. They all do it together.

To the American, the Japanese working community is exclusionary, requiring that members subordinate their other identities to that of the primary group and place the demands of the working community before all other commitments. For example, while companies are concerned about the private lives of their members—sometimes even seeing to it that employees are introduced to suitable potential mates— wives and families are almost never included in company gatherings. Americans often see this as a sign of forced conformity rather than an indication of group solidarity.

> Ed: I think a lot of them like to be with the men, you know, with the guys, I should say. But there are some of them, I think sometimes, that the company has maybe told them, you know, you should do this or that and so they'll go on this trip with us, you know.
>
> WF: How do you get that idea?
>
> Ed: Oh, some of them seem like they might be a little bit better family men and not really want to be out drinking.

The problem with the Japanese working community, as Ed sees it, is that it is not enjoyed by all on a truly spontaneous and voluntary basis. Because he believes that communities should be voluntarily chosen, he does not believe that his Japanese counterparts are experiencing these activities as the activities of a true community. Rather he sees some of them as reluctantly meeting the responsibilities of a job.

Ed was not alone in his feelings. Some American workers in his group of trainees began to avoid the outings that the company arranged, and often these workers would arrange to go to the same place later with a small group of Japanese and American friends. The totality of the Japanese workplace was beginning to wear on them and they started to feel like schoolchildren on a field trip.

The culture of friction filters the way these men see the behavior of their Japanese counterparts, and they search hard for the individual behind the group. Yet the members of the culture of harmony also filters the way the Japanese view the acts of the Americans. Japanese often perceive in acts of spontaneous voluntarism more than is intended. For example, for the Japanese managers, the reduced attendance of Americans on the field trips was a cause for concern, and they worried whether it should be taken as a sign of unhappiness and disharmony. Did the fact that the Americans would avoid the company trip, only to visit the site a few weeks later with close friends, mean that the company was doing something wrong? The Japanese worried whether they had alienated the American workers.

VI. The Cultural Limits of Moral Authority

Mr. Y is the president of a satellite company servicing a major Japanese automobile manufacturer that has made a commitment to build a large plant in the United States. He has a close relationship with the president of the larger Japanese company, whom he has known for many years. Although the automobile company has not asked him directly to open an allied factory in the States, he is aware of their wish that he do so and he is greatly concerned about managing the cultural differences between American workers and his Japanese company. Among his concerns are the different expectations Americans and Japanese have of the way work is to be governed. Whereas Mr. Y believes that American workers will require a formal understanding of rights and obligations, he is used to workers anticipating the needs of the job and doing whatever is required to meet them. He worries that he will not be able to anticipate all that will be required and to stipulate it in a contract.

> The technical problems will not be a problem between the Americans and the Japanese but the culture will be a big problem. For

example, today we hire you and we would tell you what we want
from you and you would tell us what you want from us, but for
Japanese they don't say things clearly. They don't say really what
they feel about it so that might become the biggest problem because they only tell you the main point but they don't go into the
details.

According to the Japanese way of doing things if there is a
problem in quality control, the workers realize the problem and
then after work, they will sacrifice their own time to being with
family or with their friends. They would talk about the problem
and solve the problem and they don't get paid for that time spent
in solving the problem. If this kind of problem happened with
American workers, would they sacrifice their own time to solve
the problem for the company and not get paid for it?

Another example is in Japan, you are not supposed to come to
work exactly at 8:00; you are supposed to come 10 or 15 minutes
before 8:00 and you clean up for your work. Then at 8:00 you start
work all the way until 5:00. Then after 5:00, you clean up from
your work and then you go home.

To respond to the needs of the job rather than to the regulations of
a contract requires workers to develop a consuming sense of identity
with the company, and this is related to the idea of lifetime employment.

In Japan, the more different companies you go to, your evaluation
will be lower. You'll be thought worse of. But in America it is
different. The more places you've gone to, the more valuable you
become. [Here] you work for a company; you work there for your
whole life and the company will take care of you.

Identification with the company, according to the president, extends
beyond the individual and into the family, and other roles are subordi-
nated to the needs of the company.

WF: So would not mothers and wives say [to workers] you haven't
been home before ten o'clock for a month and a half?

Y: According to what I know, they don't say that because the
Japanese wife belongs to the company.
      If she says something about you have to come home early—
one thing—she'll get in fight with her husband. The husband
would say, I'm working for the company. Also, if she would
complain about his coming home late and stuff, she'll give
an impression of a bad woman. . . .

WF: Around who?

Y: Everybody.

WF: Have you had any situations like that at all with workers?

Y: I had it a couple of times but I thought it was a joke.

WF: It was what?

Y: They were only joking. If you're not loyal to your company, people would consider you as a bad person. But, if you are loyal to your company, they will think you're a good guy. So, because of that, a lot of people will go to the company, even on a holiday. People don't take them into the group if they don't. Now they are working Saturdays and Sundays to save the cost of electricity?

I could not help but think that Y maintains his belief that expressions of worker dissatisfaction are a joke because there is essentially no public support for expressions of this kind. The culture of harmony enables such expressions to be dismissed as inconsequential even though Japanese workers display high levels of stress and experience many illnesses that are related to problems in the workplace.

Mr. Y's description of the working community in Japan supports Sam Herman's vision of the Japanese workplace and is reflected in the view held by many Japanese and Americans alike of the inherently harmonious quality of the Japanese enterprise. There are, however, a few cracks in the vision. Ed's observation earlier that some of the Japanese workers really did seem to have a conflict between the company's requirements and their concern for their family suggests that perhaps the worker was not joking to Mr. Y after all. The assumptions entailed in the culture of harmony make it difficult to tell. A joke can be a way to test the basic cultural assumptions without risking the consequences of a full-blown and possibly unsuccessful frontal assault on them.

The militancy of some nonindustrial unions, such as the transportation union and even the teacher's union, is a sign that the degree of harmony between worker and management varies significantly from situation to situation in Japan, and that the culture of harmony may be strongest in the enterprise where face-to-face activities between union and management are common. Moreover, reports of increases in stress, alcoholism, family strife and suicides among men in the prime of their working life presents a more troubling picture of the Japanese workplace, indicating certain strains in the basic cultural assumptions.[22] Even the fact that Mr. Y dismissed the complaint of his worker by explaining that it was a joke suggests that even within the accepted worker-management relationship there is some implicit acknowledgment of a voluntary principle and of the need for individuals to consciously accept the ordering of identities. To see the complaint as a joke might be an acknowledgment that were it serious, the very idea of company harmony would need to be reexamined. If it is merely a joke, the assumption of individual and group harmony may continue unchallenged.

VII. Conclusion

Moral educators frequently overlook matters of culture in the belief that virtue and moral development are the same all over the world.[23] Whether this observation is accurate in terms of laboratory studies or survey research is a matter for researchers to debate. Yet morality in everyday life is imbedded in cultural matters, and moral development requires cultural reflection. To illustrate the point we return to the views of the economic conservative and the cultural conservative mentioned in Chapter One.

Both kinds of conservatives believe the secret to the renewal of American civilization lies within the school. The economic conservative believes that the complexities of the new workplace require a more educated, competitive work force. The cultural conservative believes that the fracturing of American identity requires a renewal of our traditional symbols and ideals. Yet depending on whether the economic conservative is correct and depending on what the cultural conservative takes as "traditional" symbols, these two positions may well work against one another. Consider, for example, one of the important reasons for the success of the Japanese workplace—the ideal of lifetime employment. If the economic conservative is in fact correct that work is becoming more complex, requiring longer training and the opening of traditional work boundaries, then the practice of lifetime employment could be very advantageous for a company. If employees could count on having their jobs no matter what, then they would have less reason to fear innovation and might be more willing to perform timesaving tasks that are not an essential part of their job descriptions. Plumbers, for example, could plug the cord back into the outlet without the electricians objecting because their jobs are threatened. Moreover, if companies could invest in training without the fear that employees will use their increased skills to leave for greener pastures, then they could spend time developing the skills of their work force.

A culture of harmony facilitates these developments. The background community assumption is that harmony is the desired state, and that harmony entails loyalty. Hence, workers are discouraged from looking for greener pastures, because to do so is seen as a sign of disloyalty, and other companies are reluctant to hire potentially disloyal workers. And, for all companies, the ability to offer lifetime employment is an important part of the prestige structure. While not each and every business is able to offer meaningful lifetime employment, it serves as an ideal for which all reasonable-sized companies strive, and the community judges companies in terms of their capacity to approximate the ideal. While some of this is changing in modern Japan, the culture of harmony provides a basis for the change and is, for example, one reason why gaps between the highest-paid executive in a plant and the lowest-paid worker remains comparatively small, and why moral behavior is still a matter of the mutual obligations of group life.

However instrumental these kinds of innovations may be in furthering the economic program of the economic conservative they are not obviously consistent with the traditional American identity that cultural conservatives say they want to renew. Our tradition does not entail the cultural assumptions that seem to support this organizational innovation and this, of course, is one reason why no conservative, whether economic or cultural, has seriously advocated such a move.

Few cultural conservatives have actually addressed the nature of the moral code that the culture of friction carries into the workplace. They want common symbols, but for the most part these are the symbols that celebrate our individualism. The culture of friction is not without its moral code, as those who too easily equate morality with technological prowess and industrial productivity believe. Rather, the culture of friction is guided by a moral code in which each person is to acknowledge the right of every other person to use his or her job as an instrument of his or her own advancement. This is not the same as an "every person for themselves" morality where no rules are acknowledged. The rules of the culture of friction are clearcut and universal. Every person has the right to advance through the instrument of work. Hence, for example, it is not appropriate to use guilt to convince a person to stay at a lesser job when a better one beckons. To ask that a manager about to consider an offer from another company with a ten-thousand dollar increase think about all that her present company has done for her is inappropriate, just as it is inappropriate to ask a worker that he think of the added burden his moving on to another plant will have on those remaining behind. These are not acceptable reasons for asking a person to stay in a lesser job.

In seeking to renew an American identity, the cultural conservative needs to acknowledge this morality as one of the important features of the culture of friction, while the economic conservative needs to worry about whether such a morality is, in this day and age, good for business. After all why should the company teach workers new skills if the result is improved marketability for the workers? And why should workers allow new contracts to be written which erase traditional job boundaries if by doing so they will threaten to eliminate their own jobs? The morality of the culture of friction requires everyone to license everyone else to make the best deal they can for themselves. It does not, however, require that they contribute to that effort, nor that they self-destruct in doing so. The culture of friction may or may not be good for business any longer, but it is certainly consistent with our traditional identity.

The attention directed at Japan illustrates the nature of the problem. Our keen interest in Japan has arisen because of its success as a modern economic nation capable of surpassing our own industrial output in many areas. It is only because of this success that we have taken any note of the social organization of Japanese society, and have come to believe that in the social organization of its workplaces and its schools may be found the secret of its success. We worry that our own commitment to individualism may have gone too far, because we have begun to lose out in certain industrial areas where we have been traditionally strong. Yet we also hesitate to accept the Japanese model because we worry about where a community capable of recognizing individuality leaves off and a mere collectivity of behavior organized to accomplish an assigned goal begins. It is therefore in the discourse about Japan—in our attempts to understand their success and to explain our problems—that much of the reconsideration of our own identity has taken place. The next two chapters analyze that discourse and its implications for reconceptualizing an American identity.

3

Economic Conservatives*
and the Culture of Friction

I. Japan's Role in the New Discourse

The changing economic positions of Japan and the United States have stimulated much of the new discourse about work and education. In 1960, for example, Japan's share of the world's GNP was three percent, whereas by 1980, the figure had more than tripled to ten percent. During the same time the United States' share fell from thirty-three percent to twenty-two percent.[1] Theirs represented one of the largest increases and ours one of the largest decreases. During the early 1980s (1980–1984) Japan experienced a 3.9 percent annual rate of growth in GNP whereas the United States growth was calculated at a 1.8 percent annual rate.[2] From 1986–1990 Japan's GNP grew at a 4.7 percent rate of growth compared to 2.8 percent in the United States, and by 1990 Japan's was at 5.6 percent with the United States' barely growing at 1 percent.[3] By 1985 Japanese automobiles had captured twenty percent of the American market, up from 9.4 percent in 1975.[4] By 1989, the Honda Accord, now assembled in the United States, was the top-selling automobile in America. By 1985, Japanese steel production had surpassed that of the United States by 26,024,000 metric tons, although some small ground had been recaptured by 1989[5]; and whereas in 1985 Japan ran a 55,986-million-dollar trade surplus, the United States ran a 124,439-million-dollar trade deficit.[6]

*For a more precise statement of how this and the term cultural conservative are being used, see Appendix II.

Moreover, balance of payment differences altered considerably in a brief number of years. In 1981 Japan had only a 4770-million-dollar balance-of-payments surplus, whereas that of the United States was 6,870 million dollars. However, by 1985 Japan's surplus had leaped to 49,169 million dollars, whereas the United States surplus had turned into a 122,250 million dollar deficit.[7] By 1985 Japan was exporting eighty-two percent of its camera production, eighty-nine percent of its watches, ninety percent of its video recorders, and eighty percent of its copying machines,[8] while U.S. production in most of these areas was essentially eliminated. These differences showed up in the unemployment rate of the two countries, with Japan's ranging between 2.0 percent in 1980 to a high of 2.7 percent in 1984, and that of the United States at a low of 7.0 percent in 1980 to a high of 9.5 percent in 1982 and 1983.[9] In 1990 unemployment in Japan was still low at 2.1 percent whereas the United States rate had declined to 5.5 percent,[10] a rate that was shortly to increase due to the recession. Today many of the signs of the good life can be seen in the higher life expectancy of the Japanese and the lower infant mortality and crime rates. In economic, industrial and social terms the Japanese appear to be winning the competition. For the economic conservative the decline in the comparative position of United States industry signals a problem with the preparation of the American work force—and this in turn is taken to define the problem with American schools.

II. Educational Achievement and the Altered Discourse

It is now a commonly held, but questionable, belief that the high quality of Japanese schooling is responsible for the increasing competitiveness of Japanese industry. In one important cross-cultural study, the performance of American students scoring at the ninety-ninth percentile of their cohort in this country was only on a par with Japanese students at the seventy-fifth percentile of their national cohort. And the lowest twenty-fifth percentile of Japanese students scored in the range of the highest ninetieth percentile of American students.[11] In science the differences are similarly striking. While the Japanese do quite well in other educational areas, such as music,[12] it is children's performance in math and science that has captured international attention, and that now fuels the belief that there is a linear causal relationship between educational achievement and industrial productivity.

Educators the world over—most of whom know the difference between a correlation and a cause—have accepted the view that there is a direct relationship between the productivity of Japanese workers and the academic achievement of Japanese students. I do not dispute that there is some kind of relationship, but its character is not as obvious as commonly assumed. In some countries student achievement is relatively low and worker productivity is high. In others the reverse holds. In the United States productivity may increase in any given year without any corresponding increase in student test performance during the years preceding the rise. Moreover, the presently accepted view assumes that if there is a relationship between student achievement and productivity, it is a linear one—that increased achievement will always lead to increased productivity. This link is not self-evident.

Certainly there is some relationship between student achievement and worker productivity. Nations with large percentages of students graduating from high school generally have higher productivity rates than nations with small percentages of graduates. Yet how far will this positive relationship go? Will more achievement always bring about more productivity? Could not higher levels of school achievement at some point bring about a dissatisfaction with one's position as a worker? What is the argument for linking school achievement inextricably to worker productivity, and how sound is it? There is indeed a case to be made, and if it were accurate, it would herald a bold and progressive overview of the structure of work. Unfortunately the vision is limited and overdrawn.

III. The Development of The New Vision of the Work Place

Those who are upset by low test scores and poor academic performance are often reflecting the concerns of leaders in more technologically advanced industries. Since these industries tend to be large, with international markets, they carry more weight in the recent educational discourse. For example, the former president of Xerox, ignoring such obvious problems with American industry as under-capitalization, Savings and Loans mismanagement, or Wall Street scandals, points the finger of blame at the public schools. "At a time when our preeminent role in the world economy is in jeopardy, there are few social problems more telling in their urgency. Public education has put this country at a terrible competitive disadvantage."[13] He is not, as might be supposed, faulting education as a whole for neglecting the cultural, ethical and value education that a strong and respected business requires in its top executives—as well as its workers.[14] He is, rather, accusing the primary and secondary schools of failing the American people by developing an inadequately trained work force— one that is not able to compete on the same level with the Japanese.

The economic conservative writes as if in modern, technologically advanced countries like the United States, more routine forms of work will soon no longer be available. Some argue[15] that the less desirable jobs will be taken up by people in Third World nations, and that more complex, intellectually demanding work will remain for people in the more developed countries to compete for. New free trade agreements with less technologically dependent nations, such as Mexico, provide substance to support this view. The economic conservative argues that, without an economy that can support an unskilled, even though disciplined, labor force, the nation's schools must educate everyone to work in more intellectually demanding settings. This then sets the tone for the economic conservative's vision of schooling. It serves as a warning to an errant nation. There will still be educational winners, people who are adequately trained for complicated, interesting, and well-paying jobs. And there will be educational losers, people who will be trained for the drudgery that more civilized society leaves in its wake. The difference is that instead of winners and losers being located within a single nation, it is the nations themselves that will occupy these positions. The responsibility of the advanced nations is to avoid falling into the position of the less advanced. America must keep its place in the world through its leadership in education.

Behind this view of educational reform is a traditional American understanding of the nature of the public good. The public good, in this view, is created by the friction that is generated when people pursue their own private wants. The public is best served by people advancing their own individual goals (as circumscribed by market needs). Excellence is then the product of competition. Students compete for high grades and test scores; teachers compete for merit pay increases; and schools compete for students. The market and the regulatory forces of competition will enable the best to rise to the top, and in this way the larger public good is served. The public good is a by-product of each of us doing our individual best. It is not the conscious concern of any of us, but it is what we get when each of us, spurred on by competition, does our individual best. If American schools are demanding, then the American work force will be able to meet the international competition. With people all over the world wanting our products, then more jobs will flow to this country and our national debt will vanish.

How strong, then, is the link between educational excellence and worker productivity? And just how adequate is this view of the public good? The answer, which will be developed in this chapter, that the image of the public good, as drawn by the conservative educational reform literature, is actually incongruous with the view of the public good that is emerging in the conservative literature on work. Moreover, while the economic conservatives argue for a closer tie between school and work, what they want for the schools is inconsistent with the changes they want in the work force. However, one can still find emerging in their appeal for a new type of work force, an image of a public which, although partial and inadequate, contributes something important to our understanding of the character of a democratic society.

IV. A Case for the Link between Achievement and Productivity

An influential argument for connecting school achievement and industrial productivity rests on the view that most of the routine operations of the American factory could be taken over by robots, and that the major task of humans would then be to manage contingencies that cannot be predicted or programmed into the machine. In this view of the workplace, many different people hold the key to the successful operation of the plant, and the most important factor is the free flow of information between them.

Because of the nature of contingencies, these newer jobs cannot be reduced to simple routines, nor do they lend themselves to a well-defined division of labor. The model of work presented here is fluid and interactive. Workers interact in communicatively complicated ways both with each other and with machines. Numbing, routine work and hierarchical organizations are replaced by interesting human work and more horizontal organizations. One of the pioneers of this vision, Larry Hirschhorn, describes its impact:

> In contrast to mechanical performance, there is no predetermined sequence of actions; instead, the individual or the machine responds flexibly to environmental changes. In order to operate, feedback systems must import error, not exclude it as mechanical systems do.[16]

Older forms of mechanization required a system in which the worker's role was continuously narrowed to an ever more specified motion—the turning of a screw or the setting of a handle. The ideal was a deskilled work force that simply took over those functions that could not yet be performed alone by a machine. In the new system, Hirschhorn tells us:

> we . . . see the worker moving from being the controlled element in the production process to operating the controls to controlling the controls.[17]

Unlike the system of mechanization where the workers learned to perfect a single movement or set of movements, under the new system the workers are "defunctionalized." In a defunctionalized workplace workers give up most of the physical effort needed to accomplish a task—robots or similar devices do this—but they gain control over a wider range of the production process. Workers calibrate, program, and monitor the robots while the robots perform most of the actual physical processes such as lifting, turning, or cutting.

The vision calls not only for a new workplace but also for a new breed of worker. Rule of thumb techniques alone are not sufficient. Workers must have a theoretical understanding of the systems as a whole, and must know how to interpret and act upon unexpected data arising from unexpected sources.[18] Workers must be trained to connect a malfunction to a wider frame of reference, and to conjecture about a multiplicity of possible causes. When a rule-of-thumb formula fails, workers need to be able to search out information from other sources and to link new information to the operation of multiple systems. When workers continue to respond in a habitual manner, failing to examine possible alternative causes for a malfunction, the results can be disastrous. The breakdown in the nuclear facility at Three Mile Island serves as a warning to us all of inappropriate, habitual responses.[19]

The new cognitive demands on the work force entail a different division of labor, and a different orientation to knowledge and information. Strict and rigid hierarchies are dysfunctional in this new setting. Because there is a need to maintain a constant flow of information through all levels of the system, new forms of communication are needed. When rigid structures of rank get in the way of the flow of information, vital communication is impaired. The work requires that employees be trained in many different aspects of the system.[20]

According to this view, the insight and the feedback of the line worker is essential to the production process. Fail-safe machines are impossible to produce, and the nature and characteristics of break-downs are difficult to predict before hand. The introduction of each new program requires workers who are able to respond intelligently to any erratic behavior that the machine manifests. Thus, the new methods of production not only require new forms of knowledge for the work force, they also require a new relation to knowledge.

In the past, knowledge was treated as a scarce commodity which one person or group used to protect themselves from encroachment by another. Hence electrical skills could only be employed by electricians, and only trained plumbers could fix the pipes. One of the perennial struggles of capitalism has been between the craftsmen trying to main-tain an exclusive domain of skilled performance and the managers attempting to design work roles so that they require as few skills as possible.[21] Control of knowledge was synonymous with control over the production process, and as long as systems were relatively inde-pendent and problems could be predicted in advance, this cartel-like relationship to knowledge was acceptable. Today the increase in complexity and the need for workers to have a comprehensive understanding of production argues for a wider distribution of knowl-edge if a firm is to remain profitable and safe. The increased complexity of the new systems involved in production increases the likelihood of a serious error, one that is difficult to diagnose and correct, and which has the potential of harming a large number of people. The control room of a nuclear energy plant or the control tower of a large airport are examples with which most of us are familiar, and other examples exist, ranging from chemical plants to battery factories.

The potential for multiple and unpredictable sources of error to develop, and the need for workers who are able to diagnose problems that can issue from any number of multiple systems, suggests to advocates of the new workplace that management no longer should have an interest in monopolizing knowledge. Management goals, it is argued, are now better served by spreading such knowledge as widely as possible. The new goal for management should not be to divide worker knowledge into as many separate pieces as possible, but to devise a system of worker rewards that accommodates the sharing of knowledge.

V. Educational Implications

Is this vision not exactly what the modern educator needs to tilt the scale in favor of both better academic skills and more flexible

classrooms? Does it not show just how inadequate and outdated are
those who insist that educational institutions be fixed and hierarchical?
And does it not, in its insistence on lateral communication and reduced
inequality, approximate within the workplace the requirements for
public discourse that I am calling for in the schools? Does it not finally
seem that good education is now compatible with good business? The
vision certainly comes close to making the case. After all, if this vision
is correct, flexibility is now the key to competition. Because rigid,
mass-assembly-line processing is no longer competitive in a changing
world market, our old strength is now our greatest weakness. American businesses fail when they meet the competition because they do
blindly what they know best. They intensify the instruments of routine, assembly-line production. Because the system of mass production is precisely the problem, attempts to intensify it make the situation
worse rather than better.[22]

Moreover, good education involves understanding other cultures.
Parochialism hurts American manufacturing. In the past American
manufacturers had an

> unlimited and uncontested outlet for their products in their own
> domestic market. The home market was large, unified, and famil-
> iar. Foreign markets were small, segmented and protected not
> only by tariff barriers but also by impenetrable distribution sys-
> tems. Above all, they were foreign: operating in them required
> linguistic and cultural skills that Americans did not have and did
> not wish to acquire. Hence, most foreign markets and foreign
> competitors were largely ignored.[23]

The absence of foreign language skills is the least of the problem.
Much more harmful, according to these authors, "is the assumption
that American tastes, American ways of doing business, and American
products are universal (or ought to be)."[24]

VI. The Discrepancies in the Images of School and Work Reform

Ironically, the vision of a flexible, laterally structured workplace is
not often the image that guides school reform proposals.[25] One would
think that if the workplace required new modes of interaction, then
so too would the school. Yet this is not the lesson that is usually drawn
from business. More emphasis on the right answer, more frequent
testing, and increasing emphasis on higher test scores recreate in the

school exactly the hierarchical structure and individual competition that we are told is outdated in the workplace. If it is true that we need less hierarchical, more cooperative workplaces, and if the new kind of work requires greater sharing and less monopolization of knowledge, then the focus in schools should be not just on individual output, but rather on the quality of social relations and the patterns of interaction in the classroom as well. Consider, for example, the claim reported above that it is no longer in a manager's interest to monopolize knowledge. This claim is only true if the manager does not feel threatened by workers who have access to the same knowledge that she does. This is certainly unlikely if schools continue to teach students that individual competition is the primary condition in the workplace. If the vision of more cooperative and flexible work is correct, then conservatives will need to rethink their ideas about standardized tests and a unified curriculum.

Putting aside the need for reducing hierarchy and increasing flexibility, will the new workplace require higher academic skills? A general answer is difficult to give because there are many different kinds of jobs, even in a highly technological society. The highly computerized workplace, where robots do all the routine work and humans are reserved for the more contingent, intellectual functions, will employ only a minority of the work force. The vast majority of new jobs will open up in areas that will continue to use low technology—elementary schoolteachers, janitors, and so on.[26] Many jobs that have recently been computerized will require less, rather than more, skills from their workers. For example, cash registers now tell supermarket cashiers exactly how much change to give back. Many clerks never learn how to count change and are quite lost when the machines break down.

The argument that some nations are more productive than others because they have a stronger and more academic school system is by no means self-evident. True, schools are important at the early stages of industrialization when new work habits and widespread literacy need to be developed. However, this speaks only to industry's need for basic education. It is also true that a number of complicated research and engineering positions are required in a high-technology work force. However, these comprise a relatively small number of positions, and those who occupy them are very mobile and can move from country to country. The more important issue for education is the extent to which a high-technology industry requires a high-technology work force at all levels, and whether there is indeed a strong causal connection between school achievement and industrial productivity.

Japan, even a Japan with a precipitous stock market decline, suggests that the connection is strong. However, this may be misleading. Japanese students score higher than those of any other nation on a number of international comparisons in math and science, and Japanese industrial growth is among the highest in the world. Similarly, the test scores of American students have declined, and so has American productivity when compared to Japan. However, if even a prima facie case were to be made, comparisons with other nations would need to hold up in the same way as they do with Japan. Nations with relatively high productivity rates would need to have high achievement scores, and low productivity would need to be preceded by years of relatively low achievement. The stronger case would need to show that the relationship is causal and that other intervening factors relative to culture or to investment policy, etc., did not serve to raise both test and productivity scores. Indeed, the recent problem that college graduates have had finding jobs suggests that the problem is less with skill level and more with an economy that is not generating enough jobs. In the absence of a compelling argument to this effect, Japan may be an exception to an otherwise more haphazard relationship.

Additional suggestions that the link between school and work is weak are found in the experience of the Japanese with American workers. When Japanese automobile companies have established plants in the United States, worker productivity in these plants is frequently comparable to productivity in Japan. This rate of productivity has even been achieved when the Japanese have rehired the same work force previously employed by an American plant.

Consider the case of the joint venture between Toyota and General Motors, NUMMI, in Fremont, California. Between 1962, when the plant in Fremont opened, and 1982 the plant operated as an assembly plant for General Motors. When GM closed the plant in 1982, it had the lowest productivity rating of all of its assembly operations.[27] In 1984 the plant reopened as a joint Toyota/GM venture, and by 1986 productivity had risen by fifty percent over the GM operation. This was the highest rating of all GM plants, and was on a par with a similar plant in Toyota City, Japan. Moreover, defects decreased dramatically and the plant reported a substantial profit.[28] The new, more productive work force consisted primarily of workers drawn from the former, unproductive work force. While there was some screening, the union successfully insisted that "the company must have compelling reasons not to hire an individual worker."[29] In the end the composition of the work force of the two plants was very similar, and, as Brown and Reich report, "what emerges as impressive

. . . is not a weeding-out process of hiring, but rather the high rates of rehiring."[30] The NUMMI experience suggests that caution is needed before attributing increases in productivity to either creaming the best workers from the previous work force or to changes in the academic skills of individual workers.

Japanese companies in the United States frequently go to great lengths to select an adequate work force, and some of the larger companies even send maintenance and line workers to Japan for training. This practice supports the view that there is something unique about these workplaces that Americans are unlikely to learn in their own schools. While there is a lot of speculation about such skills, the workers themselves can provide a firsthand resource for understanding some of these differences.

I interviewed a group of these workers while they were in Japan where they were undergoing ten months training for work in maintenance and assembly-line positions. Once the training was completed they would be employed by a state-of-the-art factory that was being built in the United States. Because they were selected very early by a rigorous process, they were all highly skilled and most had come from technically demanding jobs in traditional manufacturing plants.[31] Many had taken advanced mathematics at a community college. In this sense they conform to the profile of the new industrial worker drawn by recent educational reformers, and fit the image of the new postindustrial worker. Until they were hired for work in this state-of-the-art computerized factory, none had worked in what would be considered a high-tech setting.

In contrast to what one might expect, the sample of workers I spoke to felt that their skills far exceeded the requirements of the jobs they had been brought to Japan to learn to perform. They were frustrated over the slow pace of the training they were receiving, and did not feel that the technical skills they were learning warranted the ten months they were spending in Japan. None of the workers thought that the skills required from the workplace equalled the skills they had developed in the United States, and none of them felt that academic skills were very important in the work they were being trained to do. Their words largely confirm the lesson taught by the NUMMI experience—many positions in high-technology plants do not require high-technology skills. Here is a die maker discussing his work and some of the requirements needed to perform it.

> CC: Most of what you need is to practice. It's almost like being a body man, you know, feeling for the high spots and the low

> spots in a die and then they have to weld it up or on a cutting
> edge, you're very close.

WF: Measurement—do you need to be good at measurement?

CC: Not really. In fact, the guys on the die maintenance hardly
ever use a micrometer or anything. In fact, the company has
one set of tools that everybody in the shop uses.

The emphasis is on the need for practical, hands-on experience and a certain level of trial and error problem solving skills. For most, the skills required for these new positions were considerably less demanding than those they needed for their previous job.

WF: Are you using that math in your training program here?

AD: No, not really, not very much. This is a different, a totally
different kind of work than what I did before. Part of what I
did before was tool and die making. You know, where you
get a blueprint and you actually make a machine or a part for
a machine. If something broke down for instance and they
would need a new part maybe for that machine, I would go
make it, and . . . get the thing back running. The way their
maintenance is set up here, it's pretty much you troubleshoot
the machine, find out what's wrong with it, get a new part,
put it in there, or send the broken part out and have it fixed
somewhere else. I don't think there will be as much math
involved in that. It's just a lot of problem-solving type work.
As far as the math goes for somebody in my job, I don't know
if there would be that much use for it.

Although the new job does not require much math it was an important part of his previous work.

> I did a lot of trigonometry because when you handle a blueprint
> not all the dimensions for a certain piece were on the blueprint.
> A lot of times you took the existing dimensions and had to figure
> out angles or take an angle and figure out the length of a side or
> something. There was a lot of trigonometry involved in the job I
> had before.

Work such as tool and die making, electronics, and other maintenance functions have traditionally involved highly skilled, well-trained labor. It is thus possible that the skill level of these workers is not typical, and that *most* jobs would require an upgrading of skills and an increase in the level of academic skills, as the reform literature suggests. However, this view is not well supported by my informants' observations.

> Most of the production work done on the floor does not require a very high skill level because of the repetition of it. The production people tend to do the same thing over and over and over. I think the maintenance end of it is much more complex than production.

While his report does not support the picture of the industrial worker drawn by the new educational discourse, neither does it fully support the portrait developed by the old. If academic skills are not quite the order of the day, neither is just muscle and sweat. There is indeed a feature of the new vision of work that does involve taking responsibility for quality, reducing the hierarchical levels of communication, and finding ways to cooperate on the shop floor.

> If a person detects a defect, either one he created or one created ahead of him by accident, he's not supposed to pass that on without it being corrected, which is a person-to-person quality control. I think the demanding portion of a production worker's job is keeping an eye on quality, making sure that each job is done perfectly each time, more so than the demands of any intricate mechanical skills of his hands or whatever. I think the work level and the skill level is fairly low, but the ability to recognize defects is more important.

Of course it is possible that these workers represent a narrow slice of the work force in such factories and that a broader picture is needed to grasp the qualities that will be required by the new world of work. Yet these workers' observations square quite well with the consultant in charge of hiring the entire twenty-five hundred-person work force. She confirmed the observation of the workers that academic skills are not very important for the performance of most jobs. Nevertheless, her company did test for academic performance, and the early applicants scored high—at the twelfth-grade level on reading and math tests, although some adjustments are made for the purpose of race and gender equity.

The fact that most applicants scored at this level did not mean that they were expected to perform high-level cognitive operations. The consultant provides a description of the actual skills that are used in the production process:

> Most of these jobs would not need basic algebra. The one exception might be some of these maintenance people. The reading

> skills would be things like reading training materials, procedures manual, policies, the normal . . . business of reading I guess is the best way to put it. But they don't tend to be very complex kinds of things. It's a pretty basic level again. We were thinking of giving a writing test except there are very few out there that are very valid. For the group leaders, we had them watching a videotape of a manager counseling an employee and they had to fill out a report for us much like they do in a work situation— what happened, who said what, what kind of plans were made. It's not a composition in a sense that you just start from scratch but everybody was getting very high ratings because what we were looking for was simply can a person write in a clear manner that is understandable and did they get everything that was happening on the tape that they should have. We didn't care about their grammar because what we said was they just have to be able to be understandable and express themselves clearly. And we saw some bad grammar but the writing tasks at the plant are probably more centered along the group leader levels or above.

Even though there is an expectation that everyone in a group should be able to write at a certain basic level, there is recognition that some people will have difficulty with this task and that some cooperatively decided division of labor will ultimately determine job assignments.

> But if someone in the group is less good at that and doesn't do terribly well, another member will help them. So, we didn't feel it was so critical for one single individual, if that makes sense.

The consulting firm had undertaken a close inspection of the skills that were actually exercised in the performance of maintenance and line jobs in the sister plant in Japan. Their findings support the view that there is frequently a loose or indirect relation between school achievement and worker productivity. They found a major discrepancy in the skills the workers said they used and the skills they actually did use on the job.

> What they told us is ninety to one hundred percent of the associates in maintenance at the parent factor in Japan, that's where the job analysis was performed, read operating manuals, blueprints and procedures and instructions.
> Ninety-six percent add, subtract, multiply and divide, but only thirty-seven percent do trigonometry calculations. Again this is Japanese. This is not expected here, but since we had to start the job analysis, the closest jobs that you can go get are the ones in Japan.
> Ninety-six percent do the basics—add, subtract, multiply and

divide. Thirty-seven percent do calculations with trigonometry. Sixty-seven percent say they work with mean standard deviations.

They said they did it, but when you observe, you see them adding, subtracting, multiplying and dividing or using a computer. You never saw anybody sitting there actually doing trigonometry. So the observation didn't necessarily match what they said they did either.

Some of them did use computers, but it was pretty much learning a very specific routine and using it over and over again. It wouldn't be widely based computer skills.

Ninety-six percent said they read operating manuals. One-hundred percent said they read blueprints and ninety-six read procedures and instructions.

[Our observer concluded] that yes, they read operating manuals, that kind of normal work thing. Very few had to read blueprints and the blueprints were not particularly complex.

[Turning from maintenance to production] sixty-three percent said they read blueprints or drawings, but what our observer noticed was it sort of just, oh, what's a good example, it wasn't really a blueprint, it might be a representation of something. If one of your jobs is maybe to score a handle on a coffee cup, you would have a picture of the handle and a picture of the cup and a picture of the screws maybe.

Eighty-seven percent filled in blanks or checked sheets, like a formal report that you might put a number in and that kind of thing. They did do that. Ninety-nine percent write simple reports, but they are very, very simple. It could be a hand-written note to your manager about something. It's not a highly complex document.

Ninety-one percent of the production people say that they keep counts on production. They have to be able to count.

[And our observer noted that] they did do that in some areas. Again, that is highly computerized. You're not going to be counting the finished product that you finished inspecting, because that is automatically done for you.

They might have to perform some calculation for a report, I suppose. They do a lot of mathematical graphing—like quality graphs and that kind of thing.

While there are indeed a few basic academic skills required on the production line, in the final analysis, an automobile factory is still an automobile factory and much of the drudgery remains.

Most of these jobs are boring and repetitious. A person is picking up a bumper, looking at it, inspecting it and putting it over here. He's picking up another bumper, doing the same thing.

The consultant notes that most of these jobs do not require high levels of academic skills.

> I don't know that it would take a high-school-level education to be able to do that sort of job.
>   Workers can make a lot of suggestions but essentially it's not going to change the fact that the bumper has to be inspected.
>   The Japanese worked very fast. Here you will see people kind of stopping and saying something or yelling at someone. The Japanese didn't make a sound. They only talked to people on their breaks. They concentrated on the work with a ferocity that just amazed me to tell you the truth. Frankly, I could not imagine doing something like that with two ten-minute breaks during the day and a lunch period, and being able to focus and concentrate like that.

It is not academic skills that the schools need to develop for this kind of work, she tells me, but rather "good teamwork" skills and interpersonal skills.

> I don't know what a school could do to develop good teamwork skills—good interpersonal skills, good kinds of inner problem-solving skills, which is sort of the equivalent, or good communication are more important than anything else. It's an expectation that this is how lives are conducted and it is so ingrained in their family, their communities, their schools, their religious practices. It's kind of hard to take it apart.

The observation is disturbing because it suggests that there may not be the easy relationship between the development of academic excellence and the requirement of a productive work force. If the consultant is correct, however, then such a work force will require that more attention be paid to the development of cooperative relationships, teamwork and interpersonal skills. Yet just how far we really want to go in this regard is clearly problematic from an educational point of view when one considers the pace of the Japanese factory.

The above is not meant to diminish the significance of academic skills. Clearly there will be many jobs for which knowledge of mathematics, science and other traditional academic areas will be very important. Moreover, when taught correctly, these are areas of knowledge that transcend any single job, and should be important for many areas of life and culture. Nevertheless, if there is doubt about the general applicability of the justification for emphasizing certain subjects, then it should be voiced. After all, the wrong reason for the right subject is still the wrong reason—and often results in inappropriate teaching methods.

There are also practical reasons for questioning the relationship between academic performance and worker productivity. If it is cooperation that we need, then we should present whatever we teach in a way that furthers cooperation. And if the importance of science and math, literature, and foreign language does transcend the requirements of working life, then we need to find ways to evaluate them that do not depend on their contribution to worker productivity.

VII. Why the Emphasis on Academic Performance

Ironically, neither the vision of the new workplace, with its cooperative teams and its lateral structures of communication, nor the practices of many state-of-the-art factories supports the competitive educational reform models. The first does not support it because the emphasis on a set and rigid curriculum and the competitive atmosphere fostered by the excessive use of standardized tests likely hinders the development of the kind of cooperative attitudes and communicative practices that such a workplace calls for. The second fails to support this vision simply because it does not square with observed reality. Some jobs will indeed require higher-order math and reading skills. But many other jobs will not, except perhaps as imposed, but functionally unnecessary, prerequisite for employment. What might be the reason for the excessive demands? Why do our political leaders insist on making America first among the nations in science and math? Is it simply our obsession to be number one in everything? Or is there more to it than that?

Tests do more than simply assess performance. For example, they can serve to motivate people. They tell students to study hard so that they will get into a college and then gain a good job. They motivate by depersonalizing the selection process and giving it the appearance of impartiality. They are important in helping people believe that the world is fair and that most of us get what we deserve; and they are important in tempering the resentment that might come when some otherwise competent candidates are left behind to linger in the ranks of the underemployed, while others are selected to move ahead. When tests lose this power, then selection loses the aura of impartiality, and the economic and the political structures are less secure because many people will question the way in which positions and income are distributed.

This is precisely what happened during the late 1960s and through much of the 1970s. Many people lost faith in the tests as they lost faith in the ability of economic and political agencies to provide a fair and reasonable distribution of goods and opportunities. Much of this was justified. Many of the major tests were racially and sexually biased. Testing agencies misrepresented the extent to which scores could be improved by direct coaching. As the currency of tests declined, so too did the legitimation of the authority structure that they helped support. Today in the United States the renewed acceptance of test scores represents a reassertion of that authority. Yet, as recent riots in Los Angeles and other parts of the nation suggest, legitimacy is fragile and easily fractured.

Ironically, tests can sometimes be a factor in motivating people too much. For example, during the early 1980s Korea, beset by a number of problems related to too much academic competition,[32] actually took draconian measures to curb private tutoring in order to dampen competition. That these measures would have the effect of holding down performance on tests were apparently of little concern. The government threatened tutors with six-month jail terms, and called for the expulsion of any student caught being tutored. In addition, parents with government jobs who had their children tutored were fired. The threat of six months in jail for prospective tutors discouraged some would-be tutors, but probably helped the sale of home computers and educational software. The attempt to eliminate tutoring and to soften competition was unsuccessful in Korea, and the law was eventually repealed because the root of the problem there, as in Japan, lies elsewhere—in the restrictive employment policies of the government and prestigious companies. The knowledge that the best jobs go to the graduates of a few schools serves to fuel the anxiety of students and parents. The small manipulations of symptomatic factors such as the examination system does little to change matters.[33] Our own reformers should at least ask whether the ban on tutoring had any effect on test scores and whether this had any impact on the productivity of the work force. I suspect that it did not.

The Korean example suggests that academic achievement is often used as a governor of motivation and that high test scores can be as much a problem as low ones. To say this is not, of course, to minimize the importance of math and science. It is, however, to question the rationale that is being used presently to justify their educational importance.

VIII. Conclusion: The Limits of the Economic Conservative Ideal

There is much that is appealing about the vision of work provided by the economic conservative. The jobs it outlines are more flexible and interesting than the unskilled jobs many of us have known. The vision seems to call for breaking down the class structure in the workplace. No longer will some work with their heads while others work with their hands. Mind and muscle will be one. It is a vision that holds some promise for education and for the idea of a democratic public. Preparation in school is preparation for work, and perhaps preparation for work is preparation for life in a public—a life of sharing and discourse. Here knowledge and intelligence must be widely distributed. The engineer and the manager are no longer solely responsible for interpreting and deciding. They join with everyone in the work force in sharing this responsibility. Everyone must have the skills needed to interpret and communicate information and to make decisions.

It is not quite democracy, but perhaps it is closer to it than what we have been used to on the job. Yet is the vision true? Does it actually reflect the coming world of work and the needs of the new workplace? The answer is complicated, but I think that the most truthful response is that it depends a great deal on what we demand from business and its leaders. Decisions about the nature, character, and quality of work are indeed *decisions*. They are not the unfolding of the natural order of things. Yet in a democracy the important question is who makes these decisions and what, if any role, the public has in reaching them.

The economic conservative's discourse is inadequate to the task of developing a democratic public because it has no response to this question. True, the conservative discourse does emphasize the need for cooperation among workers, and asks for a wider dispersal of information and therefore of authority throughout the workplace. In this respect the Japanese success appears to have had a beneficial influence on our emerging image of the workplace. Unfortunately, educators have largely lost some of the educational implications of this vision as they emphasize academic performance and largely ignore the quality of social relations. It is as if the appropriate social relations came quite naturally to people while the academic prerequisites required much more painstaking effort. The experience of already highly skilled American workers brought to Japan for ten months to learn new forms of social relations suggests that neither academic development nor the requisite social relations are "natural."

Yet the larger point goes beyond the question of whether educational reformers have truly achieved a congruence in their vision of work and their ideas about schooling. It involves the fact that the workers' cooperative understanding, as envisaged by the economic conservative, is constrained by "market" demands. It encourages us to improve efficiency and productivity within the workplace, but we are limited by the goals of the enterprise as determined by those who own and manage it. It is a discourse that restricts participation to decisions about means. The market and the firm itself are said to provide the ends. This is not yet democracy, because it limits the role of human discourse to matters of means and makes it appear as if our goals were set by "natural" market forces. Even the jobs that sound so appealing are a response not to human need, but to market-driven "forces." Should market "forces" change, or should the economic conservative miscalculate the requirement of the workplace, then the market "forces" will call for other, perhaps more traditional kinds of jobs.

To contain the public and its good by the "forces" of the market is a high price to pay for a little more flexibility in the workplace. It is to hand over to others, for example, the important question of just how long the working day should be or what we should hold as a proper mix between work and leisure. Given that this issue has not recently been a part of our political discourse, we might understand why some accept the limited choice. Yet if Juliet Schor is correct in her estimate that since 1948 American workers have doubled their productivity while the amount of leisure has steadily decreased,[34] there is clearly a need to understand the character of the choices with which we are confronted. Certainly most of us do want to participate in decisions about how to do our work. Companies that make work interesting and that develop cooperative relationships should be encouraged. Yet we also need to be aware of other matters that affect our own and our families well-being. These include the increasing pressure on men, women, and children to forego family activities for work and school.

The economic conservative clearly has some things right. We want better, more interesting, and more challenging jobs, but we want more than this. We want some control over the pace of our lives and the quality of our environment. We need to be told as often about the mandated five weeks' vacation in Austria, France, Finland, and Luxembourg,[35] as we are about the six weeks more each year that the Japanese worker spends over the American on the job.[36] And we need to contrast this to the eight weeks more that Americans spend on the job each year than their West German counterparts.[37] Moreover, the economic conservative rightly understands the parochial character of American business and the commercial importance of a more cosmopolitan approach to the world. Yet the educational significance of this insight is limited because it is framed in terms of technical goals and competitive advantages.

Certainly to counter the belief that the American way is always the most efficient can be a valuable educational lesson, as is the lesson that one's own goals and techniques are culturally constructed. However, this is not the reason conservatives want students to become aware of other cultures. It is not to temper one's own assumptions that we are told to look beyond our borders, but rather to find better ways to develop a competitive edge. The economic conservative admires Japanese schools not because their students learn considerably more about other cultures than do our students. They admire them because it appears that such learning contributes somehow to an effective, competitive work force, one that seems to have little question about the overall direction of things. Yet it may well be here, in its failure to encourage critical reflection, that we should be most concerned about the character of Japanese education and about American attempts to emulate it.

In this chapter I have examined that part of the conservative discourse that sees only markets and that understands public schools as instruments in an international economic struggle. The discourse is limited because it emphasizes markets and neglects democracy, but in this discourse there are important fragments that constitute elements of a democratic public. One fragment is to be found in the vision, limited as it is, of common goals and cooperative work that is thought to characterize the Japanese work force. Another fragment is to be found in the reduction of hierarchies and the need for lateral structures of communication. Of course, these are only fragments. In this vision workers do not necessarily share a common set of symbols and meanings, and therefore the collective is held together by function rather than heritage or history; discourse is limited to deliberation about means; the "goal" of the enterprise stands outside this deliberation, and must be accepted by it. Moreover, cooperative discourse is restricted to people within a firm, and does not extend to decisions that go beyond the good of a single enterprise.

In the next chapter we turn to an examination of the vision of the cultural conservative and the way that an image of the Japanese is used to support this vision. The cultural conservative understands some of the limits that the economic conservative ignores, and seeks to bind together history and purpose through commonly shared symbols. While the cultural conservatives are also impressed by the advances made by Japanese industry, it is not for economic reasons alone that they are inspired. The quality of Japanese industry is but a sign of the moral character of the Japanese nation, and it is here they believe that the United States has its most important lesson to learn from Japan.

4

Cultural Conservatives
and the Vision of Harmony

I. *Changes in American Educational Ideology*

Japanese department stores sell a home desk for students that has, on separate occasions, caught the attention of at least two American scholars. The desk was first described to Americans in a book published in 1983 as a way to illustrate the pressure that high school and university entrance examinations place on students and their families.

> Pursuing the equipment of competitive preparation and glancing through guides to colleges fascinates those caught in the exam obsession. One small but *entertaining* illustration of the general trend in this market is the student desk on sale in department stores. The deluxe models, which cost over $500, have built-in alarm clocks especially equipped with timers for speed tests, high and low intensity lights, swivel executive chairs, globes that light up, and in one case even a built-in calculator.[1]

A few years after this description was published another scholar described a similar desk. In this case the desk is an indication of the commitment of the entire nation to the education of its young and especially

> the mother's intense care and the nurturant and protected atmosphere. . . . The desk's work space is surrounded on three sides, shielding the child from distraction. There are shelves, and at the front is a dashboard-like arrangement of lights, an electric pencil

sharpener, a built-in calculator, and a small drawer for equipment. At the far right of the workspace is a button connected to a bell mounted in the kitchen for the child to summon his mother for help or a snack.[2]

The difference in the descriptions has little to do with changes in the desk or in the Japanese educational system. It reflects the recent changes in American educational ideology. The ideological change is not represented best in slogans or marches, and it is only slightly captured by the rhetoric of conservative policy-makers and politicians. It is most effectively expressed and transmitted through the ever-so-slight turn of a phrase or a change in the description of a common item like a desk. The first description connects the desk to a discourse of commodity fetish, and distances the writer from the process as an amused observer. The second identifies it with a sacrificing mother perhaps saving week after week to buy her anxious scholar the tools he needs to do the best job possible. Here the desk is a symbol of connectedness—of mother to child, of child to school, of school to nation. The description tells us that if we really want to know why Japan is on the rise and the United States is on the decline, we need only to understand the sacrifice that the Japanese are willing to make to shape a common identity, and then to reflect upon our own indulgence as amused witnesses. This desk is now connected to important concerns of ordinary American people—our sense of national malaise, our indifference to one another and our loss of national purpose.

When Sam Herman in Chapter Two spoke about the harmony that existed between the company and his father, when he related his father's feeling that the company would never let him down, he was calling upon images of family and connectedness. When, again in Chapter Two, the American mother complained about her children's unwillingness to carefully wipe the table, the complaint was a reflection of her feeling that family authority had broken down. And when she connected this breakdown to the failure of American industry to produce a reliable product, she was suggesting that the breakdown in family identity is a part of the breakdown in national identity. If we cannot take pride in what we do for each other as a family, then how can we take pride in what we do as a nation? The second description of the desk, that of Merry White, is a mirror of this concern. It is telling us just how the Japanese are able to establish and maintain this larger sense of identity. The process begins in the home with a caring, doting, mother who makes her child's success one with her own. White writes:

The Japanese mother intuits the desires and needs of the child's inner self and fulfills them without expecting the child to verbalize his own. She responds to his unexpressed signal and encourages his reading of her cues as well, thus creating an atmosphere of mutual sensitivity to mood and subtle body language.[3]

First a trust is established between mother and child, and then it is extended from the home to the schools and then to the corporation and the nation. When the American mothers in Chapter Two—all of whom had careers—suggested that the Japanese would hopefully bring back commitment and the work ethic to America, they may have had little idea of the demands that such a change could bring to their own lives. Yet they would be able to relate to White's description of the desk and what it means in terms of the bond between mother and child and between child, school, job, and nation. It is against this background that the difference between the two descriptions of the same desk is to be understood.

In this chapter I ask two questions: The first is: Just how did we get from the first description of the desk to the second? This question is of course predicated on my belief that sometimes, to counterphrase Freud, a desk is not simply a desk, and that sometimes a description of a desk is not simply a description of a desk. It is here an expression of a larger, ideological shift and of changes in the emphasis we place on competing educational goals. It represents a change from a more to a less progressive educational framework and the ascendency of the cultural conservatives' ideology. Whereas Merry White is showing us approvingly just how the Japanese achieve this larger, national identity, the first writer, Thomas Rohlen, is in his description distancing himself from the larger collective commitment. He finds *"entertaining"* an element of the testing mania that Japanese mothers take with grave seriousness, and he hints, in this passage, that the process by which businesses exploit the anxiety produced by the educational system is a corruption of the ideal of education itself. I say "in this passage" because Rohlen's ultimate stance is not clear-cut, and because his ambiguity reflects the ambiguity in our own discourse about the goals of education. Yet despite this ambiguity, there has been a crystallization of our ideas about the purpose of education, and this crystallization is represented by the thoughts of Sam Herman, the American mothers, and Merry White. Here I want to use the discourse on Japanese education to show just how our own recent educational commitments have been formed, and how this ambiguity has been resolved. The second question I ask in this chapter is whether anything is lost in this change in terms of the conception of a democratic public.

II. Introduction: National Identity and Educational Visions

Cultural conservatives begin where the economic conservatives leave off—with the emphasis on structures of communication, and with the understanding that uncontrolled markets produce centrifugal forces that threaten the unity of the social structure. Cultural conservatives seeks harmony through the manipulation of symbolic, rather than material, conditions. They believe that the unification of symbols and meanings will bring about a unified people. They appeal to the need for a common identity to counter the centrifugal market forces, and they understand the role of history and meaning in the development of a people. They seek a curriculum that will thread common symbols and unified meanings throughout the beliefs and values of disparate groups, and they call upon the schools to develop in children a sense of a common heritage. In this respect cultural conservatives have an explicit but limited appreciation of the public-forming role of education. They understand the importance of common symbols and shared meanings, but they do not understand the importance of the process by which they are achieved. They seek community, but they neglect democracy.

Historically, those who governed public education often have been guided by the cultural conservatives' vision, and in turn cultural conservatives today lament the passing of a supposedly Edenesque time when American values were secure and unassailable. It is against this Eden that they measure life in America today, believing that many groups are overly sensitive and are placing unrealistic demands on the schools. In the wake of these demands, turmoil and confusion reign and schools have lost their essential mission of developing a single American identity. The cultural conservative's goal has been to recapture that sense of mission through a reaffirmation of our common identity.

III. Japan and National Unity

Facts are important to cultural conservatives and must be taught in school because they fear that without them each group will have its own individual facts and its own way of interpreting them. Facts—

uninterpreted, naked facts—are a sign that the national identity is intact and that local cultural meanings and aspirations are under control. When facts are challenged—when every ethnic and racial group wants its own fact taught in the schools, when there are feminist facts, Afro-American, and gay facts—then conservatives worry that the school can no longer be counted on to transmit a unified national identity.

Much like the economic conservative, the cultural conservative also sees Japan as a source of inspiration, but for somewhat different reasons. Cultural conservatives see in Japan and its schools an answer to their concerns about preserving a single national identity and a uniform American set of values. They are of course concerned about questions of productivity, but they read productivity as a sign of something deeper—national morality. Economic conservatives look to the Japanese schools because they produce a productive work force. Cultural conservatives look to Japanese schools because they teach moral values such as loyalty and patriotism, and get away with it.

Because American identity is traditionally tied to its industrial prominence, in real life the cultural conservative and the economic conservative are often bundled together in the same person. For many cultural conservatives, the measure of American virtue has been its superior ability to invent, produce, and market new goods and machines, and the justification for spreading American civilization throughout the world has entailed a close relationship among industry, growth, and capitalism on the one side, and morality, democracy, and political progress on the other. To threaten the prominence of American industry is thereby to call into question its very identity as a nation. As a presidential commission put it:

> If an unfriendly foreign power had attempted to impose on America the mediocre educational performance that exists today, we might well have viewed it as an act of war. . . . We have, in effect, been committing an act of unthinking, unilateral educational disarmament.[4]

The language of threat, disarmament, and war is a sign that more is at stake than the sale of automobiles or computer chips, and that the discourse about Japanese education involves more than just talk about schools and jobs. It is a moral discourse, a discourse in which Japan serves as the goad to highlight our own moral failings, our reputed laziness, sloth, and indifference, and, as a discourse about morals, it reiterates a recurring theme of American educational reform:

A technological advantage translates into a moral advantage. As William Tory Harris, the Commissioner of Education, put it in 1889 as he justified American expansionism:

> The white man proves his civilization to be superior to other civilizations just by this very influence which he exercises over the people who have lower forms of civilization, forms that do not permit them to conquer nature and to make the elements into the ministers of human power.[5]

The history of the twentieth century has tempered faith in technology. Yet the cultural conservative shares with Harris the belief that nations on the top are there because they belong there morally. Calvanism lives here in the belief that national greatness is a sign of national morality, and it is national morality that the cultural conservative is most concerned about.

> Japan's single greatest advantage over us is moral superiority. Scholars and economists don't talk about moral superiority because it can't neatly be quantified like a trade deficit, but it's every bit as real. At its simplest it means that Japanese believe— passionately—in a job well done. It is what makes the lowest grease monkey work just as hard for the company as the president does. It drives the Japanese zeal for quality and service. Japanese at all levels work harder and care more about their work than we do.[6]

To the cultural conservative, Japanese schools represent the benefits that are derived from taming diversity and asserting traditional moral authority. The educational and economic successes of the Japanese are object lessons that the cultural conservative uses successfully to illustrate the excesses of independence, creativity, and critical thinking and to reassert the importance of obedience to institutional standards and goals.

The conservative has certainly won an important interpretive battle. Discussions about Japanese schools are not the same as discussions about other foreign school systems. Talking about what the Japanese schools are doing is different from talking about education in, say, Israel, Kenya, or Italy. When we speak about education in these countries, our purpose is usually to understand something about them, not to change something about us. When we speak about schooling in Japan, it is to exhort, to show how effective schools *can* be in a postindustrial age, and just how far our schools have fallen from an achievable ideal. Japan has become a symbol through which the cultural conservative seeks to develop a new consensus about the role of the schools. Behind this vision of morality and national prominence is an image of a public and of the public-forming character of education. Moreover, it is an image that has traveled far beyond conservative circles, and is perhaps the most influential conception of the ideal of education present in American society today. It is not, however, an adequate conception, for it sees a public as a product to be delivered rather than as a process to be achieved.

Nowhere is the recent advance of the conservative program more obvious than in writings about Japanese education. It is here, perhaps as much as in any other place, that we can gauge the advance of the conservative's ideal. Many who write about Japan would not identify themselves with conservative agendas. Indeed, many are progressive, child-centered educators who believe that one reason Japanese schools are superior to our own is because of the attention paid to the voice of the child. Yet attending to the voices of children may be seen to pay off for very different reasons, not all of which are especially democratic. In our decade-long affair with Japanese schools, these reasons have changed, and democratic ideals have steadily receded. Again, much like the economic conservative's discourse, this cultural discourse also connects to some important ideas about the nature of a democratic public, but it does so in a fragmented and perhaps unconscious way. To retrieve these fragments requires retracing the discourse, and bringing back to consciousness the changes that have occurred in it. It requires that we understand how that Japanese desk has changed from a commodity of exploitation to an expression of devotion, love, and connectedness.

IV. Discourse on Japanese Schools

The discourse about Japan is part of a larger struggle for control over America's self-understanding, and in the long run, this is a struggle about the character of the American self. This struggle is marked, in part, by a tension between the ideal of education as learning to define one's self through a dialogue with one's culture, and an ideal where the self is defined according to perceived external, institutional imperatives. The tension is also expressed in the conflict between those who believe that the primary goal of education is to further an egalitarian spirit and democratic institutions, and those who believe that the role of education is to deliver a set of common meanings and a sense of common purpose. Finally, it is expressed in the tension between those who emphasize the need for students to learn to be critical thinkers, where critical thinking involves reflection on widely adopted institutional practices and values, and those who believe that education consists primarily in learning a few "basic" foundational areas.

In the traditional educational literature, the first side of this tension is often expressed by the "child-centered" educational ideology, which seeks to determine educational goals in terms of the interests and desires of the child, and the second side is expressed by a national ideology, which seeks to define educational goals in terms of the needs of national growth, development, and morality. These different ideologies have important implications not only for what is taught, but also for how it is taught. For example, where child-centered education truly emphasizes critical thinking and individual initiative, teachers often will seek to limit expressions of their own pedagogical authority in order to teach children to develop habits of independent thinking. Moreover, where teachers seek to develop an egalitarian spirit and to further democratic participation, responsibility will likely be diffuse and shared by the class as a whole. However, where educational aims are largely predefined, authority will be centered in the teacher, with responsibility assigned separately by her to each individual child. Yet the distinction between the child-centered approach and the national model is not an absolute one. One mark of the ascendency of the cultural conservatives' program is that some educators who express child-centered values have adopted the cultural conservatives' terms, and measure the worth of child-centered pedagogy by its ability to produce a common set of meanings and a single identity.

The example provided by the "success" of Japanese schools and industry has substituted for a more deliberate national discourse about the proper aims of education in a postmodern, democratic society. Democratic progressives have often bought into this example, sometimes consciously, sometimes unwittingly, and sometimes as a compromise to save some aspect of the liberal educational program.[7] The task here is to deconstruct that consensus in order to show where progressive possibilities are hidden.

V. Commentaries on Japanese Education

Much of the popular conservative discourse simplifies the character of Japanese education by overemphasizing the level of harmony and concurrence that is to be found in Japan. Even though Japanese education is more centralized than American education, it provides a rich mosaic of very different experiences. Conservatives admire Japanese education for its harmonious character and for producing loyal, obedient, and hardworking students. Yet the Japanese have a militant, powerful, and left-leaning teachers union that serves as a strong adversary and balance to the conservative Ministry of Education. Moreover, while Japanese universities are often pictured as quiet training grounds for the economic and political elite, and for middle-level managers, the student protests in Japan during the 1960s were more militant than those in the United States and most of Europe, and resulted in the closing of some of the most prestigious institutions. Finally, while Americans have come to admire the harmony between Japanese management and labor, this harmony does not hold for some national unions, such as the transportation workers' union, which have carried on bitter and disruptive strikes. These union members are as much a product of Japanese schools as are the more cooperative, or—depending on your preference—docile company union members.

This complex picture is as true of Japanese public education as it is of Japanese industry and labor. At the end of the last century, Japanese education came under the control of the nation-builders, and teachers were expected to serve the state before serving the child. Yet the Japanese educator Teruhisa Horio notes that there has long been a countertradition, one which emphasizes the independence of scholarship and teaching. Horio reports that in the early days of the Meiji era, in the middle of the last century, the educational philosopher Fukuzawa Yukichi emphasized the need for an open approach to inquiry that would be available to all of the people. For Fukuzawa, the task for the new society was to break the monopoly of knowledge that had been established by those in power, and, through inquiry and knowledge, to empower the people. Thus, in contrast to the Imperial Rescript on Education of 1890, which emphasized loyalty and obedience to the authority of the state, Fukuzawa saw the need for people to organize their own path to enlightenment.[8] Fukuzawa's educational philosophy reflected many of the values that American educators would label "child-centered." For example, "rather than thinking of education as teaching people about things, it should be approached as an opportunity to remove all impediments to the development of their naturally given abilities."[9] Many of Fukuzawa's ideas formed the basis of the 1947 Fundamental Law of Education, which was enacted after the war to rid the schools of the militarism that had come to dominate them, and to replace the authoritarian values of the Imperial Rescript with democratic ones.

Horio's work is important in understanding that different strains also exist in Japanese educational thought. Of course, Japan has its cultural conservatives emphasizing education for loyalty, obedience, and national development. But it also has other voices which speak of education as a means for liberation, democratic decision-making, and individual development. Much like their American counterparts, the Japanese cultural conservatives will stress the uniqueness of Japan, arguing that the Japanese stand out among other peoples of the world as unique. Many of Japan's cultural conservatives believe that things Japanese are *essentially* Japanese and are not transferable to or from other nations. In this they differ from the missionary zeal of many of our own conservatives, who believe our principles of governments and markets should be adopted worldwide. Japanese conservatives generally hold that because of Japan's uniqueness, "Western" concepts such as individual rights, or equality, if they are at all applicable to Japan, must take on a special Japanese meaning. This meaning must respect traditional family values, the division of labor between men and women, the communal features of social and economic life, and Confucian values. This side objects to the "self-incrimination" implied if Japanese textbooks mention Japanese aggression in Manchuria or the forceful colonization of Korea.

More liberal Japanese thought rejects the idea that Japan is unique, argues that values are universal, and holds that Japan has no special values or qualities that should insulate it from the influence of the rest of the world. Concepts such as individual rights, equality, and fairness are good for the world, and they are also good for the Japanese. In education, this group emphasizes the importance of democracy and peace, and objects to using textbooks as instruments of national chauvinism. Its members are frequently sympathetic to child-centered tendencies in education, rejecting the idea that children should be molded to some national norm.

In addition to the various views and practices of different individuals, there are some important differences to be found at the elementary and the secondary levels of education. While pedagogical practices differ in most countries from the elementary to the secondary school, the practices in Japan are perhaps among the most extreme. The former tends toward child-centered practices, and even extreme permissiveness, while the latter emphasizes discipline, external control, and preparation for standardized examinations. This difference has affected commentaries on Japanese education. Those looking at the elementary school tend to see Japanese education in child-centered terms, while those looking at the secondary school tend to view it in terms of control and discipline.

Nevertheless, the image that now dominates descriptions of both elementary and secondary school is of a system that is in harmony with itself and with its society. What has changed among the many American commentators who view Japanese education positively is the way that harmony is interpreted, and the lessons it is thought to hold. In the process the democratic ideal recedes considerably, and in its place stands a new commitment, one which views the role of the school to be the fashioning of a common identity. The discourse is significant not only because of what it says about Japan, but because of the way the research agenda is wedded to the emerging conservative educational agenda. It is more significant because it reflects the rather haphazard and unconscious way in which educational ideals can change with a change in political fashion. I begin here with some background material in order to provide a historical context for the discussions that have developed about Japanese education.

VI. The Forgotten Discourse about Democracy

The stubborn persistence of poverty and inequality during the late 1960s and the 1970s in the United States led many American radical and conservative critics to question whether the kind of educational reform initiated during the Johnson presidency could be used to effect significant democratic social change. The Left and the Right disagreed about why schools were not meeting expectations. Some conservative critics argued that differences in intelligence along racial and class lines accounted for the "failure" of the federal programs to make significant changes.[10]

In response to the conservative argument, radical theorists proposed that educational reform is limited by the structure of the workplace within a capitalist society. Because work in a capitalist society is structured in an undemocratic, hierarchical fashion, and because the function of schools is to prepare students to work within a capitalist structure, schools are also undemocratically and hierarchically structured. Moreover, because they must prepare students to work at different levels of the capitalist enterprise, schools teach some students to be intellectually active, and others to be passive. Like the corporation and the society outside it, some people must be educated to make the rules, while others must learn to follow them. A democratic ideology, with the inaccurate belief that everyone has an equal chance to succeed, legitimizes schools in the minds of parents and students, but it does not represent reality. Schools, these critics concluded, serve to simply reproduce the class structure and to then justify that reproduction.

Despite their differences, the conservative and the radical educator agreed that schools could do little to advance equality. Both sides' arguments were partial. In addition to an overemphasis on biological or social determinism, the advances made by programs such as Head Start suggest that the conservatives were mistaken in writing off the possibilities of education. On the other side, radical reproduction theorists never successfully showed that structural limits had actually been reached by the present capitalist order, and therefore their analysis only explained inequality *as such*. It was an open question whether or not it explained inequality in capitalist *American society*. While the arguments were flawed, the concerns about equality occupied the central focus of school policy and research; the major issues of the time, such as whether busing was an effective means to achieve desegregation, were basically spirited by egalitarian concerns, which also formed the backdrop against which other educational systems, including the Japanese, were examined.

This concern was expressed as late as 1980 in a major work on Japanese schools. The author, William Cummings, drawing on research he did in the early 1970s, argued that the radical critics were wrong and that Japanese education was an example of a school system that was successfully being used to create a progressive, democratic and egalitarian society. The Japanese school,

> challenges the established hierarchies, urging that they be leveled. Rather than concerning itself with reducing the effects of social background on individual learning, it attempts to realize a situation where all can learn; rather than have pupils learn those skills and knowledge that will help them to fit into existing hierarchies, the transformationist approach urges that pupils develop a critical attitude to these hierarchies. Today's critical children will be tomorrow's adults, working in positions where they can level the hierarchies. As the hierarchies become more equal, so will the opportunities.[11]

The effect of these changes, Cummings argued, is profound. Not only is the cognitive development of Japanese students among the most equal in the world, but democratic sentiments have been strongly internalized, and these sentiments exert egalitarian pressures on adult institutions, forcing them to change. Like subsequent writers, Cummings believed that the Japanese system could serve as an example for Americans, but for him it exemplified the way education could be used to achieve a more egalitarian, democratic society—not how it can be used to advance the goals of industry. In his description of Japanese schools as child-centered, in his picture of the Japanese family as egalitarian and permissive and of Japanese mothers as flexible and responsive, he is seeing the home, as well as the school, as the training ground for the new egalitarian, democratic, social order. That Cummings' description of the treatment of Japanese children is similar to the one White provides a number of years later is an indication of the stability of the Japanese educational system. That Cummings believes he is seeing education in the service of democracy, while White speaks not at all about democracy but rather about industry and productivity, indicates the rapid changes that have occurred in the weight given to competing educational goals in the United States. Rohlen provides a key to understanding this change and to exploring the image of nationhood that lies behind our most recent infatuation with the Japanese.

VII. Schooling and National Identity

Rohlen was the first person to document the recent relationship between Japanese schools and Japanese industry. His description of the student's desk with which I opened this chapter indicates that he is able, at times, to maintain a distance from the process he observes, and that he is not completely caught up in the ideological presuppositions that underlie later works on Japan. However, he is involved in a dual discourse, one that is committed to two conflicting ideological positions at the same time. Such a discourse represents a moment in a historical dialogue that marked a change of tide. In the case of the American discourse on Japan, the currents of democracy were submerged while those of national identity and uniformity surfaced. Rohlen draws on the emerging conservative consensus as a way to display the significance of his study, but he also holds on to some progressive educational values. In this way he enables us to excavate some of the themes that were submerged with the tide of the 1980s.

Like Cummings, Rohlen uses Japan as a way to exhort American educators. However, when he does so, it is not because of Japan's democratic qualities, but because of its contribution to the development of a moral national character. In this sense he has indeed adopted the cultural conservative's program. Rohlen is deeply concerned about the United States' place among the nations of the world and about the identity of its people as a nation. In his exhortation Rohlen draws upon the emerging conservative consensus, and returns to the earlier theme that the central role of the schools is to build a morally superior nation.

> How well a population performs the basic tasks of social existence when multiplied out day after day, year after year, is the underlying basis and sense of dynamics for key institutions that in turn shape a nation's place among all nations. The historical rise and fall of civilizations, in other words, rests heavily on such assumed matters as socialization, fundamental skills, and general morality.[12]

His description of the merits of the Japanese system is weighted heavily in terms of industrial efficiency and productivity. The Japanese have developed an exceptionally efficient system for the production of human capital. In contrast to the United States, where there are wide differences between the most and the least educated populations, Japan's educational system is able to sustain an impressive level of uniformity throughout the country and to provide industry with an average citizen who is more highly educated in terms of basic skills than most other countries. Thus, whereas nations like the United States do a superb job in terms of their best students, but miserably in terms of their worst, Japan, Rohlen suggests, does a good job of educating almost all of its students.[13]

Rohlen agrees with the economic conservatives that industrial productivity is a result of the Japanese educational system, but it is the moral quality of the nation that he finds more impressive. Schools contribute significantly to this national moral character through demanding, among other things, that meticulous attention be paid to detail and by teaching students important traits such as loyalty and hard work. This, in turn, serves to develop highly disciplined workers who identify with the companies that employ them and contribute to high productivity. The school

> teaches careful, intellectual work habits aimed at reducing routine mistakes. Another crucial ingredient is a capacity to remain alert and to find repetitive work interesting. Japanese workers generally accept organizations as allies and are responsive to their requirements—including, for example, working late to solve problems.[14]

He tells us, in contrast to Cummings, that Japanese schools are highly stratified.[15] He mentions, as does Cummings, that there is greater equality of achievement in Japan than in the United States, but the Japanese school is not singled out because it teaches students democratic values. Rather, it is cited for its ability to dispose students to accept institutionalized authority and to discourage them from thinking on their own. It legitimizes existing social relations[16] and creates a group of passive, uncritical students.[17] "They are motivated by entrance exams and trained by parents to view learning as a necessary burden in preparation for adulthood. . . . They learn not to challenge authority."[18]

While Rohlen acknowledges that the practices have some disadvantages, he emphasizes their many benefits and their importance for stimulating Japanese industry. For example, Rohlen mentions the economic, social, and political advantages to teaching so many children to sit still.[19] Furthermore, he sees in the Japanese examination system an important balance to the particularism associated with a group-oriented society.

Rohlen believes that the rigid, controlled routine of the educational system is instrumental in the development of many of the more admirable features of the Japanese character:

> Are we not witnessing in all of this something highly indicative of Japanese national character? Many virtues—diligence, sacrifice, mastery of detailed information, endurance over the many preparatory years, willingness to postpone gratification, and competitive spirit—are tied together at a formative period.[20]

Even the herdlike group psychology has its moral benefits as students learn to restrain their instincts and desires.

> This desire [to achieve] . . . comes as part of a great mad rush, the product of group psychology, and it focuses on the goal of social status. . . . The entire process tests the ambitious student sorely, but the lesson learned in the cathartic experience is to knuckle down, to restrain one's instinct for pleasure and personal preference. Walking the prescribed straight and narrow path, wherever it leads, is the way of the successful student.[21]

VIII. Emerging Consensus

Although Rohlen contributes to the emerging conservative discourse, he is not unambiguously impressed by the character work of the Japanese school. Rohlen represents a dual discourse because he holds his views with hesitation, ambivalence, and implicit—perhaps even unconscious—doubt. He is a participant in an emerging political consensus about educational goals, but the consensus had still to crystallize.

Rohlen is impressed by the way the Japanese school prepares the Japanese work force, but his endorsement of this role is ambivalent because he actually holds two conflicting ideas about the aims of education. Only one of these ideas is compatible with the "character development" and nation-building that he appears sometimes to be so impressed with. Indeed, his concern about the importance of schools to industry came essentially as an afterthought to his study. As he writes in his preface:

> When I went to Japan for thirteen months of fieldwork in 1974, the country was not the hotly debated topic that it is in the world today. I had no expectation that what I was about to study would prove to be of instructive interest to American educators, or that Japanese education would begin to impress me as a significant element in American understanding of Japan's economic success. Yet during the last two years, as this book has taken shape, Japan's industrial prowess and social order have captured the attention of much of the world. Japan, whether perceived as a competitive threat or as a model of efficiency, now merits careful study.[22]

Rohlen's concern for the wealth-producing features of schooling does not, however, dominate the book. It, along with the themes about national character, is the focus of only two chapters—the introduction and the conclusion. These are, of course, important chapters, in that they frame the ethnographic and historical study which comprises the larger part of the work. Yet the dual character of the discourse is apparent in the middle chapters, which often provide a favorable comparison of American education in contrast to that of the Japanese. The ideal of American education—teaching students to be flexible, critical, reflective thinkers[23]—are praised in contrast to the dronelike behavior that he describes in Japanese classrooms. Such comparisons may suggest a familiarity with only the better American schools, but they are clearly part of the earlier educational discourse, and show the transitional point that Rohlen occupies in the discourse on Japan. Here Rohlen is scathingly critical of Japanese schools for their authoritarian character and their inflexibility. He describes a system where teachers are paid quite well and have high social prestige, but where the classroom is dull, inflexible, and uninspiring.[24] Describing his own feelings as he sat through the classes at a typical high school, he tells us that "The lectures have generally been boring. . . . I . . . find the monotony almost insufferable at times."[25] At one high-level public high school, he writes scornfully, "Many teachers . . . view themselves as experts in their subjects, especially in the kind of minutiae that can be objectively tested on university entrance examinations."[26] In these middle chapters Rohlen's description is of a system driven by irrelevant information imposed by external examinations that are virtually the sole arbiters of an individual's social standing and rewards.

When Rohlen wrote the middle chapters, his focus and concerns were similar to Cummings'. Indeed, while Rohlen's book was published in 1983 as the conservative consensus was emerging, the research was done in the middle 1970s, close to the same period as Cummings. The two writers differ a great deal about what Japanese schools are like as a matter of fact, but they often share a similar understanding of what counts as reasonable education. I say "often" because of Rohlen's mentioned ambivalence. In these chapters, when Rohlen describes Japanese education he is describing a system that is effective in deadening curiosity, imposing dated knowledge on students,[27] minimizing the need to develop higher-level interpretive and critical skills, and leading children to dwell in a bizarre fantasy world.[28] It is a system that has the effect of narrowing students to a single goal—passing the entrance examination into the university:

> With so much riding on examinations and with so many years of preparation invested by each candidate, universities recognize a responsibility to make no sudden changes. They announce plans for revisions sometimes as far as ten years in advance. If a new economic theory or new questions in microbiology are going to be included, the groundwork for such learning must be laid in junior high school. If the correct answer regarding the causes of World War II changes, then students trained to give old answers should not be penalized. For reasons like this, the reform of the content of the entrance examination moves with glacial slowness.[29]

Finally, the system he describes is one where business feeds off the education of children as a huge industry of cram schools prepare them for the examination, and newspapers and magazines provide readers the latest results. Sometimes Rohlen ingeniously struggles to place the best face on these practices, and to justify them.

> Japan . . . is a group-oriented society—neither individualistic nor socialistic. Such a society can choke on its own narrow particularism if it does not have well-entrenched mechanisms that counterbalance its powerful tendencies to allocate rewards and favors on the basis of personal affiliation. What can happen all too easily is that those responsible for selecting people for universities, jobs and so forth cannot resist personal pressure from relatives, friends, and colleagues. The weight of personal obligation requires a powerful countermechanism. An impersonal exam system that adjudicates the selection process is just the solution.[30]

With the suggestion that Japanese schools tend to reproduce the existing class structure, and that the examinations test for irrelevant information and lower-level skills, it is difficult to understand why they should be accepted as impartial and adequate selectors—unless, of course, the idea is to legitimize an otherwise arbitrary social order by teaching people to value certain ritualistic rites of passage as academically significant. (While Rohlen is unclear, there is, as we will see in the next chapter, ironical truth to his observation.)

Rohlen's ambivalence arises because he sits squarely in the middle of the two conflicting ideological movements mentioned earlier. The one, emphasizing equality and democracy, is the product of the 1960s and 1970s. The other, emphasizing competition, productivity, character development, and unreflective loyalty, was soon to become the product of the 1980s. He wants to use schools to maximize the development of human capital, so that American industry can compete with the Japanese, and he also wants them to maximize the development of human potential, so that students can become critical adults, presumably participating as citizens in a democratic society. While these two ideals may, in some places, be consistent with one another, Rohlen's description of Japanese schools unwittingly indicates that this is not the case in Japan. Rohlen manages to remain in the middle of the two movements because he does not acknowledge the contradiction. When he makes his plea that we need to learn from Japan's successes, he does so within the context of an argument about human capital. In other words, Japan can teach us how to educate a more productive work force. However, he concludes his book with a rousing appeal to the achievement of human potential as a fundamental social good—leaving the impression that somehow, despite its rigid curriculum, its brutal tests, and its mindless selection process, Japanese schools enable students to achieve their potential.[31] Yet only a few pages before his concluding remarks, he tells us about his own reservations about Japanese schools: "The well-intended teachers and well-behaved students put their efforts to purposes that are ultimately shallow and uninspired. The nation benefits economically. Society is well run. But it is a system without much heart."[32]

It is exactly this confusion, the conflation of human capital with human potential—between the investment and the enjoyment—that marks the transition from one ideological point to another. Yet of course human capital, as important as it may be, is not a fundamental social good. Human capital is what we invest. Human potential is what we achieve and enjoy when we are allowed to fulfill our own special talents. And while some level of capital is necessary to fulfilling our potential, it is certainly not the case that this is an everlasting linear relationship. At some point, if we continue to look at human beings as human capital, we reduce the extent to which they can achieve their unique, human potential. This is, of course, the principle problem with theories that insist that schools must serve to enhance national competitiveness. At some point this goal becomes educationally counterproductive. Rohlen fails to acknowledge this point and thereby he fails to see the tensions in his own analysis. He passes himself on the tracks without fully realizing he is traveling in opposite directions. He wants both democracy and efficiency, but he does not realize that the latter—as commonly understood—does not automatically entail the former, and is sometimes counterproductive for achieving it. Indeed, democracy is sometimes notoriously inefficient. This, of course, is exactly the confusion that marks the current American discourse on education. To make better, more effective workers is not the same as making more thoughtful and reflective democratic citizens. Both, of course, are important, but each must be worked at in its own right.

If one does think of the purpose of education as truly the development of individual potential, and if one believes that individual potential must entail the capacity to evaluate one's own goals, then the process that Rohlen describes as Japanese would, if accurate, surely be educationally inappropriate. It would retard the development of the intellectual distance and cripple the critical perspective needed to analyze the forces influencing one's own thought and action. In other words, it would render unlikely the ironic tone that is expressed in *his* description of the desk with which I began this chapter. However, once the conflation of potential and capital has been made, the ideological transition has been completed and we have unambiguously entered the world of the cultural conservative.

IX. The New Consensus

Recent works on Japan largely neglect education's role in the formation of a democratic public, and take it for granted that the ultimate goal of education is to effect a smooth harmony between the interests of the individual and those of industry and the state. The educational consensus appears complete, and it is now time to take it apart. We can begin by saying a few more words about Merry White's book.

For White, the Japanese educational challenge is really an industrial challenge. She believes that once we understand how the Japanese schools and the Japanese family are centered around the child, we will also understand the force behind Japanese industrial success. In so many words, a child-centered school is a good school because it produces an efficient work force. Child-centered education is not just good for children, it is also good for business.

Although White appears to update Cummings, her treatment of Japanese education is a part of a different educational consensus, one that takes for granted significantly different educational aims. Whereas Cummings addresses child-centered education in Japan because of the role that he believes it plays in creating an egalitarian, democratic society, White addresses it because of the role she sees child-centeredness playing in the preparation of an efficient, productive work force. Yet, as with Rohlen, it is not the academic skills that children learn that are of primary importance. It is the identification with institutionalized authority that ultimately makes the difference.

Japanese educational practices, according to White, teach children to "cheerfully conform to the community's expectations."[33] The result is a society determined to "help children engage wholeheartedly, and for the most part pleasurably, in their work, whether that effort leads to a life of bureaucratic predictability, small shop-retailing, or breakthrough innovations."[34] Of course, these are the traits of a happy and perhaps productive worker. They are not especially central virtues for the democratic citizen. Here reflection and critical awareness are some of the virtues we want to cultivate.

Unlike Cummings, democracy is not a central concern for White. Nor is she concerned whether the schools can be used as an instrument for justice and social transformation—at least not in Japan, where harmony and peace are thought to prevail. Indeed, she reports on a number of antidemocratic practices, but registers little criticism. For example, when she deals with Japan's concern for racial purity and cultural homogeneity, and the difficulty Japan has in accommodating culturally diverse groups such as the Koreans or the oppressed Baru-kamins, she does not develop a critical voice. Instead of challenging the chauvinistic theme about Japanese uniqueness, she notes only that it inspired many of the education programs of the pre-war period that functioned to ward off cultural colonization by the West.[35] She continues by noting that the modern curriculum functions to develop the basic moral constructs without which self-identity is deeply flawed.[36] She concludes by observing that Japanese students who have been abroad are often bullied on their return to school in Japan—a serious problem in Japanese schools—because they are not able to reconstruct this identity in the proper way. Hence, she appears to leave the burden on the returnee to adjust to the rigid cultural con-straints of many Japanese schools. When she then lists the actual character traits that she finds so admirable—learning to bear hard-ships, to have patience, to overcome obstacles, and to listen to other people's opinions[37]—she fails to explain just why she sees these as specifically Japanese. Nor does she reconcile her attribution of a will-ingness to listen to other people's opinions with her acknowledgment of the bullying that is directed at children who have been abroad.

The silences in this book are themselves revealing of the changing ideological climate. The fact is that slowly, through contact with for-eigners, Japan is becoming more multicultural. It is not the multicultur-alism that results when stranger meets stranger, but it is that which results when a family member returns home after having picked up some of the strange ways of the foreigner. In Japanese schools, the children who have gone to school abroad often present special prob-lems for the schools, and have been the objects of bullying for other students. White fails to adequately consider the problems now devel-oping because many Japanese children educated abroad find them-selves shunned by fellow students, and sometimes are mistreated by overly parochial teachers. The mistreatment is not because these returning students are unable to bear hardship or lack patience, but more because they do not sit or stand in the customary way, or because they are more ready to speak their mind in the classroom. One need only assume a different set of values—independence over incorpora-tion, critical thinking over unreflective loyalty—and one could read White's praise of the Japanese school as a scathing criticism. In neglect-ing to consider the responsibility that the school has to the returnee, she is reflecting the ideological position of the cultural conservative—the material for a unified, harmonious nation already exists in its traditional symbols and practices.

X. Conclusion

Japan has a different meaning for the cultural conservative than it does for the economic conservative. Whereas the economic conservative sees in the Japanese the vision of the future American workplace, the cultural conservative sees the image of a lost past. The economic conservative is an MIT economist seeking to learn how to organize the American economy from the Japanese experience. The cultural conservative is Sam Herman waiting for the Japanese to return to America the moral virtues and the work ethic it has lost. Cultural conservatives seek harmony and national unity through common symbols and shared meanings. They seek to effect this unity by regaining control of the cultural institutions that are critical to the formation of identity. They fear that diversity threatens the very fabric of cultural received opinions. The themes of the Women's Movement and the prominence of feminism within debates about cultural change is a sign that the traditional socialization schemes—the separation of private and public spheres, the female/male division of labor, the nature of the family, and the role of the public schools—have now entered the realm of conscious choice and deliberation. Of course, this choice is negotiated in both the "private" and the "public" spheres. Thus not only are the constitutive features of national identity in question, but also the very structures through which that identity is to be developed. As one of the leading cultural conservatives, Allan Bloom asks: "When there are no shared goals or vision of the public good, is the social contract any longer possible?"[38] Is it any wonder that Japan stands as an object of envy for conservative ideology? Were we only as clear about what it means to be "American" as the Japanese are about what it means to be "Japanese"! In clarity there is unity. The shift in the scholarly discourse on Japan in recent years is not only a reflection of this concern, it is an indication of how the concern for harmony and order has dominated much of our understanding about other peoples and institutions. And it is also an indication of the influence that the culturally conservative interpretation has gained in recent years.

Bloom's question highlights the crucial difference between conservative and democratic ideals. The first question for democracy is not whether there are shared goals and visions. Nor is it even whether there are common symbols and meanings. It is, rather, what is the process through which goals and visions are deliberated and how are conceptions of the common good developed? A democratic public seeks to maintain control over its own development by seeking a consciousness that is aware of its own symbols and of its own construction through them. Cultural conservatives admire Japanese schools because they believe that they are able to maintain control over the symbols and meanings that are transmitted to children. They forget, however, that a principle role of education as a normative enterprise is to teach children to control their own symbolic processes and the effects that symbols have on them.

It is precisely because we have some awareness that education has this important function that I must press many of Rohlen's otherwise astute observations. To say of a school that it legitimizes existing social relations[39] and creates a group of passive, uncritical students should not be to praise it.[40] To describe students as primarily "motivated by entrance exams and trained by parents to view learning as a necessary burden in preparation for adulthood," to say that in the schools students "learn not to challenge authority"[41] and that students learn to "walk the straight and narrow wherever it may lead"[42] should be to say that the schools are inadequate for the preparation of a democratic citizenry. Moreover, this kind of schooling is especially inappropriate for a multicultural society like the United States.

Cultural conservatives—commenting on American schools—see our educational crisis as a sign of a larger cultural crisis, in which national identity has fractured, civility has eroded, and the country is in danger of breaking into irreconcilable racial, ethnic, gender, and class interest groups. In this they are right, but their solution is partial and inadequate. They seek to mend this fracture by minimizing local meanings and teaching standardized interpretations. Diversity may be represented in the school, but largely as examples of the transformative power of the American ideal. History may include the stories of blacks and immigrants. However, the cultural conservative fears that we have too much diversity threatening the "unity" and the transformative power of the American experience. They fear that diversity threatens to result in a paralyzing national self-doubt and guilt.

The cultural conservative believes that, in the process of becoming American, older identities must be shed. One can perhaps maintain a nostalgic fondness for another land, whether it is Italy, Mexico, Korea, or Jamaica, but one cannot be both an American and a non-American. To become an American is to shed one identity for a better one, an identity, as one often-used, older history text put it, upon which "have been fastened the hopes and aspirations of the human race."[43]

In contrast to the cultural conservative, some critics of public schools reject what they also see to have been the historical mission of the common school—to establish and maintain a single, dominant, White, anglo, male-gendered, Christian identity. The criticism—often voiced by various minorities and feminists—has stunned many conservatives. It rejects the idea that there is a single cultural norm which all children should be taught to adopt, and proposes that what is offered as the *American* identity is simply the identity of a particular but very powerful group. When this norm goes unchallenged, it follows that the school renders some cultures invisible, and that children from these cultures are expected to define themselves and to judge their worth in the light of this norm. For example, in some instances Jewish children were expected to sing Christmas carols in school while celebrating Chanukah only at home. Even when the vast majority of students were Jewish, school remained open on Jewish high holidays although the classrooms were empty. For others, especially Blacks, the ideal meant that their culture would be displayed in the curriculum and the text, but only to illustrate the superior character and the greater charity of the dominant culture. And in this display Black culture was often distorted and degraded. One text widely used from the early 1920s to the late 1950s explained the situation of the slaves by reporting that many slaveowners dealt with unrest by treating their slaves with ever more kindness, feeding them their favorite foods, and he concludes that: "It was a rare Negro who could resist the appeal of a good barbecue."[44]

These criticisms press the difference between the economic and the cultural conservative, at least in theory. When confronted with such criticism, economic conservatives could point to their support of plans that would enable parents to choose their children's schools—pointing out that parental choice is consistent with appeals to market principles. Yet, presumably, enabling parents to choose their own child's school would also enable them to control their child's identity. If this kind of choice were fully realized, it could develop into the cultural conservative's worst nightmare—the continuous splintering of identities and the dissolution of any national unity. For the cultural conservative, nationhood requires the formation of common identities, and schools must be the place where identity work is carried on. Choice can only be trusted if there is assurance that common symbols and shared facts are transmitted to every schoolchild. Cultural conservatives are likely to respond to critics by acknowledging the merit of including symbols and heroes from minority cultures into their repertoire of common symbols, but they want to control the selection and the assignment of meaning.

The cultural conservative's vision is one where a public is controlled by common symbols and unified meanings, and where the school's role is to create this public through a common curriculum.[45] It is also to minimize the significance of local meanings. Yet to minimize local meanings is to minimize the experience they entail. It is sometimes to ignore poverty, unemployment, homelessness, and despair by substituting distant meanings as common ones. In these cases, common symbols are empty symbols. They are only common in any concrete sense if they maintain connections to the experience of everyday life. And they are educational only to the extent that they help clarify those experiences. The mistake of the cultural conservative is to assume that symbols are independent of a material reality, when in fact the two are closely related.

Even conservatives can lose control of their own symbols. For example, witness conservatives' complaints a few years ago about students' failure on a national survey to answer a simple question such as "when did Columbus first *set foot* on America?" Their concern was that too many students could not answer the question. Yet when conservatives complained about the failure of students to answer the Columbus question correctly, no one appears to have noticed the more serious issue involved in the way the question was phrased. This failure is a strong indication of just how much the question of national identity is up for grabs. In the days when people asked "when did Columbus *discover* America," there was apparently more certainty about the historical roots of the American experience.

The nature of this vulnerability underscored the difference between conservative and democratic ideals. Certainly, from the democratic perspective, the newer question is clearly preferable to the older one. However, democracy aims to achieve *conscious* control over its symbolic framework, and this means that common symbols require common work. The example also suggests that conscious control over the symbol-making process ought to be a part of the conservative's as well as the progressive's educational agenda.

I agree with the conclusion of the cultural conservative. The character of our collective identity is among the most important educational projects. I also agree that the development of such an identity must reach well beyond the concern of the economic conservative for material well-being, and must seek a deeper connection with familiar social and philosophical traditions. Beyond this point, however, the conservative comes up short, failing to see that identity is not a product to be delivered but a process to be constructed. This requires that cultures seek to understand and come to terms with their differences—both symbolic and material. This requires a commitment to a process of cultural understanding that goes beyond the efforts of the past. Without such a commitment, democracy is abstract and formal, and there is no real democratic public. Imposed meanings are not adequate substitutes for genuine communication and inquiry. Just how common meanings are achieved says a great deal about the democratic character of a society. In the next chapter the differences between Japanese and American identity are explored in terms of their implications for school and work.

5

Collective Identity and Social Practice

I. Cultural Identity and Productivity

The economic and the cultural conservatives are really asking two different questions about school and work. The first asks how schools can develop the higher-level academic skills that (they believe) are required for the new workplace. The second asks how schools can develop a sufficient commitment to the larger national collective. It is the acceptance of a collective interest that the cultural conservatives seek, and they believe that Japan has been more successful than any other industrial nation in achieving consensus about national identity and goals. The willingness of students to diligently pursue the abstract, dull, disconnected routine of the school is seen as a sign of the commitment to a collective goal, and is preparation for work that in itself may not be essentially meaningful, but which may serve a larger social purpose.

The cultural conservative rightly leaves open the likely possibility that the academic level required for different jobs will continue to vary considerably. Sometimes high technology adds to the needed academic skill level, but sometimes (as with computerized cashiers) it reduces the needed level. The economic perspective can explain productivity when many jobs require a highly skilled task force. It is more limited when, as is the case in Japan, many members of a highly skilled work force must take jobs that do not call for their skills to be exercised, and appear to do so without complaint.

II. An Alternative Conception of the Relationship between Academic Achievement and Productivity in Japan

Although Japan is regarded as a capitalist nation, the Japanese government has a much more visible role than our own in encouraging corporate investment, in coordinating industrial initiative, and in determining the sectors where growth and decline will occur. While there are very important relationships between government and industry in the United States, they are still limited and constrained by the cultural ideal of the rugged individual, unfettered and unaided by government and by the tradition which limits the coordinating role of the government.

For example, in Japan the Ministry of International Trade and Industry (MITI) plays a direct and visible role in spurring industrial cooperation, and in determining such important issues as areas of research and development to support. Thus, for example, when we read in the United States press that Japanese industry is outstripping American business research in key areas such as superconductivity, we are often not told of the large role that the government ministry plays in these developments. In many instances, productivity increases in certain areas because MITI, in consultation with major industry, has determined that such areas hold the greatest promise for the future of Japanese business, and has decided to stimulate product research and manufacturing.

Because there is a tendency in the United States to distrust business-government partnerships, believing that if one group is advantaged by government another must be disadvantaged, such coordination is more difficult. It does occur in the form of government grants to industry and universities and, more important, through the billions of dollars spent on the military budget. Yet because of this subterfuge, it is more difficult to target such research directly for commercial and consumer interests. Even though military research frequently will be cited for the side-benefits it has for the consumer—for instance, Teflon was a product of the space program—few would think of this as the primary justification or as the best means by which to promote consumer products. Yet the connection between government support of military research and consumer products is sufficiently strong in this country that the waning of the Cold War is perceived by many to be a threat to our own economic well-being, rather than an opportunity to improve consumer goods or individual well-being. Since the United States has a very limited tradition of direct government support for industry, there are few ways to pick up the slack. Moreover, because of the philosophy that stresses the role of the single individual in enhancing economic growth and that takes conflict and friction to be the base metaphors describing relations between government and groups, it is difficult to find overt ways to encourage industrial cooperation. The inability of the government to coordinate industrial development and decline places business at a disadvantage in many competitive situations with Japan. As Ezra Vogel describes the process, MITI officials

> try to restructure industry, concentrating resources in areas where they think Japan will be competitive internationally in the future. . . . MITI officials consider it their responsibility to assist companies in declining industries to merge or go out of business while encouraging new ones to move into localities and employ the personnel who were laid off. If conditions are not serious enough to shut down a whole industry, they work out a "depression cartel" agreement among companies in a depressed area to reduce production capacity, with the reduction distributed relatively equally among the companies.[1]

Abegglen and Stalk make a similar point when they note that "there seems to be no other nation in the world where even relatively low-ranking bureaucrats can, with impunity, publicly list industries that will and must phase out of the economy."[2] Indeed, the number of Japanese industries that have experienced this decline is sobering in light of American complaints about purported unfair competition. Textiles, coal mining, shipbuilding, aluminum, electric furnace steel, are all examples of once-flourishing Japanese industries that have undergone a significant, government-directed phased reduction.[3] Government-industry cooperation is a major factor in Japan's industrial development and in its rise as an economic superpower, and this cooperation includes the phased reduction of entire industries. To say this, however, is not to deny the importance of other factors—lower interest rates and taxes, a high savings rate, and a comparably insignificant military budget, for example. Nor is it to minimize the intensity of the competition that occurs between companies in the same industry. To suggest that there is significant coordination between industry and government, is not to deny the sometimes cutthroat competition that takes place between companies. It is simply to say that the Japanese will allow their government to plan and coordinate business and industry in ways that we in the United States will not, and that this coordination provides certain competitive advantages on an international level.

Consider just how difficult it is for the United States government to coordinate the activities of private industry. The textile and shoe industry, for example, were clearly in difficulty after the Second World War, and it would not have taken too much foresight to predict that cheaper foreign labor would drive most of the companies out of business. Yet each community, first in the Northeast and later in the South, had to experience for itself the trauma of a major industrial plant closing. Things are different in Japan. When MITI tells the steel industry that if it does not scale down over the next five years, lower-priced Korean steel will force huge layoffs, it is generally believed, and industry begins the unhappy process of down-scaling. Imagine the reaction in the United States if, for example, in the mid-1970s the Department of Commerce told the American automobile industry that it needed to scale down its operation, and that workers needed to be retrained, because the industry would not be able to meet the foreign competition that was about to beset it from Japan, unless, of course, it instituted restrictive ("voluntary") quotas.

III. The School's Role in the Legitimation of Collective Interest

The school system plays a vital role in the planning process in Japan. It is where the population learns to accept the authority of government ministers in units such as MITI. And it is this legitimacy that enables the government to coordinate the rise and fall of major industrial sectors. Most of the key bureaucrats in MITI come from the same university, Tokyo University, which is known by everyone as the most prestigious school in the country. Most people not only know this fact, they also know that most people know that most people know this fact. The knowledge is collectively held. That Tokyo University is a public institution available to any student with sufficiently high test scores is another important component of this collective understanding. This fact by itself is somewhat different from the American pattern, where government hiring is dispersed among university graduates and where the top graduates of the top schools will tend to take positions in high-prestige, private firms rather than in government agencies.

In Japan, the prestige of an individual's university is a sign of a person's capacity to legitimately influence and guide public policy. This legitimacy is rooted deep in the Confucian tradition, but, more important, it is reflected through a number of contemporary practices. Among these practices is the nationalized system of testing. The tests, and the role they serve in gaining access to prestigious high schools and universities, legitimize the place of the winners in the education race by ensuring that everyone recognizes they have been a part of the same competition.

Critics of Japanese schooling, and there are certainly many of them inside Japan, are especially vocal in their criticism of the examination system whereby students compete for places in prestigious colleges and universities. They argue that the questions are unnecessarily detailed, emphasizing rote learning and memorization. Indeed the emphasis on arcane detail and esoteric knowledge extends considerably beyond the formal school system. For example, the examination to license hairdressers asks the examinee to spot the error in statements such as: "A healthy adult has six to eight thousand white corpuscles per cubic millimeter of blood; that an adult's blood makes up a fifth of body weight or that hemoglobin has the function of carrying oxygen in the bloodstream."[4] It does not ask the candidates just how such knowledge will be useful to them.

While there is a great deal of madness in the excruciating detail that is required to do well on the high school and college examinations, there is a sense in which the kinds of questions asked fit into the common Japanese belief that effort counts more than ability—itself an interesting cultural difference in the way Japanese and Americans explain success. The questions are drawn from the junior high school and high school textbooks, and, as we have seen elsewhere, schools are slow in incorporating new theories and information into the tests because of the lead time needed to change the textbooks.[5]

More important than the quality of the questions on the entrance examination is the very public character of the process and the fact that all have suffered through the same experience. While there are slight variations in the process from prefecture to prefecture, the basic procedure, and more important, the idea that society is hierarchically ordered and that every one has a role in that hierarchy, is widely shared. This, of course, is the same principle expressed in the respect students are expected to give to their teachers, and in difference in status between men and women in the society at large.

The process begins in junior high school, where students start taking practice tests during their next-to-last and last year, and, on the basis of performance are advised about the high schools to which they should seek admission. There has been recent growth in the number of high-prestige, private high schools, but for most people the public school still is the vehicle for security and mobility. When most students consider private schools, it is usually the less prestigious ones that serve as a safety net for students who have failed to pass the test for a usually more prestigious, and less expensive, public, academic, high school. The fact that public high schools are clearly (although unofficially) ranked according to how many students go on to prestigious universities, means that everyone in the area will know which high school is ranked by everyone else as first, which is second, and so forth down to the last. Students are very limited in their choice of schools, and in many prefectures are allowed to take the examination for only one public school. The penalty for failure is high—either a less prestigious private school or a vocational school. Yet the penalty for failure is more than an indication of a student's lack of ability, or even of an unwillingness to exert the required effort—as the Japanese would be inclined to explain it. Since teachers spend a great deal of time calculating which students are likely to gain entrance to certain schools, students who go against the teacher's advice and fail may be seen as unwilling to accept the larger social consensus. In such cases failure may be seen as a sign that the student has not yet acknowledged the principle of hierarchy and place. And as the Japanese proverb has it—the nail that sticks out will be hammered back in.

Admission into a university is by a similar procedure, with each department in each university giving its own examination. Here, too, everyone knows the relative prestige of each university. Just as schools are clearly ranked in prestige and benefits, so too are many jobs, and the best jobs go to students from the highest-ranked schools. The fact that Japanese workers do not usually move from company to company adds great significance to the process. The company that one enters after graduating from school is, in many cases, the company from which one will retire at the close of a career. (We have seen that job switching is looked down upon as a sign of disloyalty.) As the student enters the room to take the examination, knowledge of this fact reinforces the message that personal identity is firmly rooted in one's place and membership in a group.

The fact that virtually every male student plays the same game means that everyone is aware of the standards which are used to allocate jobs, social prestige, and rewards. Ultimately each individual male, with an abundance of adult counseling, overwhelming evidence of his "proper" placement in the form of "objective" test scores, and a full understanding of the system of prestige allocation, actually "chooses" to be a student in one school rather than in another. This means that they all have "participated" in "choosing" their own allocation of prestige and rewards.[6] This process provides the system with an enormous degree of legitimacy, and this is reflected in the prestige and trust provided to its most successful members—among whom are those career bureaucrats in MITI who coordinate the rise and fall of giant industries.

If coordination is reflected within the educational system, so too is the compliance and cooperation that is reported within the factory. The school is a public place, and the fact that, as such, it belongs to all of its members is a message that is communicated in different ways. Teachers appeal to the student's obligations to others—to their family, their school, and their society, and, in doing so, they communicate a message of cooperation.[7] In their day-to-day behavior outside of school, students are thought of as representatives of the school, and, when the occasion arises, teachers will supervise that behavior. For example, rules against smoking and drinking are expected to be followed outside school as well as in, and many teachers will confront violators wherever they see the rules being broken.[8] Moreover, students are expected to take responsibility for their school. They plan many of the activities, such as the annual field day and the various club events. They are responsible for keeping both their classroom and the school itself clean, without the benefit of a janitorial staff, and often they are constantly reminded of the long tradition of the school—providing a sense of membership in an important historical process.

When American commentators look at the Japanese school they tend to see the intense competition that is involved in preparing students for entrance examinations, and assert that this competition explains the success of Japanese industry. However, by itself this would explain very little. Imagine how alienated a worker here would rightfully feel in the knowledge that three to five points on one or two tests made the difference between managing a factory and working on the shop floor. When, in Chapter Three, the hiring consultant reported that many Japanese on the factory floor said they knew trigonometry, but that few used it, she was not providing a fail-safe formula for industrial success. Traditionally, an overtrained work force has been as problematic as an undertrained one. The Japanese miracle may be due less to the high-level training of its industrial work force than to its ability to bring aspirations in line with actual opportunities.

To view the schools' contribution to quality and productivity essentially in terms of skill development is to see the relationship through Western eyes, using Western concepts. It is to make achievement a Calvinistic, individual product, and to establish competition as the basic relationship between people and firms. Certainly competition is present in Japan. But to see the relationship between school and work only in these terms is to miss a more important fact: that in the school a foundation is established which will later allow wider, cooperative, communal action to take place.

IV. Seeing is Being

Cultural identity is more than a way of being. It is also a way of seeing and a way of not seeing. For example, many American commentators seeking to understand productivity frequently miss the painstaking efforts that are taken in Japan to maintain social relations, which often means maintaining relatively equal material relations—at least within individual firms. In the early 1980s, when Americans first started to express systematic concern about academic achievement and low tests scores, and started highlighting the accomplishments of Japanese students, arguments were advanced that teachers should be paid according to their individual merit. Yet in Japan teachers are paid essentially on the basis of seniority, and competition between them is held to a minimum. Many successful Japanese companies also work to cushion failure, and it is important to note that the salary gap between the lowest-paid shop worker and the highest-paid executives in Japanese firms remains among the smallest of all industrialized countries, whereas in the United States it is among the largest.[9] Ironically, Japan, a culture that assumes hierarchy to be the natural relation between people, takes great pains to reduce distance and alienation, whereas the United States—where equality is seen as a key value— justifies the growing gap between rich and poor on the grounds that it furthers productivity.[10] When Americans want to improve performance, the initial response is to increase competition and widen differences. In Japan it is to seek the reason for a breakdown in human relationships and to work to repair the fracture. This response has roots in culture and in the way culture guides understanding.

In the United States, social relations are often seen as but the sum of individual choices, and therefore not an object for conscious concern or attention. One of our traditional heroes, "the strong, silent type," is essentially retarded in terms of his ability to attend to, much less discuss, relationships with others; and educational reformers, especially those with the interests of business in mind, are largely silent about the need to develop students who are more sensitive and responsive to those around them. Some strands of feminism have made attempts to change this,[11] but the absence of a feminist influence on the goals of educational reform is noticeable.

The Japanese reject the idea that social relationships are no more than the sum of individual relationships and that they therefore may go unattended. While competition surely exists, it is the ability to cooperate and to establish structures that maintain cooperative relations that accounts for much of Japan's industrial success. Competition is found in both societies, but in one it is defined as the essential character of all relationships, whereas in the other it is viewed within the context of a more basic harmony that needs to be attended to and maintained. Our traditional concepts make it difficult to see the attention that is being paid to maintaining harmonious relations, and we are much more likely to account for worker productivity by pointing to individual achievement rather than by the relative wage equality that is found in the Japanese firm. Yet, I think, part of our deeper concern about the direction of American society involves an uncertainty about whether our belief in competition serves us in the way that we are told. The problem is, however, that the scientific tools we have to address this concern already presuppose an answer to it.

Of course, science is supposed to eliminate the differences between cultural ways of seeing without altering cultural ways of being. The virtue of scientific concepts is that they are supposed to be indifferent to cultural variations, enabling a light to be shed on those relationships that are most useful. Hence, whatever else it is—the fluid of baptism, the cleanser of sin, the ocean of misery—water *is* H_2O. So, too, the concept of productivity. Whether a workplace is harmonious or not, competitive or cooperative, high-tech or low, whether the product is bread or ice cream, productivity *is* output over input. It is the number of units produced given the number of person-units worked. Culture, it is said, may tell us whether we prefer bread to ice cream, cooperation to competition, high-tech to low-tech, but only the science of economics, using the concept of productivity, will tell us who gets the most output from the least input. Culture lets us be different. Science lets us see the same—or so the claim goes.

Yet the concept of productivity—as used by American economists—is an essentially individualistic concept. It provides a very American (or at least Western) way of seeing. Because the concept of productivity does not count as work labor that is not directly tied to marketable goods or services, it militates against maintaining traditional relationships, including the labor of a housewife, or the teaching of a parent. Effort expended in maintaining relationships is not counted in units of production and hence will not be found on any comparable measure of productivity.

The opposite of productivity is not waste, but inefficiency. Inefficiency is the expenditure of time over and above the minimum required to produce a marketable product. Hence, many activities which are *socially* valuable, but which do not have *a market* value, will be counted as inefficient. Consider the fact that in the race for high technology, some societies will advance further and quicker than others. And those that do will, in the economists' view, be more productive than those that do not. Nevertheless, even though some countries will have a higher proportion of workers employed in high-technology industries, all countries will have a mixed labor force, and routine labor will not in fact disappear. Granted the "winners" in the high-technology race will have a larger proportion of jobs in the more advanced areas than the "losers," but no country will have a majority of jobs devoted to high technology. Thus one of the most important tasks of all societies will be to find ways to enable the different segments of the work force to labor together in reasonable harmony. Yet the standard conception of productivity has difficulty addressing this issue, because the contribution of some of the older sectors of the economy fail to conform to the economic definition of efficiency.[12]

The Japanese have learned this lesson reasonably well as they struggle, against American pressure, to maintain the socially significant, but economically "inefficient" network of neighborhood shops. Since the United States long ago destroyed most of this important small businesses infrastructure, leaving school and television as the principle socializing institutions, it is difficult for American business or economists to see the Japanese network as serving any useful purpose. Because they do not see its purpose, they view it simply as a trick of Japanese business to deny American business access to Japanese consumers. In other words, American business pictures itself as an ally of the Japanese consumer, with both standing against the "wily and clever" Japanese businessman. Yet the Japanese consumer most likely accepts the collective interest as much as the Japanese businessman and worker, and in many cases appears willing to endure higher prices and some inefficiency for the sake of a low unemployment rate.

In this regard, we are at a considerable disadvantage, because little thought goes into the reconstruction of some of our own neglected socialization structures. Since we operate within an individualistic framework that pays little attention to the structures through which social relations are maintained, we develop few ways to appraise the innovations which contribute to such breakdowns. Rather, our individualistic framework leaves us with only the moral categories through which we can condemn those who are inadequately social-ized. It provides very little to restrain us from tearing down the very structures on which healthy socialization depends.

The (American) economist's conception of efficiency does not pro-vide the tools with which to count the non-market costs and benefits of different forms of distribution systems. For example, the destruction of similar neighborhood distribution systems and family-owned small business in the 1950s in the United States left a significant gap in child-adult relationships, and reduced the amount of informal but daily interaction between adults and children and limited the community's involvement in child-rearing.

The concept of "productivity" is unable to take into account the social effects of this change because the socialization of children is not measured in market terms. Productivity is a unit that measures the marketable output of individual workers. It measures the social effects of the relationships that go into producing this output only insofar as they contribute to producing more or less of the specific product. It does not measure the effects of the social relations on the quality of social life. We know that something is wrong, of course, when juvenile delinquency increases, but we attribute the increase to drug use, or some other similar effect which we mistakenly treat as a cause. It is a problem of individuals. Irresponsible children, negligent parents, permissive teachers are its cause—not a breakdown in larger social relationships brought about by a blind application of the concept of efficiency.

We fail to consider the possibility that our scientific categories—the way we measure productivity and progress—lead us to neglect the very relationships that are needed to make delinquency an unaccept-able option for youngsters. Yet if those relationships are to be effective, they need to form a fabric that embraces and supports individuals, families, schools, and cultural institutions involved in child raising. And this may sometimes mean greater inefficiency in some econo-mists' sense of the term.

V. Social Relations and Productivity

It is likely that a conception that leads us to neglect social relations also has a negative influence on productivity. However, because we have learned not to count social relationships in accounting for output, the effect is difficult to see. Consider a simple example. I arrived at

Narita airport outside Tokyo and stayed overnight at a nearby hotel before traveling the next day to a city a few hundred miles west. When the hotel bus brought me back to the airport the next day, I hired a porter to take my many suitcases to the ticket counter of Japan airlines (JAL), and as he left I gave him the small amount of Japanese currency that I had available. When I reached the ticket counter, I was informed that I was in the wrong place and that I needed to go to JAL *national* flight counter. I was at the international counter.

The international flight office is on the top floor at one end of the building. The national flight desk is on the bottom floor at the other end of the building. Because I had no Japanese currency, I could not hire a porter, and there were no carts available in that area of the airport. Thus I had to move my two suitcases, two briefcases, a suitbag, and four bottles of scotch, which I had purchased (duty free, of course) as gifts, by myself. I began by piling up the various items as best I could, and walked as fast and as far as possible before collapsing. I did this three times and progressed, perhaps one-hundred feet—at this rate I would surely miss my connection. As I sat recovering from my last trek, I began to puzzle the situation out and a very simple, quite eloquent solution hit me.

I left half of the luggage exactly where it was, including the scotch, which was worth about eighty dollars a bottle in Japan (retail, of course) at the time, and I took the other half of the luggage down to the national flight desk. Then I left that half of the luggage there in the waiting room, while I returned to fetch the second half. Within fifteen minutes my work was finished, and I was in line waiting to receive my boarding pass. Had this happened at Kennedy or O'Hare airports, the story would have been quite different, and I clearly would have been reluctant to leave my luggage without finding a trustworthy, charitable person to watch it. (And who knows who is trustworthy these days?)

The experience illustrates a lesson about social relationships and productivity. In this case the goal was to get the suitcases to their destination in time to catch the plane. It is more productive if one person can do this in the allotted time than if two people must do it in the same time. When honesty can be assumed to be the social norm and respect for the property of others is honored, productivity can be improved. Being able to assume basic honesty and good will is a rather obvious example of the way in which social relations influence productivity. Yet honesty and respect grow out of reasonable social policies that take into account, among other things, the effects of an uncontrolled profits and large inequities and which seek to contain them.

VI. The Concept of Intelligence: A Cultural Artifact

The success of the Japanese has not only aroused a critical examination of American education, it has also promoted a small cottage academic industry which promotes the view that advances in industrial achievement are an indication of superior intelligence. In other words, it is claimed that the Japanese are not just better at making cars or television sets than are Americans, they are also more intelligent in some sense of that concept. Claims about racial variation in intelligence are suspect on many different grounds—not the least of which is that they are based on faulty concepts and frequently are aimed at the most vulnerable social groups.[13] Moreover, these particular assaults are usually covers for blaming Blacks and other minorities for our economic problems.

Even if there were something to the claim that there are racial variations in intelligence—a reason that is always readily available to explain poverty and oppression whatever the group involved—there is no reason to think that it is this difference in intelligence which explains the relative productivity of different groups. After all, it is unlikely that Japanese intelligence (as understood by those who make claims about racial differences) was any lower at the time when Japanese production was uncompetitive on world markets. Moreover, a focus on individual intelligence is counterproductive to the extent that the problem involves social relations. It restricts treatment to changing something about individuals—perhaps the way they are selected, or the birthrates of certain groups, or immigration policy, and it neglects any serious attempt to understand the components of productive social relations.

VII. Sharing in Industry

American educational reformers frequently overlook the importance of social relations, and instead emphasize the healing power of competition. Witness, for example, what had become a yearly ritual of recent Secretaries of Education—the publicizing of the famous wall chart in which each state is ranked according to the scores of its children in standardized tests. The publicity is intended to spur school officials to improving the scores of their students. The fact that test scores have largely stagnated over the last few years has not deterred the secretaries from continuing the ritual. Nor has the fact that the publicizing of test scores provides a strong incentive for educational officials to encourage slower students to drop out of schools, and pressures teachers to teach for the test. Competition among teachers, in the form of merit pay increases, has also been proposed as a way to increase the academic performance of American students.

Although competition is very much present in the Japanese system—especially as it involves the intense pressure related to entrance examinations—there is significant emphasis on cooperation and community-building, and this emphasis is clearly carried over into the workplace. One Japanese executive who had spent a number of years in East Asia and then in the United States observed that the emphasis on community enabled Japanese executives, who in some respects are competitors within the enterprise, to share information with one another which will enable the job to progress more efficiently. The willingness to share information was the one factor that he cited in explaining the advantage of Japanese industry.

His observation while clearly incomplete, does make sense. If six people all need the same piece of information and they all have to discover it by themselves, then it will take the company six times as long to have the information acted upon as it would if one person told all of the others. Sharing is important not only among similar positions in a hierarchy, but also among different positions as well. Moreover, if the differences between winners and losers is very large, if the players perceive that the penalties for failure and the awards for achievement are greater than the gains from cooperation, then they will be deterred from this kind of sharing. Another Japanese executive illustrates a feature of cooperation when he describes what he takes to be a crucial difference between American and Japanese workers.

> Americans tend to complete what they were told to do but rarely go beyond that. So I have to be clear about what I am ordering. Otherwise there will be a problem later. I'm not saying it's their faults, but it's a possible misunderstanding caused by different customs.
>
> I can give you a simple example. If I order a Japanese subordinate to take a measurement of a dimension, he will also measure another dimension since another dimension relates to the first dimension. But in case of most Americans, they take only one measurement, since I *literally* ordered them to measure only that dimension. That's it. Not everybody, but most.

To the extent that this description is accurate, it reflects many different facts of the American experience, including the intensification of the division of labor that attempts to enhance job security often entail, and a failure on the part of industry to enable workers to participate in the basic purposes of the enterprise.[14]

The executive's comment also indicates an important point about education. The ability to provide the unasked for dimension requires an understanding of the overall purpose of the request. When both the understanding and the purpose are shared, then every detail need not be specified. These American workers had learned the academic skills required to measure the angle. They presumably lacked the social structure required to demonstrate an understanding of the reason behind the request. Yet the failure to provide working-class children with such reasons, and even to discourage them from seeking them, is quite well documented in the education literature.[15]

VIII. Structuring Individual and Collective Achievement

The United States is known for its egalitarian spirit, while Japan is considered a hierarchical society. However, many features of industrial life complicate the image. In Japan the hierarchy is perhaps clearer, but in the United States it is often steeper, with the different levels more removed from one another. Lee Iacocca's autobiography captures the steepness of this hierarchy when he describes his ascent to the presidency of Ford Motor Company and then the events following his demotion. First the ascent:

> Those were the days of wine and roses. All of us who constituted top management in the glass house lived the good life in the royal court. We were part of something beyond first class—royal class, perhaps, where we had the best of everything. White-coated waiters were on call throughout the day, and we all ate lunch together in the executive dining room.
>
> Now this was no ordinary cafeteria. It was closer to being one of the country's finest restaurants. Dover sole was flown over from England on a daily basis. We enjoyed the finest fruits, no matter what the season. Fancy chocolates, exotic flowers—you name it, we had it. And everything was served up by those professional waiters in their white coats.[16]

And then the swift descent:

> On October 15, my final day at the office . . . my driver drove to World Headquarters in Dearborn for the last time. . . . The very next day I got into my car and headed out to my new office. It was an obscure warehouse on Telegraph Road only a few miles

from Ford's World Headquarters. But for me it was like visiting another planet.[17]

In contrast, Japanese executives work in more modest surroundings, taking care not to create great physical distance between workers and managers. The physical surroundings of executives are usually pleasant, but not overelaborate. Few executives have private offices, and these spaces are modest and functional. One American worker with years of experience in American auto factories described his reaction to the first day of work at NUMMI:

> On my first day, I went to lunch in the tooling lunchroom, a very nice lunchroom, and I sat down and this Japanese gentleman sat down next to me. This is the guy they described to me as the boss—Mr. Toyota himself. He is one of the sons. He just said hello, can I sit here and I said yes. He sat right down with me, wearing the same uniform I was wearing. I had never seen anything like that before.

Social relations not only play an important role in building morale and establishing loyalty, they are also crucial in the production process. Traditionally, in simplifying work, the assembly line took responsibility and knowledge away from the worker, accumulating it in the higher management. As we saw in an earlier chapter, Japanese plants reverse some of this—but not necessarily in the direction of more and higher-level technical skills. Even where the skills required for job performance remain relatively simple, as they largely do in assembly operations, they entail a cooperative effort and an understanding of the shared purpose. For example, one of the features of Japanese industry that has been adopted in some American plants is the quality circles, or *kaizen*, where workers discuss the work process and how to improve it. Instead of responsibility for job planning remaining in the office of a work design engineer, it is dispersed throughout the various positions. As one American worker who is now employed in a factory managed by the Japanese describes it:

> It's not a suggestion program. It's not the typical American suggestion box where you put in a suggestion and you may be financially rewarded. Conceptually it's that we are all in this together. If we can make changes that improve the product or improve our work base, make our jobs easier, less physically taxing, we are going to produce a better product. If we don't produce a good product, we're not going to have a job because they're not going to sell.[18]

As the factory encourages shared understanding and knowledge, more lateral communication patterns are established, fewer problems are channeled to the boss to solve, and more spontaneous interaction among the work force is encouraged. Sometimes in doing this it is useful for a member of the team to have some rudimentary statistical skills:

> We were having some water leak problems and we wanted to start statistically keeping track of where the leaks were occurring and how much time it was taking to repair them. We could feed back to the place that was of most concern—whether it was where the glass was installed or a body seam that we were having relatively consistent leaks at a point. We could go back to that point on the assembly process, look at why it was happening and make corrections. Many times we try to do it informally and not involve the branch manager—associate to associate or group leader to group leader.

In hiring American workers for new Japanese transplanted factory, the personnel consultant that we met in Chapter Three explains that they needed to reconceptualize the organization chart.

> The hierarchical model that we use in this country is not as applicable to these new plants as you might think. There is an organization chart, but from the interaction that I have noticed, lines are crossed. Consensus means that you are going to have people involved that on the hierarchical organizational chart don't look like they have any necessary involvement—you cut across those kind of things in the organization.

She is not referring to the standard distinction between formal and informal leadership within an organization. It is rather that the formal organization is structured so as to maintain loose and fluid boundaries and cooperative relations between different roles. The need for highly cooperative people who have an understanding of the larger purpose of the enterprise is illustrated by the care that goes into the selection of a work force for a new Japanese-managed factory in the United States. The personnel consultant describes the process:

> I think we need people that are much more cooperative than say the American model—more interested in teamwork, better skills, that generally means interpersonal skills too. I think it's composed of a few elements. There's trust, there's credibility, there's an

element of likability. There's a sense of fairness—certainly a lot of empathy and being very tolerant.

The selection process for this plant begins in the state employment office, with a number of standardized forms and aptitude tests which are scored in racial and gender groups by percentiles, followed by a medical examination which includes a drug test. Those who pass this part of the process are then invited to the selection center near the plant for an all-day screening that consists largely of various kinds of group work intended to test interpersonal skills. The process begins with a group of five candidates, generally strangers to one another, forming a team that is asked to do various tasks, such as designing a work apron, and giving themselves a name.

In one key situation the group is asked to build a mock robot out of various nuts, bolts, rods, and other assorted parts. The members are shown a prototype and then told to build a similar one. According to the personnel director: "There is no structure given to the group whatsoever. Part of their job is to create some structure so that they can figure out what it takes to build the robot, who is to do what and how they are to work as a group." Those who score the highest are not necessarily those who have the clearest idea of how the robot should be built or those with the most efficient notion of group organization:

> We've had some people who tried basically to just take over entirely. That's usually the type of person standing there saying well you take this and I'll do this, and its not really getting any agreement. The group usually rejects that person and chooses another whom they are more comfortable with. A good person would probably say "John how do you feel about taking this part?" and John might say "I'm not very good at that. I might be better at sorting hardware" and so the person might say "let's try that." They seem to strike a good balance between what structuring needs to be done and how much people need to be taken care of in some respects also.

After the robot has been assembled, the group then discusses ways to improve the process, and then reassembles the robot. The evaluators assess the way the members treat one another's ideas, and their general contribution to the group process.

IX. Cooperation and Sharing within the Industrial Structure

In hiring American workers, the personnel director was attempting to select the characteristics that she felt were essential for working in a state-of-the-art industrial plant. Cooperation, teamwork, and sharing were, to her, essential, and for most jobs they were considerably more important than what she saw as an inflated academic requirement. The traits she was looking for mirrored qualities she observed in Japanese workers, but she knew, too, that there were limits to the extent to which Japanese customs could be transported to the United States. Thus, while certain features of Japanese culture, such as morning exercise, quality control circles, and group safety rituals, were incorporated into either the training program or the actual workplace, there were clear limits as to how far the emphasis on interdependency could be carried. As she explains:

> A lot of attention is paid to what they call private counselling on the part of the manager. In Japan this is one of the major differences. A manager kind of becomes responsible for the whole lot of these employees. If someone had a drinking problem at a typical plant in the United States, a manager would probably be counselled not to get involved. Get the employee assistance people involved, or doctor, or someone who knows about this stuff. Your job is to get the employee to agree to get treatment and to keep your eye on performance. But in Japan it is very different. For example, the way you get a mortgage there the boss will actually make a decision about making a mortgage.

This difference is important to note, and it marks a distinction between our conception of teamwork and the more communal aspects of many Japanese workplaces. It is a limit that is important to attend to in light of methods, often noncommunal, that American companies have developed for intruding on workers' private lives. The concept of teamwork maintains a sharp distinction between what is public and what is private. The manager is advised not to involve himself in the drinking problems of his employees because of the taboo that the line not be crossed. In this country, to cross the line is interference or spying for the company. Teamwork involves one's public role and the coordination with others that is required to accomplish it. In Japan the line between our idea of public and private is more easily crossed, and management is more able to address issues that workers here would be reluctant to share with management. In part, this is because the line between management and worker is more blurred, and in part it is because employees who are guaranteed lifetime employment have security that is often not available to American workers. Yet it may also be because firms encourage their workers to develop multiple perspectives and to experience company life from different points of view.

X. Multiple Perspectives

Japan is a hierarchically ordered society. It has different forms of speech for men and women, as well as for people of different rank. There are complicated rules as to who bows first to whom and how low they are to bow. These features of Japanese society are very important, but it is easy to forget them when one looks simply at the structure and relations within the workplace. Here a great deal of attention and effort is placed on providing people with multiple perspectives and enabling them to experience different roles. This serves to blunt their identities as occupiers of any specific roles, while sharpening a shared identity as a member of the enterprise as a whole. Common dining rooms and parking lots are part of this process, but many companies carry it much further. Below, an American executive now working for a Japanese automobile company explains how future managers spend their few months on the job.

> Every university graduate who enters this company has seven months of training, and during that he has two months of working on the production line building cars. So a design engineer is going to remember when he worked on that line and tried to put this part into another part and it didn't fit quite right. Also, all graduates spend two or three months selling cars door-to-door—carrying a pamphlet saying, "excuse me ma'am, Would you like to buy a $20,000 sporty car?" And he's going to remember that, too, when he starts to design cars one day and of course they couldn't sell cars too easily—not door-to-door.

Within the Japanese company, and especially the larger, more established firms, there are significant attempts to supplement the symbolic significance of these practices with real material advances. Despite periods of intense conflict between management and labor, Japanese industry developed more egalitarian relations within firms.[19] As Gordon in his important study of Japanese labor describes this system, it involves more equal treatment between blue and white collar workers in terms of salary, status and job security.[20]

American workers are frequently skeptical of corporate attempts to create better labor-management relations because they believe that management's essential interest lies outside of the plant, with the stockholder, and eventually with itself. When management introduces human relations techniques, such as encounter groups, into a plant or factory, techniques that are intended to foster more cooperation, the results are often at best mixed, because workers understand that such groups are not authorized to effect real shifts in power. American workers know, as Abegglen and Stalk put it:

> The Western corporate pattern might be described as an alliance
> of senior management and shareholders to optimize current earn-
> ings from the company to mutual benefit. The company becomes
> a vehicle for profit optimization, or, at worst, for profit maximi-
> zation.[21]

The result is a reflection of one of the central tenets of Western political philosophy. The success of a company is really the achievement of individuals, and the company itself is but the arena in which the conflicting interests of different individuals are played out. It is an artificial entity that is vested with reality only through the acts of individual human beings. Yet as Abegglen and Stalk suggest, under this conception, there is no one to identify with the company as such:

> the success of the company depends critically on a single executive
> or small group of executives. Thus if they achieve success through
> their individual efforts their compensation should be appropri-
> ately increased. Not surprisingly then, lower ranking employees,
> especially as represented by their trade unions, also seek to max-
> imize their share of current earnings. In this process, the company
> becomes an organization external to the interests of its members,
> to be used to further their earning advantage to the maximum.[22]

In other words, this conception is a reflection of Western political philosophy, where individuals are real and organizations artificial.

The Japanese company functions differently in its allocation of mate-rial benefits, and this difference enables concern over internal relation-ships to be accepted as an important factor on the corporate agenda. Westerners frequently comment on the fact that in Japan individual personal identity is connected to corporate membership. When asked what they do, workers will first say they work for Honda or Toyota before they say they are welders or tool makers, whereas most American workers will say what they do before they tell who they work for.[23] Yet this identity of worker-for-company is not just an idiosyncratic feature of the "Japanese psychology" or a unique feature of "Japanese culture" in some abstract sense. It is also woven into the material structure of the Japanese corporation and reflected in corporate practices providing a closer identity between worker and manager.

For example, boards of directors of Japanese companies are usually made up of senior executive employees rather than external shareholders. The board's constituency, according to Abegglen and Stalk, "is the career employees of the company itself."[24] Frequently, higher management will be selected from former members of the union. Few Japanese managers hold significant amounts of shares in their company, and share price has been reported as the "least important objective in managing their companies."[25] As Abegglen and Stalk note, managers are thereby freed from short-term concerns and need not be concerned with showing a steady improvement in share earnings.[26] While the company legally belongs to the shareholders, as in the United States, the different relationship between shareholders and managers is reflected in different operating practices between companies in the two countries. For example, as already mentioned, the spread between the salaries of the highest-paid executive and the lowest-paid worker is much smaller in Japan than it is in the United States. A report in the early 1980s put the annual compensation for top executives at between fifty-thousand dollars and two-hundred and fifty thousand dollars, as opposed to the salary of over a million dollars paid to at least eighty-five American executives at that time. Moreover, this difference is not a reflection of the generally higher salary for American workers, since by 1982 Japanese workers were paid about the same as American workers.[27] As Abegglen and Stalk put it:

> The employees of the Japanese company share more equally in the cash benefits available from the company than is the case in other countries. . . . Japanese executive pay levels are set with a conscious awareness of the need to stay within reasonable ranges with regard to other levels of compensation. . . . Organizational pressures work to limit executive pay at least as much as do self-sacrificing impulses by the executives themselves.[28]

This is reflected in the income distribution of both the company and the nation as a whole, which is more nearly equal than in other developed countries.[29] Both management and workers share in the benefits and the difficulties of the company. Both receive bonuses, and usually management will reduce its own level of compensation before undertaking to approach the union for reductions in the workers' levels.[30] With the fortunes of different groups visibly and directly tied to the fortunes of the company, concern for the harmony of the work group, for the interpersonal relationships that constitute the working enterprise, is accepted as a genuine effort to better everyone's lot.

This is not to say that the Japanese company is an economic democracy, nor is it to say that a collective interest is equivalent to a public interest. Decision-making is still hierarchical, although it is also more consultative on the shop floor than one would find in most American plants; discrimination against the native Barukamin and Korean populations still exists both inside and outside the plant; lifetime employment is largely restricted to men; and large corporations play an important role in manipulating the stock market. Nevertheless, more attention is paid to the decision-making process and to the effects that decisions will have on the texture of relationships throughout the enterprise. In addition, for whatever reason, there appears to be a more heightened awareness and a greater consensus throughout the society as a whole about the character of the collective interest. Yet this is not the same as saying that a democratic public is the instrument for the development of this interest. There are many ways in which such an awareness might be achieved and, as will be seen in the next chapter, not all of them are consistent with democracy.

6

Japanese Identity

I. Strains on Identity Formation in Japan

Sumo wrestling is the quintessential Japanese sport, dating back to ancient times, and originating in prayerful rituals involving the harvest. The tradition is maintained in pre- and post-bout rituals where the contestants bow to each other and scatter purifying salt on the ring. It "has the same sort of distinctively Japanese appeal as, for example, the Kabuki theater." Sumo wrestlers are ranked according to their records and the top rank, *yokozuna*, has been granted to less than sixty men in sumo's long history.[1]

There is today a serious dispute going on in the Sumo Association, which ranks wrestlers and confers the title of *yokozuna*. The leading wrestler is Salevaa Atisanoe, a 575-pound Hawaiian American, whose sumo name is Konishiki. Given his very impressive won-lost record, many believe that Konishiki should be given the title *yokozuna*, but the Association has denied him this privilege, and many believe that the reason is that he is not Japanese. When someone claiming to be Konishiki complained on the phone to the press, the wrestler was criticized for behavior unbecoming of a sumo, and the next day he denied that he had made the call. Publicly griping about one's situation is considered not very Japanese.

The Japanese are torn, because sumo wrestling has two distinct parts which are treated as one. The first is the skill involved in pushing an opponent around the ring—a skill that likely comes more easily to a 575-pound Hawaiian American than to a diminutive 450-pound Japanese. The second is its ritualistic meaning—a meaning that reaches far back into the thousands of years of Japanese history—and that represents the virtues that have constituted the nation itself. We can judge the former easily by counting the won-lost record of the participants. But how should the latter be judged? And who should do the judging?

The episode is significant because it demonstrates that, to varying degrees, the strains that are felt in the United States about our own collective identity are felt in other countries as well, and Japan is no exception. While some may suggest that the sumo example is trivial to the many competing demands on American cultural and educational life, it is not a trivial issue to the Japanese. Something very important about what it means to be Japanese is at stake in this issue. It raises the question of whether Japan can continue to hold on to local standards of evaluation, standards which for many express the history and tradition of nationhood itself, or whether Japan must go the way of the modern world and submit itself to the standards of a "universal" international order. Thus, the yokozuna debate represents a much larger tension in Japan, a tension that reflects, as both cause and effect, its favorable position in the international economic order.

To understand what is happening in the world of sumo is to see that concerns expressed by the cultural conservative are not specific to the United States. Similar problems are being experienced throughout the industrial world, and are clearly present in Japan. To isolate the problem as peculiarly American is to misunderstand its origins, and will likely lead to the wrong remedy. The conservatives' belief, for example, that Japanese schools are models of educational excellence is wrong. Their mistake, however, is not in the belief that the schools control discord and contribute to social harmony through a common curriculum, shared symbols and the development of mutual aspiration. The mistake is the failure to understand that the tensions conservatives fear are worldwide, and that they are inevitably reflected in disputes about symbols. Conservatives fail to see that an education that seeks harmony through unified symbols and shared meanings educates people to a world that simply is passing out of existence. And they fail to understand that the role of education in a world of uncertainty and ambiguity is not just to produce well-socialized people. It is to produce people who are conscious of the process through which they and others are being socialized. This is not just a nicety of democratic principles—it is a necessity of education in a modern multicultural age.

There is no better way to demonstrate this need than to examine the very engine of Japan's educational success—Japanese women. It is the Japanese mother who takes control of the child's early identity formation providing the foundation that eventually cements the connection between the child and the school, a connection that, as White did correctly point out, later extends beyond the home and the school to the corporation and the nation (see Chapter Four). It is the early childhood teacher—a woman—who provides the young child with the first lessons about living and working in groups. It is the wife who, by attending to the educational needs of the child, frees her husband to carry out his corporate duties wholeheartedly. She negotiates with the teacher, chooses a *juku* (or cram school), arranges for a tutor, prepares the elaborate school lunch, irons the uniform, maintains the child's hair at just the prescribed length, and then stays up until late in the evening to attend to her husband's needs when he comes home. And it is again the woman who, when industry needs part-time or temporary workers, leaves the home to answer the call, and then, when labor is plentiful, returns to the life of a full-time housewife. In her capacity as part-time worker, always on call to fill the gaps, she provides the flexibility that companies need in order to maintain their policies of lifetime employment among their full-time male work force.

Yet changes are coming, and if they reach as deeply into the core of Japanese society as I think they do, they may well call for deep changes in its educational system. In this chapter, I look at the role that women play in the identity formation process, and I look at how their own identity is shaped to enable them to play this role. I explore the factors in our postmodern world that are interrupting this identity formation process, and address possible implications of this interruption for the future needs of Japanese education. I conclude that Japan needs more democratic education, not less, and that what Japan needs, we need as well. I show why education in Japan, as elsewhere, must involve a reflective understanding of the process of one's individual and collective socialization. In the final chapter, returning to the problem of education in the United States, I explore the process through which such an understanding may be achieved in a multicultural age.

II. The Importance of Women to Japanese Industry and Identity

The success of the Japanese in the international market has placed significant strains on their traditional identity. For example, the various economic and financial scandals that have rocked Japan in the last few years are sometimes taken as indicators of declining morals, and they may be, but the publicizing of these infractions results from the challenge that the traditional value system is experiencing as it seeks to meet newly introduced international business norms. Hence, what was once, perhaps tacitly, accepted as the obligation to treat a long-term client in some special way may now be identified as illegal favoritism in the financial market, and the perception of such favoritism cannot be allowed if Japan is to be an international player. As the rules of the game change, so too do traditional conceptions of relationships and obligations, conceptions which are at the foundation of human identity. In these pressures we can begin to see some of the limitations of cultures that seek harmony in the modern world, and we begin to see strains in the socialization structure of Japanese culture.

In Japan, as in other areas of the world, women do most of the identity work of the society, and are the primary socializers. This is more so in modern-day Japan than it is in most other developed societies. In Japan the schools depend on mothers to provide an array of tasks and experiences that will enhance school performance. These range, as I noted previously, from preparing the exquisite lunch that children carry to school, to selecting a tutor, supervising homework, driving the child to a lesson or meeting the teacher in the home, purchasing just the correct school uniform, and making absolutely certain that the child's hair is cut precisely to the school's prescribed length. Young children often sleep with the parents until junior high school, and so a mother's sense of responsibility continues day and night. The mothers' responsibilities are especially intense when the child is very young, and most mothers seem ready, as White correctly emphasizes,[2] to meet the child's every need. As Befu writes: "In Japan, very often there is a coalition of mother and children against father. By contrast, in the American pattern, the tie between husband and wife remains the basic coalition even after children appear on the scene."[3]

In my own travels in Japan, on buses, on trains, and in parks and other public places, I am constantly amazed by how rarely Japanese children cry out or make unruly demands. This is not because they want fewer things than American children, but because their mothers constantly anticipate their wants, and meet them. Americans would likely judge such behavior harshly, seeing it as indulging and spoiling the child, yet this would mistake some of the motivation and some of the effects of this behavior. The mothers are concerned that the child not make a nuisance of himself; the child appears to pick up this sensitivity, and the school nurtures it. As Befu remarks:

> Japanese define motherhood as an entirely worthwhile and satis-
> fying calling. Japanese women take motherhood as seriously as
> American career women take their jobs, perhaps more seriously.
> Doing a good job as a mother is widely regarded as a full-time
> occupation in the United States, too. But a woman's other interests
> and commitments are viewed as having equal, or nearly equal,
> claims on her time.[4]

Although the school is clearly responsible for keeping order, in most instances that is not very difficult to do. Children who ride bicycles to school, even in large cities, usually are comfortable leaving them unlocked during the day, and students are courteous and attentive. A lot of this is due to the work of the mother at home in preparing the child to trust and accept authority. Additional preparation is done by women who teach in the day care centers and nursery schools and take special responsibility to prepare children for working in groups.

Thus women serve Japanese society in a number of ways. First, they are the primary socializing agents, and as such, they play a crucial role in teaching children to trust authority and enter into alliance with it. Second, as the principal pre-school teachers, they prepare children to work in groups, and teach group discipline. As the authors of one cross-cultural study of pre-school report:

> The staff of Komatsudani [the Japanese pre-school] believe that
> children learn best to control their behavior when the impetus to
> change comes spontaneously through interaction with their peers
> rather than from above. Thus Hiroki's best chance to learn self
> control lies not in encounters with his teachers but in play with
> his classmates.
>
> Fukui: I told Midori and the other children that if they felt it
> was a problem, then they should deal with Hiroki's throwing the
> cards. If I tell Hiroki to stop, it doesn't mean much to him, but if
> his classmates tell him, it affects him.
>
> Tobin [one of the researchers]: But he kept throwing the cards
> even after Midori told him to stop.
>
> Fukui: Because he's so proud. He won't ever change his behav-
> ior if someone orders him to. He'll always do the opposite in the
> short run. But in the long run, his classmates' disapproval has a
> great effect on him.[5]

Finally, women render an important service within the labor force. When labor is scarce, women serve as a temporary work force to get the job done when needed and then they are returned home to prepare the supper. When labor is plentiful, these temporary workers can be released, enabling the system of lifetime employment for men in large companies to continue.

The overt socialization of women and men into their traditional gender roles remains much more obvious in Japan than in Western countries, and certainly more so than in the United States. Even though coeducation is the rule, young, unmarried men and women are not expected to socialize with one another in couples, and even though the female work force has greatly expanded in the last few years, Japanese wives still remain economically dependent and enjoy little independence and power outside the home.[6] Moreover, there is still a strong taboo against woman who have both children and careers together, and indeed, relatively few women have what would appropriately be called a "career" outside of the home.

III. Gender and Identity Formation

Identity formation is the subjective side of which socialization is the objective element. Socialization, consists of the institutions and practices that support and reinforce an anticipated identity. The subjective component involves the way in which individuals come to think and feel about themselves, and the roles they accept as appropriate for people like themselves. These two aspects serve each other. Institutional practices work to produce an identity of a certain kind, and this identity then works to maintain the practices. A well-socialized subject is a person who accepts the assignments society lays out, believing that they are just the right ones for her. A subject who is socialized to respect gendered boundaries will give a gender-relevant reason for this belief—for instance, that she is a woman and "only men can do that kind of work."

In Japan gender identity is very prominent, and is reinforced through the practices of the major socializing institutions—the family, the school, and the workplace. Parents pay considerable attention to the gender-appropriate character of different schools, but this character is not necessarily to be found in the formal curriculum which, except for minor variations, is essentially the same for boys and girls. Below a mother talks about the different educational aspirations she has for boys and girls.

M: Since my own education was in a girls school there were many, many rules. You have to fold the socks three times or the uniform had to be of a certain length. I remember being bound by rules all the way up to junior college. I think it was quite stupid, but even now if I had a daughter and lived in Japan I may choose that kind of a school for her, as stupid as it may seem now.

WF: What about for your son?

M: To be honest, whether this is good or not, I would like to send him to a school which has a reputation of sending its graduates to a prominent university because I think that if one has a good educational background one may choose his own career. In Japan now if you don't have the education, then you are doomed. If you have a good education, there are many opportunities and many doors that open. If you become a doctor and decide that you don't want to be a doctor you can become a fish merchant. If he likes books, he may even write one but if he does not have the education there are not many opportunities.

WF: Would the school that you went to enable your son to get into a prominent university?

M: Not for boys.

WF: Why not?

M: When I was younger, a person I knew decided to go to a certain public high school on the basis of the school codes. When he was in junior high school, he looked at these codes. There were many that started with sentences that began with: "you may not" but when he saw the code book for the school he chose, there was no sentence that indicated that one may not do something. I heard this maybe twenty years ago but I still remember it. But for girls maybe because of some nostalgia for those days I would put her into a school with strict rules.

The different factors that are entertained when deciding upon schools for sons and daughters are also reflected in other aspects of family socialization. Girls are expected to speak in a soft voice, and they are expected to be more tidy than their brothers. Sons are more often protected from performing household chores, and encouraged to spend their time studying. Traditionally, higher education was encouraged for sons but not for daughters. These differences are reflected in the different career aspirations of children. Men want to get into a prestigious university as the key to occupational advancement and social prestige. Lebra reports that:

> In the future autobiographies written by seventeen- to eighteen-year-old high school students . . . one finds a clear sex polarization regarding their educational commitment. For male students, admission to a good, hopefully prestigious, national university is the absolute indispensable foundation upon which to build a career identity. They are obsessed with the hurdle of the "examination war" and (in autobiographical essays) write about attendance at cram schools. . . . By contrast female students reveal much less of a myopic obsession with examination war, choose two year colleges more often than four year universities . . . and specify no college names.[7]

The different educational futures that Mrs. M projects for sons and daughters, and the different attitudes of male and female high school students is consistent with and reinforces the way in which corporations treat men and women and the different career paths that they lay out for them.

Mr. H is a high-level executive in an up-and-coming company employing about six-hundred salesmen. He has spent considerable time in the United States and is one of a few executives who gave up a permanent position with a major manufacturer to take a chance on a then somewhat risky new venture. He was referred to me because his company is thought of as among the most advanced in terms of its personnel policies, and his own views on business represent the progressive thinking within the corporate community. When asked about the role of women in Japanese business, his answer reflects the tension between the actual practices of his own corporation and his sympathy towards a more modern point of view.

> Hu: Yes, it's gradually changing these days. Z [the name of a well-known company] people will be angry after hearing this statement. Z had a certain regulation until 10 years ago that a girl [sic] who has reached the age of 30 had to quit the company. It was brought to the court and the company lost. There is a tendency, even in our company, if a girl reaches the age of 30, still unmarried, people would think why doesn't she get married or she is going to be an old spinster or something like that. So it's very uncomfortable for her. But, it's changing.

WF: What I'm wondering is why that developed—that there are so few women?

Hu: Women have a responsible job to raise children. And Japanese society hasn't reached the point to give women a lot of work. We don't have any facility to take care of children.

WF: Yes, but this would not speak to the unmarried women. That would tell us something about why married women might not advance, but is there a connection for women who are not married?

Hu: People have an idea that women are inferior to men. It's funny to say but my boss, an old Navy officer, always says that women are like animals. He is now sixty-four years old and he was educated like that.

WF: When he says they are like animals? What does he mean?

Hu: Girls are girls and what they can do is kind of limited.

WF: Referring to their intelligence?

Hu: Yes. I don't quite agree with him. But most of Japanese executive members or Japanese top management levels think that way.

The woman who reaches twenty-six or twenty-seven unmarried may find herself the object of all kinds of attention from other workers and managers hoping to introduce her to some eligible young man. Once married, or once children arrive, the woman is expected to leave her position so that some other person can fill her slot.

The message is clearly understood and frequently anticipated by young women as they search for jobs. A number of women who were about to graduate from a good, four-year coeducational university in Japan discussed their future plans with me. They have all spent a year studying in the United States in the Japanese equivalent of the year abroad program, their English is excellent and they are all in the process of interviewing for jobs. Their own identity as future wives and mothers limits the way they think about work and reinforces the expectations of the company. Most appear willing to accept a subordinate role at work and to limit their career aspirations.

WF: Did you go through a long interview? How did you get the job?

SO: I took an exam, it's easy, not difficult at all. I went on an interview twice.

WF: What did they ask you?

SO: Uh, what's my strong point or what do you want to do? Why do you want the job? What did you do during your university time? What do you think about the job? How long do you want to work?

WF: What did you say about that?

SO: I want to work as long as possible. They asked me if I had a person that you want to marry now—special person. I said no—I wanted to tell them, but I was afraid to.

WF: Why didn't you tell them?

SO: I think the company wants me to work longer, but will worry about after I got married that I would quit soon. It is typical Japanese where women tend to quit jobs after marriage.

WF: What's your plans?

SO: Now I think I want to continue the job even after marriage. I think I was influenced by American women, since they work even after marriage and even if they have a baby.

WF: What about after you have children?

SO: I don't know about that. If I think I can work, even after I have a baby and if my future husband would allow me to work, I work.

Whereas SO sees herself as more modern than many women, in that she might choose to work after having children, she accepts the fact that her husband will ultimately decide the matter.

Women who are hired by major firms adjust their expectations to fit the role that they believe the company has marked out for them. AM has just been hired by Z, the major manufacturing company mentioned earlier. It has many facilities abroad. Her English language skills could serve her well in a position in the United States where she has already spent time as a student. However, anticipating the company's response, she does not pursue this interest in her job interview.

AM: I didn't expect that I could go to other countries as a member of Z. It's impossible for a girl to go abroad.

WF: Why?

AM: Because they have to take more, very big responsibility, and they think that girls cannot do that.

WF: Did you ask them in the interview?

AM: No, I didn't.

WF: Why not?

AM: If I did, maybe they would not employ me. Just asking might be okay, but if I say that I really want to go abroad, maybe they will think that it's not a girl's job or something.

WF: Where will you be using your English, your spoken English skills?

AM: They said they don't have many foreign visitors from abroad but they have some. I hope I can guide them along when they come and welcome them.

WF: What do you picture yourself doing in ten years?

AM: I'm going to have a husband and some children.

WF: I see. So you don't intend to stay with Z forever?

AM: No, I'm not going to work for a long, long time.

WF: Could you work once you were married if you wanted to?

AM: Yes.

WF: In Z?

AM: Yes, but not for long—until I had a baby maybe.

When the women are then assigned to "women's work" there may be some disappointment, but few challenge the assignment, and other factors, such as a families' expectations that unmarried daughters live at home, reinforce the corporation's decisions. This makes the loop from school to routine job to marriage and child-raising difficult to break. One senior describes her interview.

> They asked me what do you want to do if you get the job here. I said I would love to be in the position of foreign currency exchange. They said it would be difficult for you because the job is not very often available. Usually girls and females working for banks are needed on the first floor where they are visible to customers. They asked if I liked this kind of job and I say yes.

The concept of "women's work" is maintained through a set of mutually reinforcing practices that involve the expectations of both the company and the family. The company's inclination to assign women to routine work where they can easily be replaced is reinforced by the family's concern that the daughter continue to live within its household.

> The main currency exchange and stuff like that would be located in Tokyo and my parents never want me to leave home before I get married.

And the family's desire to have the daughter live at home is reinforced by the company's inclination to assign her to routine jobs where she learns little and has little invested in a career. Hence there is considerable congruence in many instances between objective socialization practices and the formation of a subjective, gendered identity.

IV. Philosophical Congruence

Identity formation entails the development of rational structures that help make sense of the available alternatives and of the constraints that are imposed on one's choices. Hence, the choices made by these women, and the institutional practices that reinforce them, are consistent with a larger philosophical vision of the character of social relations. Women in Japan are supposed to soften the harsher elements of competition and to preserve the more tender and compassionate side of life. When high school women choose not to engage in the struggle for prestige, and aim for a junior college or a noncompetitive four-year institution, it may be because of the high value they place on the virtues of nurturing and compassion, and the belief that these are incompatible with academic achievement. When asked to describe their most memorable moments in school, many of the women I spoke to told of a teacher who helped them develop compassion and understanding.

> Mrs. H: I lived near the river at that time and there was one child who came from a rather poor family. This child did not have a mother and lived with the father. Because they were poor they could not afford all the things other children had. He wore shabby clothes and when he came to class other children would pick on him. But when he moved we all pitched in and bought him a going-away gift.
>
> There was also a boy who was very small, a dwarf. He was also being bullied and he liked to go fishing so he would go to fish early in the morning instead of going to school. Sometimes the homeroom teacher would go and pick him up at his home to go to school with this child or

one of us to go and bring him to school. Since this child went fishing early in the morning, we had to get up very early to catch him before he went fishing so that he would come to school with us.

Mrs. U: When I was in third grade, my school had a class for children with special needs—mentally handicapped—at that time I think there were two classes for these mentally retarded children and that was very memorable. It was the first time that there was such a class, and I think the teachers were really careful about it. They were able to make us feel natural about having these children around. I think the teachers were very good. They made the situation so that the children would not be prejudiced against these handicapped children and yet would help them out when it was called for. It was the first time for many of the students to be with these mentally retarded children, yet the teachers were able to make it happen very naturally.

Interestingly, none of the mothers mentioned the communal aspects of their own children's education, and most believed that the pressure to achieve high grades and to enter a prestigious university had increased greatly since they graduated from school.

These aspects of women's education are also on the minds of those who are responsible for the higher education of women. The president of a coeducational university describes his hope for the integration of women into the corporate side of Japanese life.

I think here in Japan the universities are becoming the main cause for the opening of society to women. Many of the girls who come to the university come with the expectation of their parents that they will spend four years at the university and then get married and have a child. But the parents underestimate the change during those four years. The women who do graduate frequently want to go into careers. Frequently they want to continue working after marriage. This is bringing about a change in the status of women and I would hope the university would bring this about in a graceful way, one that helps them maintain their values as a Japanese society and their strong traditional family life, and have a happy joining of career with marriage, and to be aware of the different opportunities where they can maintain their strong family values and still think of some type of career outside the marriage.

It remains to be seen whether this ideal—the compatibility of home and career—truly reflects the experience and the thinking of the graduates of his university.

This picture rests on an aspect of Japanese life which many believe is eroding—the strength of the traditional family—through the demands of the company on the father and the movement of women into the part-time work force. The ideal that the university president hopes for—of family and career working together in harmony—actually turns into an added burden for many women rather than a new opportunity. Working wives spend longer hours than their husbands laboring on the job and in the home.

Changes are occurring in both objective practices and in subjective aspirations. It is not completely unusual to meet women with strong career aspirations, but often the traditional consciousness still structures the perceived alternatives. While the number of women seeking a lifelong career is still quite small, it is growing. However, these women frequently share with more traditional women the view that motherhood and real careers are incompatible.

For example, among the graduating seniors at the president's university was a woman whose goal was to enter the Japanese diplomatic corps. She was beginning the process of examinations and interviews that she hoped would lead to a post. She knew that the chances for success were low and that they were much lower for women than for men. The idea of marriage and a family appealed to her but she felt they conflicted seriously with her career goal. As she explores her choices and explains the constraints that have been placed on her, she demonstrates that both future mothers and future career women accept the idea that there are strong boundaries between family life and careers for women. We have been talking about the relatively small number of women who enter the diplomatic corps and I ask:

> WF: Why are so few women hired in the diplomatic corps?
>
> YH: I think that there are two reasons. One is that women may quit the job and second one is so many Moslem countries . . . women are outside of society and women maybe can't work as well as men in those countries.
>
> WF: Do you want to get married eventually?
>
> YH: I don't think marriage will be the prime thing in my life. I'll never quit a job for marriage. Almost all men want their wives to stay home, so maybe I can't marry because I want to work from early in the morning to late at night and no husband

would want me to work like that. Marriage is important but
I don't think I have to marry.

WF: What about children?

YH: Well, I want to have children but I think a baby needs a
mother.

YH comes the closest of any of the graduates to challenging the
collective consensus by seeking a nontraditional career. Yet her challenge is limited to alternatives that, while uncommon for women, do
not challenge the structural constraints that make this choice different
for women than for men. She believes, for example, that the small
proportion of women eventually accepted into the diplomatic corps
can be explained on more or less functional grounds. She does not
ask whether other countries assign women to Moslem countries or,
to take an analogous position, whether countries should avoid sending
Black diplomats to South Africa because of the then existing policy of
apartheid. Nor does she ask why so many women might quit their
jobs. Instead she is willing to accept the idea that the government
must have its reasons. Both YH and her more traditional classmates
accept the idea that women may wish to pursue careers, and both
view career and motherhood as mutually exclusive—a judgment they
do not make about careers and fatherhood. Her choice is an uncommon one but it is not taken in the spirit of a significant challenge to the
collective consensus that renders careers and motherhood mutually
exclusive.

V. Strains in Japanese Identity Formation

Potentially, one of the largest sources for intensifying the tension
in Japanese already strained identity is to be found in an unlikely
source—wives of plant managers, engineers, and executives, who
have spent some years in the United States or other Western countries.
The great success of Japanese industry means that an increasing number of managers, executives, and engineers and their families have
spent time working, studying, and living aborad, and this results in
an awareness of alternative gender roles. It also adds to the strain
already felt within Japan itself, as an increasing number of women are
entering the labor force as part-time or temporary workers. Within
Japan, however, women workers are expected to remain in subordinate positions, and there are only a very few models of successful
women. The women who have spent time outside of the country

arrive back in Japan with experiences that could add to challenges to the existing order.

However partial may be the advances of American women, the progress brought on by feminism in the United States provides the wives of Japanese businessmen with powerful models, and many take the opportunity while in this country to expand their interests and develop themselves in ways that would not be quite appropriate in Japan. Moreover, these women, used to a restricted identity as daughter, wife, and mother, not only see in the United States more women in executive roles, they also see more men working around the home. Ironically, the same Japanese executives who describe American workers to me as somewhat lacking in initiative are often described to me by their own wives in the same way. They don't do a thing around the house.

When they return to Japan, these rather privileged women often come to experience their role in a more marginalized and distanced way. They see the ever-present concern for harmony as confining and restrictive, and seek, from their marginalized perspective, opportunities for their own individual development and growth. Much like the American workers employed by Japanese firms, they have experienced both the culture of friction and the culture of harmony and as "education mamas" (the Japanese term to indicate the time and devotion many mothers put into their children's education) who have momentarily stepped outside of the Japanese system, they are often able to objectify their own cultural experience and to express the educational incongruities that can make living in the two cultures difficult.

They come from a place where harmony and concorde are supposed to prevail, but they have experienced a place where they are *told* everyone is supposed to develop their own interests, to satisfy their own goals, and to grow as an individual. Moreover, unlike many Americans, they have the material resources and the time to undertake new activities and interests. Many are able to speak insightfully about the way their own thoughts and feelings have been formed and about the pressure to behave "appropriately" once they have returned to Japan. Even more important, some of them begin to experience a conflict in their own identity, a strain that represents a crack in the ideal of harmony so basic to Japanese corporate life. These women begin to question the received definition of Japanese womanhood and the roles and experiences that are associated with it.

Some Japanese mothers who have spent a few years abroad return to Japan and pick up where they left off, but many do not. At least a

few experience considerable difficulty returning to Japan and accepting their role in Japanese society. Their conflict is between the
identity developed abroad and the role they are now expected to
resume at home. Unable to reinternalize the expectations of Japanese
society, they experience its values as marginalized participants in a
collectivity rather than as members of a community. The experience
is described by one mother as she explains just how she comes to
behave according to the norms of the collectivity, and why she spends
so much time preparing her child for participation in a system whose
values she has come to seriously doubt:

> I don't know why. I think every mother faces that same thing and
> if every mother wouldn't do that, I wouldn't do it either. But every
> mother thinks that it is important and so every other mother does
> it. So the mothers kind of create their own reality—their own
> world.
>
> Society expects us to do it and that's what it means to be a good
> mother and also to be ready for the competition we prepare our
> children for. Education is an important thing in Japan. I don't
> agree with it but I have to do it because I cannot change the whole
> society so I have to change.

Some find it very difficult to accept once again the role of Japanese
mother, and they have great difficulty readjusting to life in Japan. For
example, while Americans marvel at the low divorce rate of Japanese
families, many Japanese mothers often feel as if they are running a
single parent household because the father is rarely home. Of course
many Japanese mothers do adjust to their return, but for many others
it is not easy, and some come to feel as if they are being called upon
to make a very large sacrifice. Endurance, a very important ideal in
Japanese society, turns into longing and regret. Here is one mother
describing life after she returned from the United States to Japan.

> WF: When you make supper, is your husband usually home?
>
> MU: Never.
>
> WF: What time do you go to bed?
>
> MU: About 12:00.
>
> WF: And then you're both up again at 6:00. Do you get tired?
>
> MU: Yes I'm tired. . . . I'm not happy in my life.
>
> WF: Do you see each other very much on weekends—Saturday
> and Sunday?

MU: Sometimes he works Saturdays too.

WF: All day Saturday until 11:00?

MU: Yes, sometimes.

WF: What about Sundays? What are Sundays like?

MU: He goes to play golf sometimes.

WF: Do you play golf?

MU: No.

MU: I need more freedom. In Japan, I have to think all around.

WF: You have to think what?

MU: I have to think what the other people are thinking, what the neighborhood is thinking and feeling.

   I'm forty but when I went to the United States I could forget my age and do anything I wanted to.

   I did a lot of things so I thought my ability was developed.

WF: What kinds of things did you do?

MU: I liked writing. I was making a family newspaper—what was happening in my family. I was using a computer—making one hundred copies. I mailed them to my relatives and friends. I didn't like to speak to audience but I had an opportunity to do that though at my elder son's school. I was so nervous. I spoke to the American people telling them about Japanese culture. I was surprised about myself and it came out okay.

WF: What other abilities did you develop?

MU: I didn't swim at all and one day the children had a field trip and I went to the park with them and some little boy fell in the water by himself. I went in the water to pull him out and after that experience, I had to learn how to swim. And I was diving.

WF: A high diving board?

MU: Yes.

MU: So I was thinking about the United States after I came back to Japan as to what should I do and now I feel very old. People think I'm a housekeeper, I'm forty years old and I'm a woman so I have to behave in a certain way.

WF: You have to behave the way forty-year-old women housekeepers behave?

MU: Right. American people gave me lots of energy.

WF: I wonder how? Do you know how that happened?

MU: They like challenges and creativity.

WF: But don't Japanese people like challenges and creativity?

MU: I think not so much. They don't like failure.

MU: I'm still missing America so.

Mu describes her feelings as an alienated Japanese wife and an "education mama" who must still behave as that system requires. Her fractured identity has made her more conscious of demands and expectations that other wives and mothers may take for granted and obey in unconscious silence. Yet MU has experienced another life, and for her these demands and expectations are no longer second nature—if they ever were. Whether she is right and it is her experience with Americans that freed her, or whether it was just the opportunity to be away from her traditional obligations, we do not know. Nevertheless, she is now *aware* of the need, as she puts it, "to think all around," to take account of what others expect from her, and to find ways to meet those expectations. There is no doubt that she still performs her duties as a responsible Japanese mother, but she has become aware of her own motivation for doing so, and in this awareness is to be found a tear in the idealized seamless cloth of institutional practices and subjective aspirations.

VI. Developing Strains in Subjective Attitudes and Objective Practices

Although Americans have become very critical of their own public educational system and have come to think of Japan's schools as exemplary, Japanese mothers who have sent their children to school in this country often view matters differently. Some are unhappy about the importance placed on order and conformity in Japan, and they often value the emphasis on individuality that they find in American schools. In these cases their subjective identity has divided from their institutional socialization.

Mrs. K is a jewelry designer who came to the United States with her husband, who was involved in developing a Japanese plant. She is one of a small percentage of women who, after attending a rather ordinary junior high school, entered an elite public high school and then went on to an elite public university. As she describes her experience in the junior and senior high schools, we see the range of socialization that can occur in Japanese schools. First the junior high school:

> The school started about 8:30, and we would be out in the courtyard, and we would do exercises, and the principal would say a few words everyday. When the speech was long on a hot summer day, some children fainted because they had to stand in the sun for a long time. This was not unusual. There were about one-thousand students and I think on a very hot day maybe five or six people would faint. The other students would keep on doing the exercises while a teacher came over to help.

Her high school, one of the elite public schools in the city, was very different. Unlike most other high schools, students were not required to wear uniforms and, much like elite schools in many other countries, academic achievement and individuality were important aspects of the goals of this school.

> In high school, I think there was a lot of respect for the individual. It was a public school well known for its reputation in sending its graduates to top notch universities. I think there were about three times more boys than girls. The school respected individualism and the teachers would respect the students and let them do what they wanted to. We had uniforms but we did not have to wear them. It was unusual for the schools not to require that the students wear the uniform.

However, she is critical of both schools. The first school she sees as stressing collective values and the second individual ones, but neither emphasized communal ideals.

She elaborates on the difference between collective and communal values as she compares her daughters' schooling in Japan and in the United States. She distinguishes between schools that encourage students to take initiative for themselves—as she was expected to do in high school—and ones that encourage them to take initiative as a member of a group that has developed a common goal. She begins by linking the development of community and the development of communication skills.

> In Japan there was no encouragement in the classroom to express yourself or be yourself. I think there is more emphasis on keeping the rules or learning skills. For example, show-and-tell does not exist in Japan to help enhance communication skills. You would

not see things like "she has good communication skills" on the
report card. In the U.S. I think the communication skills and
working with others are taught in the classroom but in Japan there
isn't anything like that.

She continues by distinguishing between an active, individual learner
and an active learner engaged in the work of a learning community.

In high school we were told to take initiative but it was very
difficult to come together as a group, especially because everyone
had their own goals of entering a certain university. In high school
I realized that there were a lot of interesting people but not very
much cooperation. They were not trained to do so and even as an
adult they are not. They have not learned to live as one part of
society. Japanese people emphasize groups a lot but I don't think
they really know how to do that. It is not that they have a common
goal or feeling towards something and want to develop it. It is
more like a group that is imposed by someone. They will do it if
they were told to do it but there isn't really a relationship that
develops among the group. The schools do not emphasize development as a person, true communication, and I think that hinders
the formation of a natural group relationship.

In her notion of "true communication," Mrs. K is seeking a communal
relationship between the individual and the group, but she is unable
to find this in Japanese education.

Mrs. K's criticisms of Japanese schools are not unique, and are
voiced by others whose children have spent some time in American
schools. Take, for example, one of the features of Japanese education
that has impressed many American commentators—the number of
years that Japanese students devote to a foreign language—especially
English. The study of English usually begins in the seventh grade
and continues throughout secondary school. Moreover English is an
important component in most entrance examinations into high school
and universities. But surprisingly, it is not uncommon to find junior
high and high school English teachers who are unable to carry on a
conversation in English. This is because in Japan there are two different kinds of English. There is the language as it is spoken by native
speakers, and then there is the language as it is studied in school. It
is not unheard of for children who have spent a few years in the
United States to be ostracized by other students and the teacher for
speaking English too well. A mother who had returned to Japan with
her child from an extended stay in the States reports with despair the

steps that had to be taken to hide the children's knowledge of English from both fellow students and the teacher.

> My children after coming back to Japan wanted to hide the fact that they had lived abroad in junior high school. One day my son told me when he was in junior high school that his teacher told him that his English was so bad that he wanted to laugh. His teacher asked some questions. Of course he knew but he did not speak out. He told me he tried to pronounce English the way Japanese people speak English even though he knew the way Americans spoke English.

In relating this story the mother reveals a countereducational ideology—she is aware that there is a real difference between English as taught in Japanese schools and English as a real language of communication. Moreover, she is critical of the school's assigned goal—to teach youngsters to excel in school English.

It is frequently assumed that the Japanese are, by virtue of culture or character, more group-oriented than Westerners, and therefore tend more naturally toward a uniform, collective educational system. This is a controversial issue, but it is not difficult to find Japanese people who are as critical as the most individualistic American of educational uniformity, and criticism of Japanese schools for neglecting individual differences is common among parents who have lived in the United States. When they look back to the Japanese schools, such parents may become quite sensitive to the uniformity demanded by some classroom teachers.

> Coming here and looking at the education that my children are receiving it seems as though they are getting noticed for a certain ability or talent and the teachers actively encourage that. But in Japan it is not like that. I wish the Japanese school would take more individuality in consideration. [In Japan before we came here] in my older son's class, when he was in third grade, there was a new girl in the class who had spent six years in the U.S. The teacher noticed that this girl was different. She worked too much at her own pace. The teacher was very disturbed by this child and said at one point that it is very difficult to conduct a class where there is somebody that is not at the same level. The teacher in a conference with other parents had said that this girl was very outspoken and deviated a lot from the class and that she had great difficulty in handling the girl. Plus the mother would call the school and complain.

Japanese mothers, at least those who have spent time abroad, are often quite critical of their children's schooling back home. That they may continue to serve its ends when they return says less about their critical ability, or the extent to which they value individuality or uniformity, than it says about the power of institutions to structure and mold behavior.[8]

VII. Compliance and Agreement

Revolution is not, however, around the corner, and most mothers upon their return to Japan, do reconnect with the educational system. While many of the mothers I interviewed would prefer an education that pays more attention to the specific needs of their children, when they return to Japan they are likely to behave in ways that reinforce educational uniformity. This is not primarily because their preferences change, although, as we will see, the issue of preferences is complex. It is rather because they are aware of the objective, structural conditions that determine success and failure in Japanese schools, and, regardless of their own ideals, they learn to respond in ways that both conform to and reinforce these conditions.

For example, mothers whose children were presently attending school in the United States were asked to respond to the following hypothetical situation:

> Toru is in his second year of high school . . . and has a good chance of passing the entrance exam to Tokyo National University. His older brother, who has been working in the United States for five years, has just returned home for a short visit. Toru has been listening with great interest to his brother's description of his life in the U.S. When the brother is alone with his parents, he informs them that he would be returning to Japan in about a year and before he does he would like to invite Toru to live with him and attend a good high school in America. He tells them that he believes that the experience would be good for Toru, that it would widen his experience and knowledge of another culture. He knows that Toru had been planning to take the entrance examination at Tokyo University the next year and wants to know if the parents think that this invitation is a good idea. As Toru's parents what would you tell the brother?

Most of the mothers who prized the fact that their children were allowed to develop their own individual interests in the American schools would discourage the child from leaving and few were enthusiastic about the opportunities such a visit might provide. Mrs. U's response reflects the dilemma that the mothers felt.

> If it were someone else's son I would just say, yes, its a great idea; it would be good for Toru. But if it were my own son—he may lose his confidence and not do well in English here.

Mrs. U's reluctance is typical. To let the child take a year off from high school would be to endanger his opportunity to be accepted to a high-ranking university, and this would reduce his future opportunities. Were the child to persist in his request, she would try to arrange it so he could delay graduating from high school and take the test a year after he returns from the States. Mrs. N. represents a similar response—it would be a great experience—but not for my child.

> It is hard to come up with a conclusion right away . . . as a third person I would probably say that would be a great experience, let him go. But as a parent, if he's already in the university and he really wants to go, then he could take a leave of absence from school for a year, and let him go even if his brother is no longer in the States. At this point it may be a good experience for him but he still has to worry about entrance exam. After he gets into the school and his will to go is strong, not because his brother is there or anything like that, then OK.
>
> As long as you have to look for a job, the name of a school has a lot of influence on whether you get that job or not.

The concern over the consequences of exercising an uncommon choice, of choosing a different educational pattern, influences not only behavior, but thought as well, and it is here that the issue of preferences becomes complicated. For educational preferences eventually are concretized within the structures that exist, and when they are, initial wishes may be altered.

Recall that earlier in the chapter Mrs. K had introduced a number of important distinctions into her criticism of Japanese schools. These involved the differences between collectivity and community, passive and active learning, and school knowledge and real knowledge, and she voiced a clear preference for active, communal learning. Yet when presented with a question about how to respond to the child who refuses to study English, a subject that Mrs. K admittedly views as suspect—as taught in Japanese schools—her answer indicates the influence that objective socialization still maintains. Despite her critical distance on Japanese education, and her ability to make crucial distinctions between real and artificial groups, as well as between school knowledge and useful knowledge, Mrs. K still indicates that her choices would be made within the constraints levied by the system.

> WF: Takeo is 14 years old and has just returned after three years in the U.S. During those three years, Takeo learned to speak English almost perfectly and reads a good deal of English literature. However, upon returning to Japan, his teacher has noticed that his knowledge of the rules of English grammar are inadequate compared to other children in the class. The teacher informs the parents that unless this is corrected, Takeo will not be able to enter a good high school. If you were Takeo's parents, how would you advise him and why?
>
> Mrs. K: I would probably tell him to study.
>
> WF: He's stubborn. Takeo tells his parents he doesn't see why he should study. In fact he knows English better than his teachers and that books are only teaching him rules and he already knows how to use the rules even though he doesn't know how to say them.
>
> Mrs. K: It's a problem.
>
> WF: Tell me, why is it a problem?
>
> Mrs. K: In Japan teachers teach them impractical English. If we use English in their way it is not practical, you cannot communicate when you go to other countries, but in Japan they have to pass the entrance examination for high schools. Their English is a bit different from spoken English but that is the fact.

When pressed to explain her decision Mrs. K gives three reasons for supporting the entrance examination. The first involves the benefits she sees in overcoming obstacles through personal struggle. With the right children the examination builds both confidence and character.

> In one sense I think it is good that they put in a lot of effort in studying and conquering the entrance exam.

She also believes that the examination serves Japanese industry by teaching students to attend to minute details, although she finds that the price for this benefit is high.

I think there are both positive and negative. For the positive like manufacturing goods the Japanese are able to come up with good quality and I think that is good, but in everyday life it could be burdensome to have to deal with details all the time. I hear that there are a lot of bullying in schools. I think the schools have become too interested in sending their students to higher education that they have lost interest in them as human beings and really caring about their personality. I think that becomes a problem. I think that is a form of perfectionism.

Yet in the end she believes that the examinations are justified, because otherwise teachers and schools would not emphasize these areas. Responding to a hypothetical question about a proposal to eliminate the required science section from the high school entrance examination, because it emphasizes memory over inquiry, Mrs. K responds:

> Mrs. K: I think if they exempt science from the entrance exam, the school would not put an emphasis on science any more so I don't think that would be good, and I think that you learn a lot from science and science is an important subject. And I believe there are many students who like science.
>
> WF: The criticism here was not that science was not important. It was that the tests were more involved with rote memory than really doing science.
>
> Mrs. K: Is it that the teachers have to help the children memorize things because they would be taking the entrance exams and therefore would not be teaching science but teaching them how to pass the science test?
>
> WF: Yes. . . .
>
> Mrs. K: I'm not sure if they eliminated the science from the entrance exam the teachers would be able to teach science.

While Mrs. K is aware that the value of spontaneity and individuality does not fit easily with the uniform entrance examination, she sees little way out of the dilemma. She knows that the examinations help establish the relative importance of different subjects and despite her appreciation of "the American way" she maintains a strong belief that some areas of knowledge are fundamental and that the examination maintains the integrity of these areas. The tests may encourage uniformity, they may dampen spontaneity and discourage inquiry, self-expression and individuality, they may fail to distinguish between

school knowledge and real knowledge, they may foster passive learning, but they do maintain the integrity of an undefined but important
conception of adulthood. Ultimately the role of the tests is character
development—to help make good adults.

> The idea of testing them to see if the children know because in
> order for them to become good adults it is necessary. I think
> education until high school is something very fundamental—
> knowledge that you need. So I am against eliminating something
> and not having the opportunity to learn. So if you think of a better
> method of testing then I would fully support it.

Mrs. K. straddles two educational ideals—One is the world of engaged, spontaneous, communal learning, the other is the world that is
preparing children for adulthood as it is conceived in modern Japanese
society—a conception that she does not see as spontaneous, active or
communal. She wants the school to pass on both worlds, community
and collectivity, to the children. Yet there is an important difference
between Mrs. K's response and some of the other mothers. Presumably, she will not just submit her children to the discipline of the
school because that is what Japanese mothers are expected to do by
those around them. She will take her action as a choice that considers
the importance of others' views but is exercised with relative independence. Presumably, if she does see a better system of testing—one
that encourages inquiry and reflection as well as perseverance and
hard work—she might well find it attractive. Clearly, her behavior
still conforms to standard educational practice, but the character of
her choice is significantly different from MU, who, as we heard from
earlier, "has to think all around."

VII. A Note on the American Schools

The American schools that these mothers were using as a standard
against which to judge their Japanese counterparts were, as I have
mentioned, not especially unusual for American schools. I did observe
some truly outstanding teaching, but then again I also observed some
rather mundane classrooms. There were many features of the schools
that I found very pleasing—the helpfulness of the staff and the willingness of teachers to talk to me and to let me observe their classrooms.
However I would not especially single these schools out for attending
to the individual needs of most students, although, as will be seen in

the next chapter, there were certainly teachers who did indeed do this.

I mention this because the reader may need some context in order to understand the Japanese parents' appraisal of the American school. Many Americans are very critical of their schools for being too bureaucratic, but these schools would deserve no added criticism on this score. They may be better than most, although not as good as those at the top. That I would not provide any special citation for their attention to individual needs, and that the Japanese mothers do, is related to the different educational contexts, and should help the reader to understand the different points of comparison. Japanese schools are highly structured in many ways, and do not allow for some of the variation that is found in most American schools. Yet there is also another factor involved in the mother's perception. *Their* children were indeed treated as special. Their arrival in the community was a big deal—after all it is not everyday that a plant worth hundreds of millions of dollars is built. Hence the school, supported by the state and the local community, set up many special programs to do what it could and what the law allowed to help these children and their parents adjust to their new home. Courses were taught by the local university and the library to help the mothers learn English and to enable them to get along in the community. Japanese-speaking teachers were hired by some schools to enable the children to learn English quickly, and summer programs were established for the same reason. Moreover, the state sponsored the development of a Saturday Japanese school to enable the children to maintain their Japanese identity while they were in America. What the mothers saw as typical of American schools was therefore a somewhat distorted image, and the attention that their children received was not received by all newcomers.

For example, in a mostly middle-class and professional school a few miles away from the school many of the Japanese children attended, I heard of a fifth-grade American girl, who had moved with her family into the community from the Appalachian region. Her father was unemployed, but I was told that the mother made ends meet by caring for infants and small children in her home. The child spent much of her time after school helping her mother care for the young children, as she and her family tried to cope with difficult times.

Her teacher saw the girl as bossy, said that she lacked certain social skills, and reported that she was behind the other students in academic work. She was transferred out of the school into a special class for mentally "challenged" students. Once assigned to this class, a student stood a small chance of being transferred back into the regular class-room. Yet while the school defined her as mentally challenged, it was aware that her behavior at home was quite mature and sophisticated. As the social worker explained when asked about her home behavior:

> She was very helpful to her mom with babysitting and she was functioning at a different level than she does at school. She was very independent, kind of took charge and was a leader in the home. It seems that outside of the school she functions very well. While I was talking with the mother, one of the other mothers who brings a child for babysitting pulled up outside the house. June ran out to greet the parent and picked up the child and brought the child in, changed the diaper, got the baby dressed and instructed her brother to come out and bring baby clothing over to her. Also, she was answering a lot of questions that her mom could not.

Yet the school did not see this behavior as a sufficient indicator of maturity to override the teacher's recommendation—backed up by "objective" test scores. The girl was removed from the classroom.

Ironically, this student's occasional pushing in line was interpreted as "aggressiveness," and treated much more seriously than that of a new Japanese child in the neighboring school who had pushed a classmate off the top of the slide, breaking his arms—an event which the teachers attributed, probably correctly, to cultural miscommunication. The Appalachian child, however, was labeled socially inept and a slow learner, and removed from the regular classroom to a program of "individualized instruction," where she would most likely stay until her schooling ended. Whereas the Japanese mothers were pleased to find schools that encouraged their children's individual abilities and treated their deficiencies as problems to be overcome, the American's schools did not accommodate the maturity and responsibility that the child from Appalachia displayed at home, did not provide coaching in social skills, and possibly appropriated the categories of "needing individual attention" and "mentally challenged" as a way to get her out of the school and maintain a reasonably uniform, homogeneous classroom.

IX. Additional Tensions

Japan's international success as an economic superpower has brought with it additional tensions as well. Not only are more high-prestige women experiencing life in other cultures, but more women are working outside of the home in order to meet the world demand for Japanese consumer goods. Pressure to restrict the work force to native Japanese, and the commitment of many companies to lifetime employment maintains a large segment of the male work force in their existing positions, and creates a niche in the work force for women who come and go as the demand for extra labor arises. Women comprise over eighty-five percent of the part-time work force, even though they are less than thirty-seven percent of the work force as a whole.[9] Part-time, usually female employees receive only half the hourly rate of full-time, male employees[10] and thus it might justly be said much of the advance made in Japan in the computer and technological revolution (as in the United States) "succeeded through exploitation of the female work force."[11]

When married women participate in the work force they are still, as in the United States, expected to carry on their household work. Hence, while more women are entering the work force, the overwhelming responsibility for household work and child-rearing remains their responsibility. A Ministry of Labor survey found that men spent only thirty-one minutes a day on household work and child care.[12] When outside employment and household work and child care are taken into account, Japanese women work six hours more a week than men.[13]

In addition to their roles as part-time and temporary workers, women play another major role in the success of Japanese industry. They provide the nurturing and care that ensures industry of a highly motivated future work force, and they provide the continuity and stability at home that enables industry to move male employees from city to city and country to country almost at will.

Hence, women play a crucial role within the corporate economy of Japan. They provide a flexible labor force that enables corporations to maintain a high level of solidarity among their permanent male work force. Women enter the work force after leaving school to serve in routine jobs with little opportunities for advancement. They frequently leave the work force after marriage, and return, again, to routine work after their children have been raised. When business is good, they provide a supply of inexpensive labor, and when business slows down, they can be let go without greatly disrupting the permanent work force. They serve a role that is similar to the "guest worker" in Western Europe, or to that disproportionately served by Blacks and other people of color in the United States. They provide the flexible laborers who are required to accommodate their lives to ups and downs in the business cycle. Even though women are exploited in other countries, the situation for women wishing to remain employed is considerably more difficult than in most other industrialized countries.

> In most countries, a close, positive correlation exists between a woman's level of education and an uninterrupted or only briefly interrupted work life. In Japan . . . because of the employment system, women college graduates have the greatest difficulty in finding and keeping employment and in receiving wages commensurate with their education. Like many other industrial countries, Japan has established in its law the principle of equal pay for the sexes. As in other countries, the discrepancies between men's and women's earnings are wide, but in Japan they grow wider with the length of employment. Indeed, given the traditional views that most Japanese, male and female, hold about women's roles in the family and at work, the Japanese employment system probably exploits women more extensively than is the case in any other industrialized country.[14]

Moreover, in periods of recession, such as that experienced by Japan from 1973 to 1977, women, along with older members of the work force, are pressured to leave their companies.[15] Thus women serve to enable the corporation to maintain its policy of lifetime employment for permanent (usually male) workers by providing the cushion a company needs to cope with difficult times. The changing composition of the workplace and the increasing need of business for cheap, temporary workers are important factors affecting relations within both the work place and the family.

The development and growth of the part-time labor force could well result in a more independent relationship between the worker and the company, and a reduced sense of loyalty. Some Japanese believe that the temporary, female work force will develop a more adversarial relationship with the company than the more privileged male labor force has done. Since the newer, growing, high-tech industries depend more heavily on temporary, female labor than do the older, stagnant, heavy industries, the changes may accelerate, thereby having a significant impact on both work and family structures. Nevertheless, the mechanism for changing women's consciousness is uncertain. For the most part, they are not unionized and usually are outside the implicit union-management partnership that typifies most industries. Yet, should change develop in the workplace, the consensus that guides identity development in the schools may be renegotiated, and Japanese educators will need to develop, much like their American counterparts, new understandings and institutional arrangements. Indeed, this pattern of employment is already changing early socialization practices significantly, as one out of four Japanese preschoolers now attends a full-time child care institution.[16] Although it is difficult to predict the implications of such changes for Japanese identity, the development is as significant as any recent changes in American child-rearing.

Recently, a Japanese woman won the first successful sexual harassment case in Japan, a victory which suggests that the Women's Movement has made inroads in Japan. Given the entrenched position of men in Japanese society, this victory represents a very important change. It suggests that the strains on the identity formation process are indeed being felt in Japan, and it certainly points to the need to institute educational reform that enables people to consider these changes intelligently. There is another aspect to this situation that reaches very deeply into the nature of Japanese identity and Japanese character. Discrimination against women in Japan is similar in many respects to discrimination that occurs in other nations, but is different in one important respect. It is an expression of a fundamental aspect of Japanese tradition—the general sense that hierarchy, harmony, and mutuality are natural components of the human condition.

In the United States the Women's Movement is in part an expression of the principle that people should be treated equally for equal talent and equal work. It is also an effort to break out of paternalistic and hegemonic interpretations of social and political relationships, and to collectively acknowledge an independent, gendered identity. While conservatives may voice concern that different rights movements— civil rights, gay rights, women's rights—will overload the system, they must also recognize that demand for equality is an important feature of our traditional value system.[17] Equal status is not something to be *given* by one group to another; it is something that, by its very nature, must be struggled for, and the general recognition of this process provides an awareness that friction is a part of our collective identity formation. Indeed the need to institutionalize friction is an important element of the Madisonian philosophy—perhaps one of the few uniquely American contributions to conservative social thought— and the acknowledgment of its place in social life is itself a crucial component of our national identity.

The context of the Women's Movement is considerably different in Japan because the role of women is but one element in an ordered set of relationships. Order, harmony, and hierarchy are as important to

the Japanese sense of national identity as is individuality, independence, and friction to our own.[18] To question one of these elements
has the potential to challenge the social foundation itself. One of the
female students that I interviewed suggested how strongly imbedded
is the idea of place and order in the Japanese identity, as she talks
about her concern for her boyfriend.

WF: Did you tell your boyfriend that you have a job?

SO: No, not yet.

WF: Why not?

SO: I think I should wait to talk to him about my job after he has
one.

WF: Is he feeling bad?

SO: Yeah, kind of bad. I think it's the Japanese culture. He is the
first-born male baby so he has to keep and help the family in
the country. The male has to help the family. He has to go
back to his house in the future. So if he has to go back to his
family—it's very far—it's two or three hours by train or car
from here.

WF: You say go back—do you mean to live forever?

SO: Yes, I think so. He wants to work here because it is a big city
and they have a lot of companies. But the companies know
that he is a responsible male and that he will go back, but the
companies want him to work until he retires.

WF: Do the companies ask him if he is the first-born male?

SO: Yes, the companies know his condition.

WF: What is he going to do about that?

SO: He is getting a complex about it, because his family wants
him to work where they live.

WF: So the family wants him to work where they live and the
companies want him to stay here until he is able to retire. Is
the company less likely to hire him because of this?

SO: Yeah, I think so. That is his weak point.

WF: How is his relationship with his family, given that he has this
conflict between his obligation to his family and his desire to
work in a company. How is he feeling about his family?

> SO: He knows he has a responsibility to his family and maybe
> will need to take care of them in the future, but in the future—
> not now! He told me that he had an older brother, but he
> died when he was young. He was not supposed to be the
> older brother.

The conversation with SO suggests that hierarchy and subordination exists within a social and critical context, and that gender is only
one ascribed characteristic among others used to allocate roles. While
her own aspirations will be formed around her future role as a wife
and a mother, her boyfriend's aspirations and career are likely to be
formed around his role as the oldest son of a rural family.

Gender hierarchy and its implicit rejection of the inherent equality
of individuals goes beyond the simple allocation of positions in Japan,
often penetrating deeply into the interactions of everyday life, and
hence into ideals about human relationships. Indeed, the distinction
drawn between gender roles is so pervasive that texts teaching the
Japanese language frequently follow the formal lessons with practices
that involve men's conversational form and women's conversational
form, thus emphasizing that the distinction is built strongly into linguistic norms.

Distinctions go beyond the different status of men and women, or
older and younger sons. At one point in my research I asked my
Japanese assistant to ask the parents to rank certain educational goals.
These included such things as "cooperating with others," "learning
the basics," and so on. These needed to be translated into Japanese
before they could be put to the parents, and I expected to see my
assistant the next day with the translation. She did not appear, however, for a few days, and when she did she told me the trouble she
had translating one of the items. She said that she simply could not
find a simple way to translate "teach students to be critical of authority" without it connoting a negative disposition. While she eventually
found a rather convoluted way to get across the idea, the fact that a
native speaker of Japanese, fluent in English, would have such difficulty suggests that there is a very different conception of hierarchy at
work in the two cultures. It also suggests that the different roles of
men and women are but an instance of a larger ideal about the natural-
ness of hierarchies. If I am right and there are large forces that now
challenge the basic principles of Japanese identity, forces that are the
result of Japan's very successful position in the international economy,
then the Japanese people will need an education that will enable them

to confront and guide these changes. This can only be done in a culture that has learned to address its own identity formation.

X. *Implications for Education*

If these changes do indeed cut deeply into the fiber of Japanese culture and across the grain of existing cultural assumptions, then what implications can be drawn for Japanese education and for education in general? To answer this question, I want to return to a sub-theme of this chapter, and to the continuing lament of many of these Japanese mothers—the extent to which they are swept up in a process with which they do not basically agree. It is not only the mothers who have deep reservations about existing educational practices; teachers, government ministers, and university educators often feel as if the whole country is swept up in something that is ultimately harmful. Yet just what is the nature of that harm? Surely hard work by itself is not a bad thing, and can well be an element in building character. I think the biggest fear is a social one; that children will learn good skills, but will fail to understand how to engage one another in a reflective discussion about the ends to which they will put those skills. It is perhaps here that one must wonder about the character of the public-forming process of Japanese education.

While the cooperative aspects of the Japanese industry provide important elements of public life, and while members of a public must be willing to engage in cooperative inquiry about the achievement of communal goals, more than this is involved in the development of a public. A public must also be concerned—indeed, must be especially concerned—about the spaces beyond the workplaces where the quality of life affects us all. It must be concerned about its physical and psychological environment and about the impact that business and governmental policy has on the well being of the planet. The engagement of a public in a discourse about goals must be an engagement that involves the quality of the goals as well as the means to achieve them. To be swept up in anything that endangers that reflective moment is to endanger the public-forming process of a democratic society.

The Japanese educational system has been responding to many of the changes that the society is experiencing. Most specifically, it is setting up programs for children of company employees who have been abroad and who would be "behind" other Japanese children in terms of the normal curriculum. There is also an extensive correspondence program for children who are overseas with their parents, to help them keep up with their peers back in Japan. Some universities have developed special admissions—a kind of affirmative action—for university-age children returning to Japan. Yet I cannot help but feel that the problem with these programs is much the same as the problem with our affirmative action policies. It treats difference only as a deficit to be overcome rather than an asset to be engaged. This problem becomes more serious if I am correct about just how deep the changes in women's experiences penetrate into Japanese identity. For if basic cultural assumptions are being challenged, then the engagement with difference becomes even more important. In such cases, education that prepares children for a reflective encounter with the agents of their own socialization is essential.

The lesson of all of this for the United States is quite obvious and simple. The "Japanese model" is of limited use in both the school and the workplace. Our own problems of work and education will have to be addressed on our own terms, and with our own needs and ideals in mind. This, of course, brings us back full circle to the issues raised in Chapter One. In a world in which identities are changing, and where we are grappling for a new understanding of who we are, just which terms are we to accept as "our own," and what does the answer to this question entail for our understanding of the aims of work and education? I turn to these questions in the concluding chapter.

7

Education, Work, and Democratic Identity

I. The Goals of a Democratic, Multicultural Education

The problem facing the Japanese is similar to, but not exactly the same as, that confronting the United States. Whereas in Japan external norms are pressing the fundamental, internal assumptions of harmony and hierarchy, here the extension of internal principles of equality and individuality are pressuring the public-identity-forming institutions such as schools. The basic assumption of equality was once interpreted in a restricted sense as simple equality of opportunity, and was applicable largely to White men. Today this bounded interpretation is being pressed, first, in terms of the exclusion of minorities and women, and second, in terms of the restriction of equality to economic and political equality. Equality is now expected by some to involve cultural as well as political and economic matters, granting different groups the right to have their own stories told in the space reserved for public discourse, a space that has traditionally been restricted.

This is a truly important breakthrough, but its educational implications have been often restricted to the development of cultural or gender-related pride, and to the development of assertive behavior associated with economic or political success. It is said, for example, that Black children need to hear about their own history and about successful Black adults as a prerequisite to their own achievement. Yet this is a very restricted sense of the aims of multicultural education. It accepts as unproblematic the understandings of larger and more dominant groups about the meaning of "success," and, more important, it also accepts market-driven identity formation as the educational norm.

Missing from this account is the desire of all groups to tell their stories not just to their own members, but to those outside the group as well. Since we want our stories not just told, but told to others, we want them to be heard—implicit in the pride of the teller is the education of the listener. We do often tell our cultural stories with the hope and expectation that they will be heard and understood by someone from a different culture—that they will command recognition by others.

Ultimately, what is involved in multicultural education is much the same as what is involved in the development of a democratic public. We are learning how to listen and how to discourse about our differences, where the rules of discourse—both our own and others' rules— are part of what we are listening for. Yet different groups need not listen for the same things. Although both dominant and subordinate groups need to learn about the ways of different cultures, they do not always need to learn exactly the same things. In the example below, consider the different lessons that are being learned by the Japanese and the American children in the first-grade classroom.

A new group of Japanese children arrived with their parents in Cornton, a middle-sized American city. Their fathers were sent to the community as managers and engineers to set up a large factory that would employ a work force in the thousands. Two of these children were assigned to Mrs. Fields' first-grade class and much of Mrs. Fields' time was spent helping the two new Japanese first-graders feel comfortable in their new school. She deliberately sat the Japanese children next to students who were bright, friendly, and popular, to ensure that the children would have someone to play with. During the early weeks of school, Sara, who sat next to Kayoko, was placed in Kayoko's low reading group, even though her skill would have placed her in the advanced group. The arrangement seemed to be acceptable to Sara's parents, who said they thought it was a good experience for her, and it helped Kayoko feel comfortable.

The Japanese children were seated so that they could communicate with their American partners and with each other if they choose to do so. The children usually were seated in rows. Each row had two desks grouped together. Hence while Takeo and Kayoko were each paired with an American child, they sat next to each other with an aisle separating them.

For the first few weeks Takeo and Kayoko never spoke to each other, even in Japanese. Hanna Watanabe, a local Japanese American whom the school hired to work with the children and their families, reported that Takeo had been teased by his older brothers when it was learned that a Japanese girl was coming into his class, and she thought that this might explain the silence that existed between them. Although Mrs. Fields reported that Sara and Kayoko communicated with a combination of gestures, smiles, nods, "almost by magic," English words were not available to either Takeo or Kayoko, and neither was willing to break the ice, and communicate in Japanese. The language they could speak was no longer perceived by them as legitimate for this classroom, while the language that had legitimacy in the school was unavailable to them.

This silence was disturbing to Mrs. Fields. While she was pleased to see Kayoko and Sara communicating with each other by whatever "magic" they used, she wondered about the adequacy of her own efforts to encourage the Japanese students to speak, and she reported with delight the process that had finally broken their mutual silence.

> Paula came up this afternoon to complain that Takeo had said something to her in Japanese and she didn't know what he said, but she didn't think it sounded "nice." She said it sounded like "swat." Paula wanted me to ask Takeo what he said. I thought he had probably told her to sit down and I said "suwatte" and he nodded yes. Then to practice my Japanese I said "tatte" and he stood up and nodded that was correct. Paula watched this, fascinated, and then commented that Takeo and I had understood one another and that I could speak Japanese. She then asked me to teach her too.
>
> Then others in the room said that they wanted to know Japanese so that they could talk to Takeo and Kayoko. Sara said that her sister even knew a word in Japanese and why wouldn't I teach them. I had wanted to wait awhile . . . but I decided that I had the "teachable" moment right then. We stopped what we were doing and I taught "Konnichi-wa" and "dewa mata." The American kids were . . . all raising their hands wanting to respond. . . .
>
> The Japanese kids were watching almost in disbelief because the others were so excited about learning Japanese. Then some of the kids asked me to call on Takeo and Kayoko. I did and the class was pleased when they responded. Before we went home we practiced the words again, and most of them told me good-bye in Japanese when they left. I said good-bye to Takeo and Kayoko in Japanese and they replied in Japanese (with a smile)—so it's OK for me to speak Japanese to them if I am saying the same thing to everyone. It makes sense because now I am not singling them out.

Prior to this episode, the children had been reluctant to respond when Mrs. Fields attempted to address them in her limited Japanese. They were comfortable speaking Japanese only when they were working with Mrs. Watanabe in a separate room, and Mrs. Fields had never observed them speaking to each other in her classroom. The day after Paula's complaint things had changed.

> What a day. My aide and I had Takeo teaching us to say the parts of the face in Japanese. Then I checked his and Kayoko's math papers, counting in Japanese (to practice my Japanese). After that the whole class practiced saying "good afternoon," "see you later," and "good evening" in Japanese. I told them that now they could greet their Japanese friends and their parents at our ice cream social tonight. A little later Sara came up to tell me to come back and listen to Takeo and Kayoko talking in Japanese. This was a first! There they were chattering away in Japanese and not paying one bit of attention. This was the first time I had heard them speak to one another. I wondered if it was because we were all speaking Japanese now (even if it is a very little bit). Anyway, Japanese doesn't seem so different anymore and they feel comfortable enough to speak now.

Once they felt that they were no longer being treated as special, Takeo and Kayoko felt licensed to speak to one another in their own language. However, it was not always easy to reach this point. Mrs. Fields experienced the struggle constantly:

> I am finally getting so I don't overreact when the Japanese kids read or respond—it's hard for me—I am so pleased for them. This is the hardest part of having them in the room. It is hard to just treat them like others knowing how hard it must be for them.

The balance between taking the children's different cultural background seriously and yet not treating them differently from other children requires a great deal of patience and practical wisdom. By meeting with parents, by inviting them to share their food and culture with the classroom, by printing her name in Japanese as well as English on the classroom door, by taking an active interest in the children's own language and culture, Mrs. Fields enabled the students to enter the community without requiring that they discard their own identity as Japanese. She did not do this by singling out the children for special treatment. Rather she simply used the right moment to involve the class as a whole in the children's culture.

Mrs. Fields' teaching reveals a model for multicultural education.

She believes that the expression of alternative identities should be encouraged, but not forced by the teacher. In the process of enabling the children to express their identities, she makes many mistakes, and is critical of her tendency to overrespond to the Japanese children. She tells me that she needs to monitor this. What makes the important difference in this case is her ability to engage the children on their own cultural and linguistic grounds, providing the security they need to enter the group as equals. This ability had been developed over time, and required a passing familiarity with Japanese culture and a modest understanding of the Japanese language. She had only started to study Japanese a few months before this episode, when she learned the children would be entering her class. The skill she had obtained in a few months was not enough to carry on a full conversation with the children, but it was sufficient to allow her to take advantage of "the teachable moment" when it appeared.

These Japanese children have been introduced to an important feature of democratic education. They have been accepted into an established community with their own cultural identity intact, and they have been acknowledged for their ability to teach as well as to be taught. They have been allowed to make a difference in the community itself. Of course, democratic education is a long-term affair, requiring more than simply the acceptance of cultural difference. Mrs. Fields has made a start with these children, but her aim is not, I believe, to teach the Japanese children exactly the same lesson as the American children. In part she is teaching the former group that it is perfectly acceptable to be Japanese while also teaching them how to operate competently in American society. The American students are hopefully learning that their taken-for-granted behavior is a cultural product, and Mrs. Fields is teaching them an understanding of another culture's ways. While she may not voice it in these terms, she is indeed sensitive to the differences in status and power that these two groups occupy in this classroom.

Someone might observe, quite accurately, that the position of these children is only temporary, and that in the long run the status of the Japanese children in the community would, because of their fathers' positions in the plant, be at least as high as that of their classmates. The observation is important because of its suggestion that dominance and subordinance are complex concepts, and that their application itself often requires a reasonably subtle discourse. Power is indeed multilayered. However, the episode in Mrs. Fields' classroom is still significant for at least two reasons. First, it demonstrates that power relations do need to be considered in determining what the aims of instruction should be in specific situations, and second, it highlights an important distinction in intercultural education—a distinction between competence and understanding.

All too often the lower-status students are expected to become competent in the ways of the dominant group, whereas no such expectations are placed on students from the more advantaged situation. This is not the case in Mrs. Fields' classroom, where there are mutual, although different, expectations. The Japanese students will become competent in many of the ways of American culture, but the American students will also achieve a certain level of understanding of Japanese culture.

Competence and understanding are related, but they are not the same. The American students will not be able to navigate Japanese culture, while the Japanese students will soon learn how to cope in American society. They will be able to shop for their parents and converse with friends and teachers in English. They will come to know that when they enter an American's home, they need not remove their shoes, and they will learn to be more assertive in the classroom. They will likely acquire some understanding of American culture as well, but their competence level will not always parallel, or even be related to, their understanding level. The American students are not gaining a great deal of competence in terms of Japanese culture, but they are traveling on the track of understanding, however limited or extensive this trip may eventually be. Yet just what is entailed in this journey, and what constitutes the kind of understanding that we have when we understand another culture?

II. Competence and Understanding

The problem of understanding other cultures is complex, but it is not, as some theorists suggest, impossible, and it constitutes an essential element of democratic education in a multicultural society. Moreover, because the first step in such understanding involves viewing one's own activity and behavior as a cultural product, understanding is usually more difficult for members of the dominant culture, who learn to take their own behavior as modeling a cultural norm. Nevertheless, we do not, contrary to some recent arguments,[1] need to have a native's competence to understand other cultures.

There is a distinction between having a native's competence and having an understanding of the culture. A native's *competence* enables us to navigate the culture—to know what to expect in response to certain behavior and gestures, such as eye contact or a smile. An *understanding* of the culture enables us to place this behavior in a social and historical context. It helps us to understand just why such behavior evokes the response it does. A person may have native competence without much understanding, as is the case with many intuitive people who respond with amazing appropriateness to people from other cultures but cannot say exactly what the behavior they are responding to means, or why it has the meaning it does. Similarly, a person may have a great deal of understanding without having any practiced competence. Historians who have studied the customs and practices of an ancient people in significant detail have acquired much understanding but no competence. They are somewhat like the Japanese graduate student who, upon first being introduced to my wife in Tokyo, gave her a big hug. He understood the behavior reasonably well—a hug does not necessarily mean desire or deep affection. He just didn't know when it was appropriate to perform it. His behavior was most likely similar in kind to the many inappropriate bows that I have given to Japanese, although, as the old song goes, "I know not where or when."

It takes an awareness of another culture to have a conception of one's own behavior as a cultural expression—this is the beginning of understanding. The native can tell us just what the eye movement means in her culture, because she is aware of our culture, and because she knows that different cultures interpret some behaviors differently.

However, there is more to understanding than simply being able to say what a particular slice of behavior means. For example, an anthropologist might tell us about some culture where looking a person in the eye is an indication of honesty, because of the strong value that is placed on equality. The anthropologist might continue that dishonesty is thereby interpreted as a stain that will lower one's standing, making one less than equal, and that people in this culture believe this lowered standing will inevitably be expressed in one's posture and manner. The eyes are taken as the window to the soul, and failing to look another person in the eye is thereby taken as a sign of wrongdoing, because it is seen to indicate the fear that if the window were open, the stain could be seen. Dishonesty has literally reduced her standing in the eyes of others, and in her own eyes as well. Here the interpretation given to the downward glance is an indication of a deeper set of beliefs about the nature of human beings and their relationship to one another. It is a sign of a well-formed set of beliefs that is embedded within the practice of the culture. To say that a person understands a culture is to say that she has access to such a set of beliefs and is able to reconstruct them when required.

This meaning of cultural understanding is the same whether or not the culture is our own or that of someone else and it is not the same as learning to operate competently—even at the highest levels—in a culture. To be able to decode a piece of behavior—one shows respect by glancing away—enables a person to navigate the culture. A person who is completely competent can navigate the culture intuitively, participate in its music, enjoy its stories and carry on many conversations. A person who is fully competent can participate in the culture from the inside. However, even this level of participation is distinguishable from understanding the culture.

When we understand another culture, we understand its deepest assumptions about what it means to be human—its core set of beliefs about self and other—and we are able to translate these beliefs into particular patterns of behavior. For example, where a glance to the side or to the floor is accepted as a sign of respect, it is likely an expression of a set of beliefs that is quite counter to the one that insists on "looking the teacher in the eye." Here looking the teacher in the eye may be a sign of disrespect, because it presumes an equality which the culture requires be earned through the wisdom that comes from many years of experience. The essential relationship is one of inequality of experience and wisdom. The person who learns only to translate the behavior—to take a glance at the floor as respect, not as dishonesty—has learned an important lesson, but nevertheless may be still quite ignorant about the culture. She knows how to show respect, but not why she is showing it or when it is appropriate to show it.

Behavior is the gateway to participation. Meaning is the gateway to understanding. To stay only at the level of proper behavior is to lose an opportunity to use the practices of the other culture to learn something about the deeper meanings of our own. To develop this understanding requires an openness to the practices of the other culture without exclusively interpreting them through one's own immediate aims, even though any fruitful dialogue will eventually involve bringing those aims back into focus. Nevertheless, one's own aims are often the reason for the dialogue to take place, and their reassessment may well provide a reason for altering the dialogue's nature. The way we see Japan may eventually tell us something about the way we are, and may enable us to better evaluate our future possibilites. Here, in the momentary suspension of some of our own cultural assumptions, is the core of cultural understanding. It is this act of suspending our own taken-for granted cultural assumptions and of coming to terms with otherness, that is one of the major tasks for the education of a democratic public in a multicultural society.

Both cultural competence and cultural understanding are important elements of multicultural education for all groups. However, because their behavior is taken as the norm, understanding is more difficult and therefore, more in need of systematic development, for members of the dominant group. One would hope that such understanding will be accompanied by certain positive attitudes, but no education can fully prescribe how one should feel about what one has come to understand. Education can at least further attitudes of patience and openness towards people from another culture by advancing the reflective insight that the norms and behavior of contrasting groups are historically and culturally constructed. However near or far along the trail of cultural understanding students may travel, the lessons of patience and openness toward the other—along with a willingness to both sincerely press ahead with one's own cultural assumptions and to change them when appropriate—is the core of multicultural education.

III. Work and Education

It should be recalled that the economic conservative was also concerned to develop a broader level of cultural awareness among American students, but between the conservative and myself there is a significant difference. The conservative believes that the parochial nature of American business is limiting competitiveness in the international market. I believe that democracy requires the encouragement of different voices within a larger communal understanding that respects differences. There are, of course, many occasions when the conservative's and my concerns intersect, and there are some practices that we both would applaud. However, there are important differences between us and there are times when the conservatives and I must part company, because behind our surface similarity is a radically different conception of educational aims in this postmodern age. They seek harmony. I seek a community that can encourage the development of individuality and that serves to enrich the public discourse through the inclusion of multiple voices and different cultural expriences.

An important difference between harmony and community is that harmony refers to the nature of a performance. Community refers to the nature of a process. In music, "harmony" is the combination of sounds as they are heard. "Community" is a particular kind of process through which a combination is achieved and future combinations formed. Where harmony is achieved through threat, deception, or pressure, community does not exist. Where harmony is developed through honest consultation with respect for different points of view and a concern for future development, then it reflects a communal process.

The American educational philosopher, John Dewey, in defining community, correctly rejected the idea that cooperation alone is the mark of a community. He wrote:

> The parts of a machine work with a maximum of cooperativeness for a common result, but they do not form a community. If, however, they were all cognizant of the common end and all interested in it so that they regulated their specific activity in view of it, then they would form a community.[2]

The definition is useful for highlighting the difference between unintelligent, mechanical coordination, on the one hand, and human community on the other hand, and it goes some way in elaborating the distinction between community and harmony. Yet there is more to the story. Harmony may also involve cognizance of a common end, and the adjustment of individual activity accordingly. Community requires that the process through which the common end is developed involves collaborative participation, and that it minimize various forms of coercion.[3]

Of course communal action is collective in some contexts. When a flooded river threatens a small town, the action taken to divert its course is collective action. However, it is the relations that the people have to each other that determine whether the collective action is communal action. At the very least we expect members of a community to have a history of common interests, and to hold expectations that they will participate in the development of a shared future. Members of communities are bound to each other in important and enduring ways, through structures that are mutually maintained and nurtured. As members of a community, they come to share histories and symbols. However, in any modern or postmodern society, what they share is not all that they are. Community requires that they also seek agreements based as much as possible on a reasoned discourse that takes into account different histories, symbols and traditions, and seeks educational policies that enable individuals to maintain and enhance their present and multiple identities.

This ideal is considerably different from the harmony that serves as the goal of the cultural conservative's enterprise. Contrast, for example, Mrs. Fields' treatment of Takeo and Kayoko with Mr. Y's dismissal of his workers' complaints, described in an earlier chapter. Here we have two different conceptions of commonality and difference. To view complaints about long hours as a joke is to reflect the distinction between community and harmony. The inaccurate conflation of harmony with community is at the heart of the conservative's appeal, and explains the attraction that Japan has for the culturally conservative thinker. Community as I conceive it, involves taking *serious* differences *seriously*, and this is precisely what Mrs. Fields sought to achieve in her classroom, and it is what Mr. Y found so hard to do.[5]

If he had to take the complaint seriously, then Mr. Y would be forced to entertain the possibility that, no matter how weak its expression, his workers do have a significant identity beyond the workplace—that there is a potential discord between their roles as workers and their roles as husbands, fathers, and sons. To read complaints as only "jokes" perhaps allows the assumption of harmony to be maintained without acknowledging that identities other than "worker" are being sacrificed. The assumption could not as easily be held if community were the goal.

An education that aims to achieve a level of community will be different from one that seeks mere harmony. Contrast, for example, two English classes held in the same Japanese *juku* (cram school). In the first, two or three hundred male students are listening intently to an instructor who is explaining to them in Japanese the subtle difference between the English phrases "getting into a car" and "stepping on to a plane." With the exception of the English words "getting into a car" and "stepping on to a plane," and a few other similar examples, the entire lesson is conducted in Japanese, and the students are attentive but totally silent. Most have failed their first examination into the university and are diligently preparing for their second chance. Some will graduate from college and enter industry with rudimentary knowledge of English grammar and usage, and, with the right assignment, will be able to develop a useful linguistic skill. At this point, however, it does not appear as if any of the students are learning English as a living language, spoken by real people in order to accomplish real purposes. This is *school* English—another test of endurance and character.

In the next building there is a small group of women sitting in a carpeted room, discussing with an instructor an English story they have read. The conversation is conducted entirely in English, and involves much concentration and struggle on the part of the students. For the most part these students do not expect to go on to high-powered universities. Although some may hope eventually to be good enough at English to serve as translators, others are there just to learn the language, but all have the experience of participating in a linguistic community.

The difference between these two groups is not simply that one is governed by educational concerns and the other by status and job concerns. It is likely that some of the women in the group enrolled to make them more desirable wives, just as it is likely that some of the men felt that they must pass the English section of the examination in order to receive a ticket to a real educational experience. The difference is that one is a closed society whose purpose is assumed, and which doggedly pursues it, while the other is an open and spontaneous one, whose members are willing to try on a different linguistic identity. In recent years the pressures to link work and education have been enormous, but if such links are to be true to the spirit of education, then work will need to become more open, communal, and reflective about ends as well as means, and will need to acknowledge and accommodate culturally different people.

IV. Identity

A. THE CONSERVATIVE FALLACY

Cultural conservatives seek harmony, but they neglect community. They appeal to the nation's founders and to the Enlightenment tradition to anchor their own idea of culture and standards, but their articulation of that tradition bears little resemblance to the dynamic interpretive struggle out of which it developed. Instead people, dates, and events are abstracted from all determinate social relations—from cultural and historical tradition—and are provided equal but separate status. Individuals and cultures are legitimate insofar as they conform to the principles of the Enlightenment vision, but the cultural conservative's articulation of that vision provides us with a prefabricated culture. The public can assimilate this culture but cannot participate in its creation. On this view, human nature is fixed. The Enlightenment thinkers discovered its laws a few centuries ago, and it is the schools' job to teach people to follow them as best they can. When we break the laws of nature, as women do when they follow the guidance of feminism, and as universities do when they adopt the latest educational fad, it is warned that we invite retribution. Children grow up scarred, and students graduate miseducated, with impoverished souls.[6]

Cultural conservatives fail to provide the kind of moral vision which could be used as the foundation for an educational renewal because their conception of education diminishes the value of reflection and dialogue, abilities that postmodern societies require in order to consciously control the strains brought about by both changing economic and cultural relationships.

This image of a passive public helps explain the cultural conservatives' general indifference towards issues of pedagogy. They seek to create a unified public by having students taught a common tradition or a common set of symbols, but they are interested in results, not in the process through which those results are achieved. Hence, if a common set of symbols can be achieved through interesting discussions or through entertaining pageants, then that is acceptable. However, it is also acceptable for children to memorize long lists of unconnected facts if those facts correspond to the requirements "needed" to establish an American identity.[7]

This indifference to pedagogy tells us much about the cultural conservatives' conception of the public. The idea that a nation's identity can be formed through a passive appropriation of prescribed symbols implies that the ongoing life of the child—the identities formed outside the school—is quite incidental to the educational process. Cultural conservatives wrongly believe that a public is created by transmitting a unified body of fully interpreted cultural material to a new generation. This mistakes the means for the end, and leads to an overinterpreted view of the cultural content which comprises the intellectual furniture of the public. In their view, each new generation is destined to accept the meaning of the old.

This view fails to acknowledge that a public is created in the discussion over its own constitution—over the struggle to give meaning to past and present events, and in the self-conscious and mutual awareness that a common self-definition is at stake. The fact that different individuals happen to share, in some isolated way, the same cultural material does not mean that they constitute a public. The cultural conservatives fail to understand that the development of a public involves the entrance into a critical dialogue, in which respect for the interpretations of others is a part of the norms of inquiry, and in this failure they provide an overinterpreted view of the products of cultural transmission.[8]

Education as an induction into a democratic public involves an active engagement with the materials and symbols of a society, and that engagement often requires that communal symbols be connected to meanings that are familiar and significant. A democratic public is always in the process of constituting itself, and the imposition of unexamined meanings retards the self-formative process. Certainly the ability to identify some significant people or events is important, but so, too, is the need to enter into the different cultural experiences and interpretations of these events.

This is important not because the ability to identify such events is necessary or sufficient for the creation of a unified nation. Rather, the inability to identify certain events and people suggests that youngsters may be losing the will to actively participate in the cultural experience of their community and to develop the skills required to deliberately negotiate and guide its future conduct.

In a democracy the product is the process. For example, Israeli educators are said to be concerned because a disturbingly high percentage of Israeli youth cannot identify Adolph Hitler or give the years that the Holocaust took place.[9] The complaint sounds similar to the American cultural conservative's reasonable concern that American students do not know when the Civil War was fought or who Benedict Arnold was. Yet the fact that some Israeli students cannot identify Hitler or give the dates of the Holocaust is a symptom; it is not the problem. The problem is to engage them in an intelligent discussion about the meaning of their past and the possibilities for their future. Their amnesia is a symptom of this failing.

Cultural conservatives are driven by an impulse to rest education on a solid, uninterpretable basis—one not subject to different and conflicting interpretations. The idea is that there is a preestablished standard that can be used to determine membership in the public. It is the function of education to see that everyone is given the opportunity to learn to act in accordance with that ideal. To provide a world whose interpretation is complete is to avoid the uncertainty of a world whose meaning must continuously be explored.

What is appealing about cultural conservatives' views is the recognition that education does have a moral dimension, and the correct belief that much of that moral dimension has to do with the creation of a public. What is unfortunate is the misunderstanding of both the nature of that moral imagination and of the character of a democratic public in the latter part of the twentieth century.

B. THE NEED FOR A DEMOCRATIC PUBLIC

A democratic public is engaged in a common discourse about difference, where the rules of discourse may become a subject for discourse.

This kind of discussion is especially important in a society whose identity is uncertain, as it is in the case of the United States, or in a society whose ideological underpinnings are under threat from contradictory tensions, as is the case in Japan. The challenge for Japanese education, for example, is to teach people how to address constructively the deeper cultural principles that present-day tensions threaten. An educational system that is examination-driven will have difficulty doing this because so much rides on getting the answer right that little time can be devoted to deciding what questions are important to ask.[10]

The demands of an internationalized economy are changing the character of social and economic relationships in Japan in ways that are unsettling to the basic assumptions of harmony, hierarchy, subordination, and place. The changing situation of women, described in the last chapter, is perhaps the most significant manifestation of the changes. The great and largely unacknowledged need in Japan is to provide an educational experience that will address this change in a way that will inform the larger set of cultural assumptions. Such an experience would require that students actually become conscious of the tacit rules governing their own socialization—such as those that limit discourse between boys and girls in the classroom—and that the reasons for these rules become part of a critical educational discourse. This is the only kind of education that makes any sense in a world where cultural interaction is rapidly increasing, and where the basic principles of social life are called upon continually to accommodate new and unanticipated situations. In Japan, education aimed at the development of a democratic public would be the prudent as well as the morally proper thing to do. For Americans, however, the concern about Japan is ultimately a concern about ourselves, and the understanding of Japan has a reflexive aim—the understanding of ourselves through an understanding of the other.

Yet precisely what does this understanding entail? What role do other cultures play in it? And to what extent does exploring my identity in this way mean, as conservatives might fear, that I am changing my identity and diluting my commitment to its formative principles? To respond to these questions we need to probe deeply into the consensus that constitutes the apparent harmony of Japanese society and that is so admired by American cultural conservatives.

The problem for the cultural conservatives is actually two-fold. On the one hand, they want harmony, but they are unable to accept the principles on which Japanese harmony is constituted without accepting a way of life that is too foreign and hence quite unacceptable to them. On the other hand, the basic principles of American life tend to place individual difference and even friction above harmony, and seem unable to produce the desired concordance. Of course, this dilemma is not just that of the conservative, but belongs to all of us. Its resolution requires a probe into the character of our own identity, and I begin this probe with a reflective analysis of our reactions to some of the collective features of Japanese life.

C. AN AMERICAN ENCOUNTER WITH JAPAN

To approach the question of self-understanding I want to begin with the reaction of some American teachers to a somewhat outdated, but not extinct form of Japanese behavior. The situation involved a Japanese couple who had moved into Cornton where the husband was to help set up a factory, and whose children were now enrolled in the school. The teachers thought it odd that the wife always walked a few paces behind her husband whenever they came to school events, and one teacher commented that when alone she was usually the more garrulous of all the Japanese mothers, but when she was with her husband, a very taciturn man, she fell silent while he did the necessary talking.

Although the teachers agreed that the mother's behavior was extreme and did not represent that of the more modern Japanese who had come into the community, they found it more than quaint. In some way it countered their Westernized sense of equality, even though they granted that the wife seemed to be quite comfortable walking behind her husband.

As Westerners, inclined toward a rights-oriented, individualistic view of democracy, there is an inclination to see situations like this as involving domination and subservience. Many would find this behavior difficult to accept, even if the wife herself rejected our judgment and told us that she was simply showing her husband respect. Our received conception of democracy makes it difficult for us to see this description as accurately reflecting the significance of her behavior. Even though we tend to give priority to people's own understanding of their behavior, many of us would be inclined to say that in this case the wife was mistaken about the meaning of her action. She was, as the Marxist might say, simply exhibiting her own false consciousness, and a few might even see in this behavior evidence of the "fundamentally" undemocratic character of Japanese society. And, of course, many conservatives would agree that the behavior is exceedingly undemocratic, and not appropriate for a democratic society. The teachers in this school reflected these reactions. They tolerantly described the behavior as exotic, but they also seemed relieved that the vast majority of Japanese parents in the community did not behave this way. Their relief was likely based on the fact that those parents were behaving more like us, and reducing *visible* hierarchies.

Some Westerners who view these relationships as undemocratic would defend their description of the wife's compliance as false consciousness by noting that, when women are assigned to and accept a subordinate social position on the basis of ascribed (gender) characteristics alone, they have failed to come to terms with the modern notion of individuality. Western liberals hold that modern conceptions of individuality require that respect be granted on the basis of achievement, not gender, and they require that opportunities to achieve should be open to all. When external influences—even those that have been incorporated into the socialized self—retard this, then we fall short of the desired form of social organization. Clearly, we frequently honor this ideal more in the breach than in the practice, but to point out the violation is to acknowledge the ideal.

D. A JAPANESE CHALLENGE TO INDIVIDUALISM

Our commitment to independence is expressed in more than simply the political realm. For example, the noted Japanese psychoanalyst Takeo Doi writes of his earliest experience in America:

> [One] thing that made me nervous, was the custom whereby an American host will ask a guest, before the meal, whether he would prefer a strong or a soft drink. Then if the guest asks for liquor, he will ask him whether, for example, he prefers scotch or bourbon. When the guest has made this decision, he next has to give instructions as to how much he wishes to drink, and how he wants it served. With the main meal, fortunately, one has only to eat what one is served, but once it is over, one has to choose whether to take coffee or tea and—in even greater detail—whether one wants it with sugar, and milk and so on. I soon realized that this was only the American's way of showing politeness to his guest, but in my own mind, I had a strong feeling that I could not care less. What a lot of trivial choices they were obliging me to make—I sometimes felt almost as though they were doing it to reassure themselves of their own freedom.[11]

Doi's reflection on his own response to American society is taken as a mirror, indicating to him something that is a key to understanding Japanese society. This is the concept of *amae*, which the translator tells us refers to the feeling that all normal infants harbor toward the mother. It is described as the "desire to be passively loved, the unwillingness to be separated from the warm mother-child circle." In contrast to our own quest for independence, which we take to be a universal drive, *amae*, which Doi sees as a characteristic drive expressed in Japanese practices and personality, could be appropriately described as the quest for dependency. Yet if Doi is correct, if *amae* does express a characteristic drive, then the concept represents a powerful challenge to Western ideas of identity and democracy.

The thinkers who formulated the American concept of democracy believed that independence was one of the few values that could be attributed to all members of the human species. It was the only value that could be taken as foundational to any association. Even the family, which serves to protect dependent children, is implicitly expected to raise children to be independent and self-sufficient. Doi's view of the Japanese, then, raises very strong doubts about the reported universal foundations of Western democracy, and if we read Doi reflexively, he also raises important doubts about the very scientific categories through which we seek to understand ourselves and others.

Doi argues that the value of independence is embedded in the categories of Western psychoanalysis, which is unable to acknowledge the drive for dependency. He writes of the overemphasis in psychoanalysis on self-reliance, and of the indifference among analysts to their patients' sense of helplessness, and he questions whether self-reliance and independence are the overwhelming driving force that psychoanalysis suggests they are.[12] To adopt Doi's view would presumably lead not to a quest for independence, but to acknowledgment of the need for help.

The same shortcoming that Doi finds in Western psychoanalysis may be found in Western economic theory. Because economists insist on viewing the basic economic entity as isolated individuals (either people or firms) seeking to maintain or maximize their own profit through market rationality, they are unable to acknowledge, as anything other than inefficiency and waste, efforts to preserve nonmaximizing structures. As was mentioned earlier, this bias leads American economists to view the Japanese networks of small shops and markets, and the duplication of inventory that takes place at the wholesale level, as both inefficient and designed to keep American products off the Japanese markets. Of course they do function in that way, but some of these practices also serve to preserve significant social relationships. A comprehensive economic theory would need to take this into account. Yet this does not happen, and the importance of these structures for maintaining intimate social contact, small neighborhoods, adult role models, and an effective structure for adult-child interaction goes underinvestigated. It simply is difficult for social scientists using traditional Western economic categories to ask some of the appropriate questions.

E. REFLECTIONS ON THE PRINCIPLES OF OUR IDENTITY

We come to a pause in the reading. For in our encounter with Japan, we have experienced a serious encounter with our own judgments and our own categories of understanding. Our encounter with Japan has turned out to be an encounter with ourselves. We have rubbed against our own cultural foundation of equality and individuality, freedom and choice, the very foundation that appears to be licensing the emergence of the multicultural experience. Is the solution to the conservative's dilemma to be found in the belief that Doi expresses, that individuals, when left to their own accord, seek hierarchy and dependency? Must we thereby accept the cultural conservatives' point of view after all, and come to renew our oneness and to license a dominant culture which, like a conductor, constructs harmony out of difference? Or is there more to this encounter than just a roundabout way into the conservatives' symphony? The questions to be asked, therefore, are whether Doi is right about Japan, and if he is right about it, then is he also right about us?

F. THE ANSWER FROM WITHIN JAPAN

One response to this reading comes from within the Japanese intellectual tradition itself. Here it is suggested that the Japanese are not the anomalies that Doi and others suggest. Instead, some Japanese and some Western scholars argue that the values of individuality and independence are not just Western values but are shared by Japanese as well. According to this view, the idea that Japanese value their independence any less than other people or that they value their group any more highly is a distortion of the true Japanese point of view. For example, Mouer and Sugimoto, in reviewing the post-war scholarly literature on Japan, see Doi as overemphasizing the dependency concerns of the Japanese. They claim that similar distortions will be found in social psychology, political theory, sociology, and other disciplines. The authors are critical of these areas for emphasizing the unity of the Japanese character, and for overemphasizing the importance of paternalism, group solidarity, and the consensus mode of decision-making. In summarizing this literature, they challenge the assumption that the Japanese derive any more pleasure from serving group interests and conforming to group norms than most other people, and they are critical of the literature for assuming that such pleasure can be taken for granted and needs no demonstration.[13] They argue that many of the comparisons of Japan with other nationalities are based on inaccurate information, and even on a misunderstanding of the extent to which the traits of individualism really do characterize Western society. To support their view they argue that much of what is "commonly cited as examples of spontaneous consensus in Japanese society is in fact produced by a fine blend of manipulative and coercive controls."[14] For example,

> One tab on people is the family registry. . . . These are part of an elaborate system of files which record information on each family. The file lists convictions, previous addresses, marriage particulars and other information; behavior is recorded on a family basis so that the peccadilloes of each individual are recorded with those of other family members. Despite a person's desire to assume individual responsibility, his indiscretions will always affect some other people. The consultation of these records in decisions relating to marriage and employment are well known, although public pressure has, in recent years, resulted in some restrictions being placed on their accessibility.[15]

Similarly, they argue that much of what passes for company loyalty, and much of the willingness of Japanese workers to go the extra mile for the company are explained by the large number of regulations and the high level of surveillance that are to be found in many companies. Employers often require a personal guarantor's statement and written proof that the new worker does not have a criminal record. New workers are often provided with a book of a hundred pages or so containing the company's regulations, which they are expected to memorize and may be tested on.[16] Thus, according to these authors, much of what passes in Japan for group loyalty and as a rejection of individuality and independence is in fact behavior that is manipulated or coerced. They grant that Japanese may express their individuality differently from Westerners, but they argue that it is held in equally high regard.

If the authors are correct, and what passes for spontaneous, group-oriented behavior is controlled from outside the individuals immediately involved in the group, then the material for a rereading of our own tradition and its universality can be found within the Japanese tradition itself. Yet this argument is somewhat beside the point. Doi did not exactly claim that the Japanese were any more inclined toward dependency than other people. He simply claimed that Japanese culture and Japanese social science were able to give voice to this need, in a way that Western culture and science could not, and that this was indeed an important need. Moreover, one may grant the truth to the claim that much of what appears to be spontaneous conformity is really the result of institutional constraints and procedures without abandoning Doi's basic point. A family register in the hands of the police would certainly affect behavior in societies where family ties were strong. Yet the strength of family ties can also be taken as an important indicator of the recognition of dependency on and identity with the family. When police are able to appropriate family shame to maintain control, or when corporations are able to appropriate family pride to develop a productive work force, they may well be seen as illustrating Doi's point. Hence the important question is not whether more control is exerted by the police or the corporation; it is to what extent do individuals and groups voice objections to such appropriation, and to what do they appeal in doing so.

Teruhisa Horio, in his important book *Educational Thought and Ideology in Modern Japan*, suggests that dependency is not embedded in Japanese character, tradition, and culture, but is the product of a planned bureaucratic drive. Horio sees two important educational traditions vying for influence and power in Japan. The first is a highly centralized system, controlled by the state and serving to produce a work force that is docile, regimented, and controlled. The second is a democratic system in which the state plays a relatively minor role in education, and where control is entrusted to the people most closely associated with the schools—namely the teachers and parents. He views the strict control of textbooks, the heavy emphasis on the examination system, and the centralized control of the curriculum as expressions of the first tradition, but he traces both to the early days of the Meiji revolution in the late 1800s, when Japan was breaking its feudal isolation and emerging as a modern nation.

He believes that one can find within the Japanese tradition the same commitment to equality and human rights that one finds within the

West and he quotes from "An Outline of True Government," a document written by Kato Hiroyuki in 1870, to support his point: "Since all men are equally endowed by nature with the right to exist, no one is therefore inherently obliged to submit to the orders of another."[17] From this Kato argued that the state should have a minimal role in the organization of national life, and that "all political authority should be entrusted to the people themselves."[18] Armed with Enlightenment principles and natural rights theory, Kato went on to attack all remnants of Confucian thought. Other major intellectuals and educators, including Mori Arinori, a leading educator of the early Meiji period, embraced these ideas. However, Mori was later to become a major figure in supporting state-organized education. Horio tells us that eventually those who embraced the Enlightenment ideals split into two groups—those who continued to advocate enlightenment from below and those who argued that the people needed to be enlightened from above—from a state-controlled educational system.[19] Horio sees in the latter group a disguised attempt to use the Enlightenment as an ideology to assert bureaucratic control and subvert the authority of the people, and much of the rest of his book is designed to explore how that control works in today's educational system.

The struggle in Japan between centralizing and decentralizing forces, as Horio describes it, is not unlike similar struggles in this country, and if he is correct, then it is likely that Western notions of individuality and independence are not inconsistent with the Japanese tradition. If this is the case, it may well be possible to establish a point of judgment and criticism from within the Japanese framework that is quite consistent with Western ones. However, this approach, while helpful, does not completely resolve *our* problem. It tells us that there may be at least two traditions in Japan, but it does not tell us how important individuality is to democratic forms of association. (It is important to note that in this country the justification for a more powerful central government is usually made on the grounds of necessity and fairness, and not on the basis of inherent dependency.) It tells us that of the two traditions, one is just like our own. However, it does not tell us how to assess the other tradition in terms of its implication for democratic life, and it is, after all, the other tradition, the tradition of Doi, which appears to challenge our notions of individuality and independence. To respond to this challenge it is not sufficient to show that there is another tradition just like ours that is to be found in Japan. We must confront the problems raised by the tradition that seems to deny what we hold so firmly—that individuality and independence are essential to democratic association. To begin by accepting Horio over Doi without investigating further is to already import Western ideals in as a template to determine the value of competing foreign traditions. A more fruitful approach might be to begin at the other end. Instead of seeking ideals in the Japanese tradition which are similar to the American ideals, we might seek that in American tradition which is compatible with Doi's description of the Japanese.

G. "AMERICAN INDIVIDUALISM" AND "JAPANESE COLLECTIVISM"

Doi's presentation of the concept of *amae* is an opportunity to look at familiar practices in unfamiliar ways and to reevaluate some of our own educational goals. For example, how are we to take the idea that there is a strong drive for dependency within the Japanese personality, and how are we to take the possibility that this drive accounts for what appears, to some Western eyes, to be an uncommon degree of docility and willingness to follow the lead of the group? If this drive does exist, then, as we have seen, it provides a major challenge to the idea of individuality and independence that—even when honored only in the breach—forms the basis of American conceptions of democratic social life and education. The challenge is even stronger if, as Doi suggests, the drive for dependency manifest in the Japanese language is also present in the longings of those who are not Japanese. If he is correct, and we are hindered by the fact that Western categories make this drive very difficult to see, then it is *our* educational, social, and political institutions that rest on an inadequate understanding of human nature.

We could, of course, take seriously the Japanese critics of Doi, accept the idea that he is underemphasizing the explicit forms of control that actually generate conformity, and reject the idea that Doi has really captured anything important about the Japanese personality. This response appears too easy because, as a starting point, it is too Western, already advancing the conclusion that we feel most comfortable with, allowing us to overlook otherwise neglected aspects of our own character. As one American worker remarked, trying to sum up his self-learning after many months in Japan: "We (Americans) feel a great deal of pressure to be independent." To put the matter somewhat differently, Doi offers a challenge that cannot easily be dismissed with charges of repression and false consciousness. To say that what we see in Japan is just a matter of domination, subordination, exploitation, and false consciousness is to assert the primacy of the very system that Doi is making problematic—our own.

We do know that some possible interpretations of Doi, some understandings, surely must be wrong. If the Japanese love their dependency so much, then why do we not hear slogans like "inequality, paternity, and dependency," adopted by any political party? Why do Japanese cultural critics not write books lamenting "The Escape from Dependency," and why do Japanese children not appeal to their "inherent right to be dominated by their parents"? Of course there is something quite contradictory about some of those appeals—for something to be a "right" means that it gives a person the opportunity to decide on her own—that it gives her the right not to be dominated.

Yet it is more than logic that leads us to pause. We do not hear such appeals in Japan because *amae* is not basically a political concept. It is, as Doi's profession would lead us to suppose, a psychological one, which is likely to be manifested in interpersonal relations rather than in political ones. Given this understanding, what we most likely have in *amae* is an important motor force of behavior in the sense that Freud understood libidinal forces. If this is the proper view of *amae* then there may well be a connection between it and political and other forms of dependency. However, rather than viewing the connection in terms of a denial of freedom, we would now view it in terms of the overarching trust that we might place in someone whom we believe will always act out of care and concern for our own well-being. *Amae* would then be understood not in terms of a negation of an aim such as freedom, but rather as an assertion of the need for a relationship of care. When we know that someone cares for us completely, we need not deny our freedom, but we often feel little need to assert it just in order to assure ourselves that we still have it. We may even reveal our childlike qualities of playfulness and irresponsibility with the understanding that, at least in this situation, we can still be accepted. This interpretation is consistent with Doi's reaction when he thought that perhaps his American hosts provided so many trivial choices in order to assure themselves of their own freedom. Perhaps when *amae* prevails, such continuous assurance is not required.

If *amae* is to be understood as a basic psychological drive, then we should be able to find a sensible connection with our own experience, with our wants and longings. When we do touch base with the concept of *amae*, we will do so, as Doi suggests in his critique of Western psychoanalysis, by announcing needs that we feel but often fail to acknowledge.

Yet if we have come this far in our acceptance of *amae* as a potentially positive force, and if we have found something promising in Doi's critique of Western psychoanalysis, are we then still able to hold on to our own standards of judgment, standards that constitute the means for evaluating our social, political and educational systems? Here it seems to me that as we explore the meaning of *amae*, our own values become vulnerable to interrogation, and our own institutions are indeed opened up for change. What is provided is not only a criticism of Western psychoanalysis but also an implicit critique of the ideal of independence which serves as the *telos* guiding the psychoanalytic process. Independence is the goal, as psychoanalysis sees it, of all normal forms of development. Doi speaks of the overemphasis in Western psychoanalysis on self-reliance, and of the indifference which he noted among analysts to their patients' sense of helplessness. He speaks of Freud's neglect of expressions of infantile desire for love and attachment. He mentions the distortions that arise in understanding when the foundation of identity is located in the separation associated with the "Oedipus complex" while overlooking the need for tenderness and the quest for attachment that precedes it.

This critique suggests that the issue does indeed involve more than interpretation. For if we were to develop our own sense of *amae*, then we would become sensitive to features in our own culture which facilitate or block its expression, and when these are absent, we might find ourselves appealing to the need for *amae* in the same way that, for other reasons, we would appeal to the need for freedom or equality. Were this to happen, then *amae* would serve as a force for changing our cultural foundations; it would serve to challenge some of the standards that we use for judging development, and especially the excessive drive for independence and the neglect of communal socializing structures.

As we elaborate the concept of *amae* in order to find new interpretive grounds on which to build an understanding of Japanese society, we come close to an important aspect of Western feminism. That is, we approach those forms of feminism that have stressed an ethic of care, that emphasize the importance of connectedness, and that seek to reconstruct our understanding of autonomy and control. As Evelyn Fox Keller writes:

> Constant vigilance and control are the telltale marks of a conception of autonomy that in fact belies its own aims. They reflect not so much confidence in one's difference from others as resistance to (even repudiation of) sameness, not so much the strength of one's own will as the resistance to another's, not so much a sense

of self esteem as uncertainty about the durability of self—finally, not so much the security of one's ego boundaries as their vulnerability.[18]

Yet there is still a difference between *amae* and the feminists' reevaluation of autonomy that is difficult to ignore. For along with a philosophy of connectedness and care is feminism's insistence that the public and the private realms (social constructs to be sure) be open to all, and that the role of caretaker not be distributed on a gender-specific basis. To hold on to this principle is to establish a strong boundary for the penetration of certain aspects of Japanese culture into American educational and economic institutions. It is to announce the need to resolve the conflict between care and opportunity, dependence and independence, in new and unique ways, but not in ways that reinforce traditional patriarchical hierarchies. In other words, it provides a temporary boundary that sets the sights for the self-directed evolutionary process to be unfolded. In this case, Japan and its culture maintain the status of the other, serving to reflect back our own self-interpretation and standards, and providing a standpoint from which to review and reconsider the goals of the educational process itself. It provides a reflective moment upon which conceptions of education can continue to be developed, and notions of personhood and community can continue to evolve.

V. Conclusion

Nevertheless, there are limits to this decentered, postmodern temper. To mimic William James, life is not *just* one damned interpretation after another, and there comes a time when we must answer the traditional Confucian parent who asked in the first chapter "What is the object of this reason?" and "Who is its beneficiary?" Ultimately we must tell the parent that we agree that the son should not turn his back on his family and his community, and we might add that we, too, object when reason is used as a club to smash commitment and destroy community. Nevertheless, we must also say that democracy must separate respect and obedience, reason and commitment, if the conversation about what we are to become is to continue in an age where not all symbols are shared, not all meanings are common, and not all ends are fully communal. In this kind of world the task of education is to further neither individualism nor collectivism alone. It is rather to promote a process of critical yet respectful participation in which both communal and global ends can emerge. When this process includes local symbols amplifying their meanings for other cultures and for different groups, and when it explores international connections in terms of justice as well as wealth, then such an education is democratic. Given the fragile ecological condition of our planet, a democratic education will require, contrary to the belief of the economic conservative, not that the schools teach children to produce more but that they help their more privileged students learn to consume less.

APPENDIX I

Notes on the
Structure of Japanese Education

The modern structure of Japanese education is the result of changes brought about through the American Occupation following the Second World War, and the developments that have taken place within Japan since that time. The basic structure, with six years of elementary school, three years of junior high school, three years of high school, and four years of university resembles a common version of the American system, and has not undergone significant change for many years. There are slight differences, however, in that Japanese students begin the first grade a little later than their American counterparts. Moreover, only elementary school and junior high school are compulsory, and so Japanese students who wish to enter the work force may legally do so at the age of about fifteen. Only a few students choose this option, however, and the vast majority stay in school at least until they complete high school.

There are also some important differences between the structures of the Japanese and the American educational system. Perhaps the most important of these is that in Japan, in contrast to the United States, the curriculum is centrally designed and controlled by the Ministry of Education, as is textbook approval. Moreover, Japan has had a very strong, socialist-influenced, teachers union, which provides teachers with considerable leverage in negotiations about salaries and other educational matters. Interestingly, Japan has no waiting period for tenure. When a teacher is hired, it is assumed that he or she will not be subject to dismissal, except for serious breaches of behavior. Another important difference is teacher salary compared to other professions and occupations. Whereas American teachers have traditionally been low-paid, starting salaries for teachers in Japan are higher than the starting salaries of businesspeople and engineers with the same level of education, and has been rising compared to other occupations.[1] This has led one Japanese researcher to conclude that "there are few occupations that pay better than teaching." The advantage of teachers grows even larger in their early fifties, when their salary continues to increase while those of most other Japanese level off.[2] Teachers in Japan rank quite highly in prestige—above architects and mechanical engineers, although below doctors, business executives, university professors, and high bureaucrats—and teaching is considered more desirable work than a number of occupations that are actually ranked above it.[3]

Whatever differences exist between American and Japanese education, relating to the structure of schools or the conditions of the teaching profession, are perhaps less important than those that exist in the transition from one level of education to another. The most striking difference between education in Japan and education in the United States lies in the transition from junior high school to high school and from high school to the university. There are variations from prefecture to prefecture in the transition process from junior high school to senior high school, but the key element in the process is the entrance examination that students take during their last year of junior high. In many prefectures the examination is the single determinant of high school placement, although some may give certain weight to school performance and teacher evaluation. Students may choose to take the examination for any high school in their school district, but they, in conjunction with guidance from their teachers, must choose the school that they wish to attend carefully because if they fail the examination for one public, academic high school,[4] they cannot then turn around and take the examination for another public, academic high school. Students who are rejected find their choices seriously narrowed.

In Japan, all high schools, as well as all universities, are ranked according to their academic reputation, and while this ranking is informal, there is very wide agreement among people in a given prefecture about the ranking of individual schools. This informal agreement is substantiated by the publication in major newspapers and magazines of the success that seniors from different high schools have in entering prestigious universities. Success then breeds success, as the higher-scoring junior high students want to enter the senior high schools whose graduates are most successful in competing for places in prestigious universities.

The fact that junior high school students are usually limited to taking the examination for only one (or one cluster of) public high school gives the examination a special significance. This significance is enhanced by the fact that, with the exception of a few (although a growing number of) very elite private schools, the alternative to the public, academic high school is a lower-prestige, more expensive, private school or a still-lower-prestige, public, vocational high school. Students also may leave school at this point to enter the job market but very few choose to do so. Because the examinations are so significant in the life of the Japanese student, a large industry has developed to help students get ready for the entrance examination. The industry includes private tutors, as well as a large network of "cram schools," called *juku*, which has grown significantly in recent years. It also includes magazines and other reading materials that publish detailed information on each school and university.

The transition from high school to university is similar in many respects to the transition from junior high to high school, and the ranking of universities and their various departments parallels the ranking of the high schools.[5] At the top of the ranking is Tokyo National University, followed by Kyoto. At the bottom are a number of private universities which will accept almost any student who can afford the tuition. A few private universities such as Keio and Waseda rank high, but they still fall below the ranking of the most prestigious national universities. In general, the highest-ranking national universities not only have the advantage of greater prestige, but they are also less expensive than the private universities. However, given the costs of attending cram schools, or tuition at elite private schools where one has a stronger chance of entering a National University, it is unlikely that the cost of the whole process is cheaper for students at high-prestige universities. At the end of the educational process, there is a very high correlation between the status of the university one attends and the status of the company one can expect to work for after graduation.

Entrance into the National Universities and the better private universities is by examination. Other factors, such as high school record, teachers' recommendations, or extracurricular activities, are usually not counted. Recently the government has introduced a national preliminary examination to enable universities and students to better determine their suitability for each other. However, each national university still gives its own examination in addition to the preliminary exam, and each department determines the scores that will be acceptable for admission. Until recently students could only take the examination for one National University during any single year; now they can take the examination for two. It is very important for the student to choose carefully. A successful student is then admitted into a particular department and is not allowed to change departments during the course of study without essentially beginning the process over again. The high stakes, the precise rankings of the university, and the singular importance of the examination make the high school years intense ones for most students, and there is a much more serious, studious climate in the average Japanese high school than in most American schools. However, the high school is only one of the sites in which preparation for the examination takes place. Many of those who are serious about entering a prestigious university will attend a cram school to prepare for the examination and a significant proportion may also employ a private tutor.[6] Indeed, there are some highly prestigious cram schools that require students to take an examination before they are admitted, because their reputation depends on the percentage of students who pass the examination to the university. A few of the very elite schools will urge the child's mother not to work outside of the home during the period in which the child is enrolled.

The examination itself requires a great deal of factual recall, and hence the schools tend to emphasize memorization and rote learning. However, the high school curriculum, especially in math, science, and foreign language, is significantly more advanced than that taken by most American high school students, and knowledgable commentators report that Japanese high school seniors probably have the equivalent knowledge in these areas of American college graduates. The intense pace does not, however, continue at the university, where most students seem to take the first two years to relax and recuperate from the ordeal that they have just been through. The structure of the Japanese educational system is useful to keep in mind when claims are made about the important connection between education and work. While Japanese productivity in certain industries has improved dramatically over the years, much of the educational structure has undergone no significant change. More students are attending college than before, but the Japanese university is notorious as the weakest link in its educational system in terms of the development of academic skills.

APPENDIX II

Terminology

A brief word about terminology to clarify my use of the label "economic conservatives." As I use the term "economic conservative," it actually matches the profile of many liberals who call for more coordination between school and work, and for the development of higher-order skills in order to make United States' industry more competitive in the international marketplace. This broader understanding of the term is appropriate if one thinks in an *economic* framework. In this case, the significant difference between the economic conservative and the economic liberal is a tactical one, involving how much direct influence the federal government should have on the coordination of school and work. Conservatives think that much of the job can be done through exhortation and example. Economic liberals will argue for more direct federal dollars for education. On this issue I take my stand with the economic liberal, and would argue, for example, that the failure to provide adequate funding to education renders many potentially innovative proposals, such as parental choice, largely a charade. However, I am not concerned to argue this point here, but rather to explain how I am diverging from conventional usage of the terms "liberal" and "conservative." The important point is to distinguish the term "liberal" as it is used in an educational, as opposed to an economic, framework.

The liberal tradition in education has many different manifestations, but the primary concern of all of them is to free the student from obstacles that stand in the way of self-realization and enlightenment. To the extent that this enlightenment is thought to be found in performed insights and traditions, it forms much of the educational program of the cultural conservative. In this usage the terms "liberal" and "conservative" are not necessarily contradictory, since the child is thought to be liberated through appropriating performed cultural material. Yet in a deep sense there is a tension, because the individual self is "freed" only by submerging its interests, desires, and lesser identities in the universal self, represented by the larger, dominant tradition. A more progressive strand of liberalism seeks the conditions for different traditions to grow and interact with each other.

As I have pointed out elsewhere, the progressive side of the liberal tradition in *education* is grounded in two competing ideals—one is equal opportunity and the other is the need to respect the child's interests and potentials. The concern for equal opportunity is both a concern about fairness in an ethical sense, and a concern about the conditions for economic growth and development. This latter concern is the single emphasis of economic liberals leading them to seek coordination between school and work. While many educational liberals also want to see a stronger match between the school and the workplace, there is a strand in *educational* liberal ideology that speaks to the need to develop individual potential, to respect the nature of childhood and to attend to the needs of individual children and their cultural differences.[1]

Here I use the terms "liberal" and "conservative" in an educational, rather than strictly an economic framework. I use the term "economic" to isolate elements of tradition that see the school *primarily* as an instrument for economic policy, and I used the word "conservative" to indicate the tradition that sees the purpose of schooling to be fixed either by the imperatives of economics or by the imperatives of national identity. I reserve the term "liberal" to indicate a body of thought that seeks in part to connect children to the larger political and economic adult society by attending to, and celebration, individual and cultural differences.

Notes

Introduction

1. These rankings are taken from Carnegie Forum on Education and the Economy, *A Nation Prepared*, 1986, p. 16.
2. David Henry Wang, *M. Butterfly*, N.Y.: William Craver, Writers and Artists Agency, 1988, p. 15.
3. Appreciation to Bert Powers for this distinction.
4. In contrast, say, to an expanded public realm where shared facilities reduce dependency on private wealth.

An American Identity Crisis

1. For a description of the way these changes are affecting the school curriculum see Joseph Berger, "Arguing about America: A Common Culture or a Land of Diversity? That is the Curriculum Debate in New York," *The New York Time National*, June 21, 1991. In New York State, where Blacks, Hispanics, Asians, and Native Americans now make up 31 percent of the population, there are dramatic changes being proposed for the curriculum. For example, "Thanksgiving would not be described simply as a joyous national holiday. It would be presented as a day that some cultures have come to see as a cause for celebration but that other groups believe should be a day of mourning. School children would be encouraged to discuss why this is so." Sam Howe Verhovek, *The New York Times National*, Friday, June 21, 1991, p. A10.
2. James Fallows, *More Like Us: Making America Great Again*, Boston: Houghton Mifflin, 1989, p. 38.

3. Ronald E. Yates, "Overworked Japanese Begin Demanding Fruits of their Labor" *Chicago Tribune*, Sunday, June 16, 1991, Section 1, p. 1.

4. In this book "American" is sometimes used as a shorthand for a citizen of the United States and "America" sometimes indicates the United States of America.

5. Verhovek, *New York Times*, op. cit.

6. Michio Morishima, *Why has Japan "Succeeded"?: Western Technology and the Japanese Ethos*, Cambridge: Cambridge University Press, 1984, pp. 1–19.

7. Takie Sugiyama Lebra, *Japanese Patterns of Behavior*, Honolulu: University of Hawaii Press, 1982, p. 158.

8. F. H. Bradley, "My Station and its Duty," in *Ethical Studies*, London: Oxford University Press, 1962.

9. Chie Nakane, *Japanese Society*, Tokyo: Charles E. Tuttle Co., 1986, p. 10.

10. Thomas P. Rohlen, *For Harmony and Strength*, California: University of California Press, 1974, p. 47.

11. Quoted in Robert J. Smith, *Japanese Society: Tradition, Self and the Social Order*, Cambridge: Cambridge University Press, 1983, p. 50.

12. Rohlen, op. cit. p. 47.

13. Takeo Doi, M.D., *The Anatomy of Self: The Individual versus Society*, Mark Harbison, tr., Tokyo: Kodansha, 1986, p. 51.

14. Alasdair MacIntyre, *After Virtue*, South Bend: University of Notre Dame Press, 1981, pp. 30–31.

15. See Alasdair MacIntyre, *Whose Justice? Which Rationality?* Notre Dame, Indiana: University of Notre Dame Press, 1988, pp. 241–260.

16. Adam Smith, *The Theory of Moral Sentiments*, D. D. Raphael and A. L. Macfie, eds. Oxford: Clarendon Press, 1976, p. 7.

17. Adam Smith, ibid., p. 137.

18. William E. Connolly, *Identity/Difference*, Ithaca: Cornell University Press, 1991, p. 85.

19. Michael J. Sandel, *Liberalism and the Limits of Justice*, Cambridge: Cambridge University Press, 1982, pp. 58–59.

20. Lebra, op. cit. pp. 22–37.

21. *Ibid.*, p. 3.

22. *Ibid.*, p. 11.

23. *Ibid.*, p. 11.

24. *Ibid.*, pp. 12–13.

25. *Ibid.*, p. 14.

26. Samuel Bowles and Herbert Gintis, *Schooling in Capitalist America: Educational Reform and the Contradictions of Economic Life*, New York: Basic Books, 1976.

27. See for example, Paul Willis, *Learning to Labor: How Working Class Kids Get Working Class Jobs*, Westmead, England: Saxon House, 1978, pp. 1–6; Michael Apple, *Ideology and Curriculum*, London: Routledge & Kegan Paul, 1979, pp. 1–25.

Japan and the American Quest for Moral Authority

1. One of the most recent and influential expressions of this line of argument is to be found in John Rawls, *A Theory of Justice*, Cambridge, MA: Harvard University Press, 1971, pp. 60–65.

2. Alexis De Tocqueville, *Democracy in America*, New York: Mentor, 1956, p. 193. De Tocqueville thought that there were mechanisms, such as elections for many public offices, that could mitigate the potential neglect.

3. *Ibid.*, p. 193.

4. *The New York Times*, Thursday, June 28, 1990, p. 1.

5. Alasdair MacIntyre, *After Virtue: A Study in Moral Theory*, Notre Dame: University of Notre Dame Press, 1981, pp. 1–35.

6. Robert Bellah, et al., *Habits of the Heart: Individualism and Commitment in American Life*, New York: Harper and Row, 1985.

7. *Ibid.*, p. 37.

8. *Ibid.*, pp. 57–111.

9. This conception is advanced by E. D. Hirsch, Jr., *Cultural Literacy: What Every American Needs to Know*, Boston: Houghton Mifflin Co. 1987.

10. See A. MacIntyre, *After Virtue*, Notre Dame: University of Notre Dame Press, 1981, pp. 169–210.

11. *Ibid.*, pp. 65–66.

12. *Ibid.*, pp. 68–69.

13. Thomas Rohlen, *For Harmony and Strength*, Berkeley: University of California Press, 1974, p. 14.

14. *Ibid.*, p. 15.

15. *Ibid.*, p. 16.

16. *Ibid.*, p. 18.

17. *Ibid.*, p. 35.

18. *Ibid.*, p. 39.

19. *Ibid.*, p. 55.

20. Takie Sugiyama Lebra, *Japanese Patterns of Behavior*, Honolulu: University of Hawaii Press, 1982, pp. 23–24.

21. See MacIntyre, *After Virtue, op. cit.*, pp. 22–60.

22. "The High Price Japanese Pay for Success" *Business Week*, April 7, 1986, pp. 52–53.

23. Lawrence Kohlberg, *Essays on Moral Development: Vol. One, The Philosophy of Moral Development*, Cambridge: Harper & Row, 1981, p. 126.

Economic Conservatives and the Culture of Friction

1. *Japan, 1986: An International Comparison*, Tokyo: Keizai Koho Center, Japan Institute for Social and Economic Affairs, 1986, Chart 1–7, p. 9.

2. *Ibid.*, chart 1–11, p. 11.

3. *Japan, 1992: An Economic Comparison*, Tokyo: Kezai Koho Center, Japan Institute for Social and Economic Affairs, chart 1–9, p. 11.

4. *Japan, 1986*, chart 3–6, p. 22.

5. *Ibid.*, chart 3–7, p. 23. Also, *Japan, 1992*, chart 3–13, p. 26.

6. *Ibid.*, chart 4–4, p. 33. In 1989 some ground has been gained when Japan's balance-of-payments surplus was 57,157 million dollars and our deficit had fallen to 106,400 million dollars. *Japan, 1992*, chart 5, p. 46.

7. *Ibid.*, chart 5, p. 46.

8. *Japan, 1986*, chart 4–6, p. 35.

9. *Ibid.*, chart 8–9, p. 73.

10. *Japan, 1992*, chart 8, 9, p. 71.

11. Delwyn L. Harnisch, *Achievement and Motivation Patterns of Secondary Students in The United States and Japan*, Unpublished seminar paper, presented University of Illinois, Fall, 1987.

12. Thomas P. Rohlen, *Japan's High Schools*, Berkeley: University of California Press, 1983, p. 3.

13. David T. Kearns and Denis P. Doyle, *Winning The Brain Race*, ICS Press, 1988, p. 1.

14. It is important to note, as one business executive has recently remarked to me, how little ethical training goes on in the nation's business colleges, and how susceptible new executives are to the ethical climate of the company. Although some companies have begun to institute "ethics" in their own training sessions, these often take the form of lessons in what not to do in order to avoid hurting the company and getting into trouble. The workshops have little that involves how to decide what the right thing is to do or how to refine the larger social purpose of the company.

15. Carnegie Forum on Education and the Economy, "A Nation Prepared," 1986, p. 16.

16. Larry Hirschhorn, *Beyond Mechanization: Work and Technology in a Postindustrial Age*, Cambridge: MIT Press, 1984, p. 31.

17. *Ibid.*, pp. 72–73.

18. *Ibid.*, pp. 91–93.

19. *Ibid.*, pp. 74–90.

20. *Ibid.*, pp. 81–83.

21. Harry Braverman, *Labor and Monopoly Capital: The Degradation of Work in the Twentieth Century*, New York: Monthly Review Press, 1974, pp. 129–130.

22. Michael L. Dertouzos, Richard K. Lester, Robert M. Solow, *Made In America: Regaining the Productive Edge*, Cambridge: MIT Press, 1989, pp. 46–47.

23. *Ibid.*, p. 49.

24. *Ibid.*, p. 50.

25. There are exceptions, of course; see for example, John I. Goodlad, *A Place Called School: Prospects for the Future*, New York: McGraw-Hill, 1984. Also, Theodore R. Sizer, *Horace's Compromise: The Dilemma of the American High School*, Boston, MA: Houghton Mifflin Co., 1984. These have limited connection to industrial goals and to the aim of improving productivity, and are best thought of as educational rather than industrial documents.

26. Martin Carnoy, "High Technology and Education: An Economist's View" in *Society as Educator in An Age of Transition*, Chicago: The University of Chicago Press, 86th Yearbook of the National Society for the Study of Education, 1987, pp. 88–111.

27. Clair Brown and Michael Reich, "When Does Union-Management Cooperation Work? A Look at NUMMI and GM-Van Nuys," *California Management Review*, Summer, 1989, p. 28.

28. *Ibid.*, p. 28–29.

29. *Ibid.*, p. 31.

30. *Ibid.*, p. 32.

31. The workers in this group were sent to Japan for ten months, probably the longest training period abroad for any program of this kind. The more than two dozen workers, ranging in age from early twenties to early forties, had worked for a number of different American companies in a variety of different capacities. Some were experienced die makers, one invented special tools for a small machine shop, another had worked in a meat-packing plant, others had worked for a large, heavy equipment company that had laid off a large number of its work force as orders fell in the early and middle 1980s. The workers were selected after a rigorous screening process, and were sent to Japan to be trained as workers in a new, heavily automated plant that was being built in the United States. In Japan they were to be trained in a similar plant using similar equipment. The workers provide some insight into the kinds of demands that are being made by the newer industries, especially those that are heavily

computerized, relying on robotic technology, and attempting to adopt Japanese management style.

32. These included physical problems such as deteriorating eye sight, slower growth, as well as social and educational ones: Teachers left teaching to enter the more lucrative private tutoring field, and children from wealthier families who could afford tutors were doing better on tests, hence setting back a commitment to improve education as an instrument for upward mobility.

33. Taiji Hotta, "Examination Hell," Urbana: Unpublished paper, April, 1988.

34. Juliet B. Schor, *The Overworked American*, New York: Basic Books, 1991, p. 2.

35. *Ibid.*, p. 82.

36. *Ibid.*, p. 153.

37. *Ibid.*, p. 153.

Cultural Conservatives and the Vision of Harmony

1. Thomas P. Rohlen, *Japan's High Schools*, Berkeley: University of California Press, 1983, p. 102. [emphasis added]

2. Merry White, *The Japanese Educational Challenge: A Commitment to Children*, New York: The Free Press, 1987, p. 145.

3. Merry White, op. cit., p. 95.

4. The National Commission on Excellence in Education, *A Nation at Risk: The Imperative for Educational Reform*, Washington: U.S. Government Printing Office, 1983, p. 5.

5. W. T. Harris, "An Educational Policy for Our New Possessions," *Educational Review*, 1889, p. 115.

6. Jared Taylor, "The Moral Superiority of Japan," *Chicago Tribune*, April 14, 1987.

7. This was one reason why a moderate like T. H. Bell created the National Commission on Excellence in Education that issued the report, *A Nation at Risk*. Bell was in part working to save the Department of Education against attempts to close it by more reactionary elements of the Reagan administration. See T. H. Bell, *The Thirteenth Man: A Reagan Cabinet Memoir*, New York: The Free Press, 1988.

8. Horio, Teruhisa, *Educational Thought and Ideology in Modern Japan: State Authority and Intellectual Freedom*, Steven Platzer, tr., Tokyo: University of Tokyo Press, 1988, pp. 52–54.

9. Quoted in Horio, op. cit., p. 56.

10. Walter Feinberg, *Understanding Education: Toward a Reconstruction of Educational Inquiry*, Cambridge: Cambridge University Press, 1983. Part One

provides an analysis of this debate. For a sample of the relevant works see Edward Banfield, *The Unheavenly City: The Nature and Future of Our Urban Crisis*, Boston: Little, Brown, 1970; Arthur Jensen, "How Much Can We Boost IQ and Scholastic Achievement," *Harvard Educational Review*, Vol. 39, No. 1, Winter, 1969. For the other side see Samuel Bowles and Herbert Gintis, *Schooling in Capitalist America: Educational Reform and the Contradictions of Economic Life*, New York: Basic Books, 1976.

11. William K. Cummings, *Education and Equality in Japan*, Princeton: Princeton University Press, 1980, p. 4.

12. Rohlen, *Japan's High Schools*, op. cit., p. i.

13. The evidence he uses to support this claim is impressive. For example, even though high school is not compulsory in Japan, over ninety percent of its students graduate compared to about seventy-five percent for the United States. Moreover, in international comparisons of achievement in mathematics and science, Japan consistently ranks first among major nations. Variation in performance among Japanese children in comparatively very low, hence supporting the conclusion of a very highly educated average. The system helps produce a more orderly, controlled society, with an exceptionally low crime rate, high life expectancy, and more efficient workers in many areas.

14. *Ibid.*, p. 323.

15. "Neither teachers' recommendations, nor grades in secondary school, nor extracurricular activities, nor personal character, nor special talents contribute to acceptance by Japanese universities." Rather, Rohlen reports that the entrance examination is the only factor and that "the exam questions are easily graded, as might be expected. Short-answer and multiple choice questions prevail. Few, if any, essay or interpretive questions appear. . . . Emphasis is on mastery of facts, control over details, and practical skill in the application of mathematical and scientific principles." *Ibid.*, pp. 94–95.

16. *Ibid.*, p. 135. The reader should note that there is a significant difference between Cummings and Rohlen on this point. My point, however, is not to settle this conflict but to point out the tensions within Rohlen's own depiction of Japanese education.

17. *Ibid.*, p. 245.

18. *Ibid.*, p. 246.

19. *Ibid.*, p. 271.

20. *Ibid.*, p. 108.

21. *Ibid.*, p. 109. Rohlen is, of course, assuming that the institutional practice determines student outcome.

22. Thomas P. Rohlen, *Japan's High Schools*, Berkeley: University of California Press, 1983, p. ix.

23. Rohlen, *Japan's High Schools*, op. cit., p. 245.

24. *Ibid.*, p. 247.

25. *Ibid.*, p. 13.

26. *Ibid.*, p. 36.

27. *Ibid.*, pp. 95–96.

28. *Ibid.*, p. 110.

29. *Ibid.*, p. 95. Also consider the following passage: "The ideal of the well-rounded scholar-athlete has become unthinkable given the present examination pressure. Reluctant bookworm though he may be, it is the pale and under exercised exam 'pro' who is going to succeed and make his family proud." *Ibid.*, p. 189.

30. *Ibid.*, p. 62.

31. *Ibid.*, pp. 325–326.

32. *Ibid.*, p. 320.

33. Merry White, *The Japanese Educational Challenge: A Commitment to Children*, New York: The Free Press, 1987, p. 4.

34. *Ibid.*, p. 5.

35. *Ibid.*, pp. 15–16.

36. *Ibid.*, p. 17.

37. *Ibid.*, p. 17.

38. Allan Bloom, *The Closing of the American Mind: How Higher Education has Failed Democracy and Impovished the Souls of Today's Students*, New York: Simon and Schuster, 1987, p. 27.

39. Rohlen, op. cit., p. 62.

40. *Ibid.*, p. 245.

41. *ibid.*, p. 246.

42. *Ibid.*, p. 109.

43. Allan Nevins and Henry Steele Commager, *The Pocket History of the United States*, New York: Pocket Books, 1956, p. V.

44. Ralph Volney Harlow, *The Growth of the United States: Vol I: The Establishment of the Nation through the Civil War (rev. ed.)*, New York: Henry Holt and Co., 1943, p. 320.

45. E. D. Hirsch, *Cultural Literacy: What Every American Needs to Know*, Boston: Houghton Mifflin, 1987, pp. 152–215.

Collective Identity and Social Practice

1. Ezra F. Vogel, *Japan as Number 1: Lessons for America*, New York: Harper Colophon Books, 1979, p. 71.

2. James C. Abegglen and George Stalk, Jr., *Kaisha: The Japanese Corporation,* Tokyo: Charles E. Tuttle, 1985, pp. 31.

3. *Ibid.*, pp. 21–29.

4. Ronald P. Dore and Mari Sako, *How the Japanese Learn to Work,* London: Routledge, 1989, pp. 121–124.

5. Rohlen, *Japan's High Schools,* op. cit., pp. 95–98.

6. For a description of the process in a French context see Pierre Bourdieu and Jean-Claude Passeron, *Reproduction in Education, Society and Culture,* London: Sage, 1977, pp. 141–177.

7. Rohlen, op. cit., p. 196.

8. *Ibid.*, p. 197.

9. For an explanation of the reasons for the high level of compensation, see Graef S. Crystal, *In Search of Excess: The Overcompensation of the American Executive,* W. W. Norton, 1991.

10. *Ibid.*

11. See Carol Gilligan, *In A Different Voice,* Cambridge, MA: Harvard University Press, 1982; see, also, Nel Noddings, *Caring: A Feminine Approach to Ethics and Moral Education,* Berkeley, CA: University of California Press, 1984.

12. That economic models may actually encourage selfishness is suggested in an intriguing paper by Robert Frank, "The Battle for Human Nature," *American Academy of Arts and Science,* July 1992. In studying the response of economics and noneconomics majors to "prisoner dilemma" games, it was found that the economics majors were twice as likely to defect (act noncooperatively) as were noneconomics majors and that the difference between the two groups widens from the beginning of college to the end.

13. I have argued this in detail in *Understanding Education: Toward a Reconstruction of Educational Inquiry,* Cambridge: Cambridge University Press, 1983.

14. See Shoshana Zuboff, *In the Age of the Smart Machine: The Future of Work and Power,* New York: Basic Books, 1988, pp. 246–248.

15. Nell Keddie, "Classroom Knowledge," in E. Bredo and W. Feinberg, *Knowledge and Values in Social and Educational Research,* Philadelphia: Temple University Press, 1982, pp. 219–252.

16. Lee Iacocca, *Iacocca: An Autobiography* (with William Novak), Toronto: Bantam Books, 1984, pp. 95–96.

17. *Ibid.*, pp. xiii–xiv.

18. Resistance to these programs is obviously present, as the Fucinis discovered when interviewing workers training for a Mazda assembly plant in Michigan: "They were going to kaizen out this and kaizen out that, so we could be more productive. The more they talked, the more it sounded like this whole team thing was just a way to squeeze more work out of every worker, and with a good dose of old-fashioned paternalism thrown in to

keep everybody happy." Joseph J. Fucini and Suzy Fucini, *Working for the Japanese: Inside Mazda's Auto Plant*, New York: The Free Press, 1990, p. 87.

19. For a history of the movement of Japanese labor, see Andrew Gordon, *The Evolution of Labor Relations in Japan: Heavy Industry, 1853–1955*, Cambridge: Harvard University Press, 1985.

20. *Ibid.*, pp. 2–3.

21. Abegglen and Stalk, *Kaisha*, op. cit., p. 184.

22. *Ibid.*, p. 184.

23. Takie Sugiyama Lebra, *Japanese Patterns of Behavior*, Honolulu: University of Hawaii Press, 1982, p. 23.

24. Abegglen and Stalk, op. cit., p. 185.

25. *Ibid.*, p. 187.

26. *Ibid.*, p. 188.

27. *Ibid.*, p. 193.

28. *Ibid.*, p. 195.

29. *Ibid.*, pp. 195–196.

30. *Ibid.*, p. 197.

Japanese Identity

1. *Japan As It Is*, Tokyo: Gakken, 1985, p. 143.

2. See Chapter Four.

3. Harumi Befu, "The Social and Cultural Background of Child Development in Japan and the United States," in Harold Stevenson, Hiroshi Azuma and Kenji Hakuta, *Child Development and Education in Japan*, New York: W. H. Freeman and Company, 1986, p. 14.

4. *Ibid.*, p. 25.

5. Joseph J. Tobin, David Y. H. Wu, Dana H. Davidson, *Preschool in Three Cultures: Japan, China and the United States*, New Haven: Yale, 1989, p. 28.

6. Liza Dalby, *Geisha*, New York: Vintage, 1985, pp. 108, 159–160.

7. Takie Sugiyama Lebra, *Japanese Women: Constraint and Fulfillment*, Honolulu: University of Hawaii Press, 1984, p. 57.

8. See Merry White, *The Japanese Educational Challenge: A Commitment to Children*, New York: The Free Press, 1987, pp. 95–110.

9. Women and Work: The Facts and Figures: Women Get on the Job" in *Look Japan*, September 1990, Vol. 36, No. 414, p. 8.

10. *Ibid.*, p. 9.

11. *Ibid.*, p. 10.

12. "Women and Work: The Equal Opportunity Law," *Ibid.*, p. 6.

13. *Ibid.*, p. 6.

14. Alice H. Cook and Hayashi Hiroko, "Working Women in Japan" in Oki-
    moto and Rohlen, eds., *Inside the Japanese System,* Stanford: Stanford Uni-
    versity Press, 1988, p. 136.

15. Thomas P. Rohlen, "Permanent Employment Policies in Times of Reces-
    sion" in *Ibid.*, p. 140. Rohlen also points out that, as the recession is
    ending, many companies begin to hire women instead of permanent male
    workers as a hedge against the next turndown.

16. Byong-Ho Chung, *Childcare Politics: Life and Power in Japanese Day Care
    Centers,* Urbana: Unpublished Ph.D. Thesis, 1991, p. 1.

17. Gunnar Myrdal, *An American Dilemma: Volume 1,* New York: McGraw-
    Hill, 1964, pp. 3–26.

18. This difference is explored in James Fallows, *More Like Us: Making America
    Great Again,* Boston: Houghton-Mifflin, 1989.

Education, Work, and Democratic Identity

1. Alasdair MacIntyre, *Whose Justice? Which Rationality,* Notre Dame: Notre
   Dame University Press, 1988, ch. XIX.

2. John Dewey, *Democracy and Education: An Introduction to the Philosophy of
   Education,* New York: The Macmillan Co., 1965, p. 5.

3. Dewey himself understood this and spent much of his life constructing,
   with varying degrees of success, a fuller and more adequate conception
   of community.

4. See Chapter 2.

5. Allen Bloom, *The Closing of the American Mind: How Higher Education has
   Failed Democracy and Impoverished the Souls of Today's Students,* New York:
   Simon and Schuster, 1987, pp. 82–137.

6. See E. D. Hirsch, Jr., *Cultural Literacy: What Every American Needs to Know,*
   Boston: Houghton Mifflin, 1987, pp. 146–215.

7. *The Christian Science Monitor,* Monday, December 14, 1987, p. 12. See also
   Feinberg, "The Moral Responsibility of Public Schools," p. 179.

8. These points are discussed in Walter Feinberg, "The Moral Responsibility
   of Public Schools" in John I. Goodlad, et al., eds., *The Moral Dimension of
   Teaching,* San Francisco: Jossey Bass, 1990, pp. 155–187.

9. See discussion of Rohlen in Chapter Four.

10. Takeo Doi, *The Anatomy of Dependence,* trans. John Bester, Tokyo: Kodan-
    sha International, 1981, p. 12. For an extended treatment of this issue
    within the context of the philosophical debate about relativism and abso-
    lutism see Walter Feinberg, "A Role for Philosophy of Education in Inter-
    cultural Research: Presidential Address." In Ralph Page, ed., *Proceedings*

of the 45th Annual Meeting of the Philosophy of Education Society, San Antonio, 1989, pp. 2–19.

11. Ibid., pp. 22–23.

12. Ross Mouer and Yoshio Sugimoto, Images of Japanese Society: A Study in the Social Construction of Reality, London: KPI, 1986, p. 54.

13. Ibid., p. 235.

14. Ibid., p. 241.

15. Ibid., p. 255.

16. Teruhisa Horio, Educational Thought and Ideology in Modern Japan: State Authority and Intellectual Freedom, trans. Steven Platzer, University of Tokyo Press, 1988, p. 24.

17. Ibid., p. 25.

18. Ibid., p. 31.

19. Evelyn Fox Keller, Reflections on Gender and Science, New Haven: Yale University Press, 1985, p. 102.

Notes on the Structure of Japanese Education

1. Misao Hayakawa, The Quality and Socioeconomic Status of Teachers in Japan: Final Report, Aichi Japan: The Japanese National Institute of Education contract no. NIE-P-85-3045 February 1986, pp. 106–107.

2. Ibid., p. 109.

3. Ibid., pp. 112–114.

4. In some prefectures two schools may be clustered together for the sake of the exam, but the same general principle holds. A failure means the student attends a lower-prestige private school.

5. Rohlen's Japan's High Schools (see Chapter Four) provides a very useful discussion of the process (especially pp. 77–111).

6. Michio Morishima, Why has Japan "Succeeded"?: Western Technology and the Japanese Ethos, Cambridge: Cambridge University Press, 1984, pp. 177–178.

Terminology

1. Walter Feinberg, Reason and Rhetoric: The Intellectual Foundations of Twentieth Century Liberal Educational Policy, New York: John Wiley, 1975, for a treatment of both elements of liberalism.

Index